Struggles for Multilingualism and Linguistic Citizenship

MULTILINGUAL MATTERS
Series Editors: Leigh Oakes, *Queen Mary, University of London, UK* and
Jeroen Darquennes, *Université de Namur, Belgium.*

Multilingual Matters series publishes books on bilingualism, bilingual
education, immersion education, second language learning, language
policy, multiculturalism. The editor is particularly interested in 'macro'
level studies of language policies, language maintenance, language shift,
language revival and language planning. Books in the series discuss the
relationship between language in a broad sense and larger cultural issues,
particularly identity related ones.

All books in this series are externally peer-reviewed.

Full details of all the books in this series and of all our other publications
can be found on http://www.multilingual-matters.com, or by writing to
Multilingual Matters, St Nicholas House, 31–34 High Street, Bristol, BS1
2AW, UK.

MULTILINGUAL MATTERS: 173

Struggles for Multilingualism and Linguistic Citizenship

Edited by
Quentin Williams, Ana Deumert and Tommaso M. Milani

MULTILINGUAL MATTERS
Bristol • Jackson

DOI https://doi.org/10.21832/WILLIA5317
Library of Congress Cataloging in Publication Data
A catalog record for this book is available from the Library of Congress.
Names: Williams, Quentin, editor. | Deumert, Ana, editor. | Milani, Tommaso M., editor.
Title: Struggles for Multilingualism and Linguistic Citizenship/Edited by
   Quentin Williams, Ana Deumert and Tommaso M. Milani.
Description: Bristol; Jackson: Multilingual Matters, [2022] | Series:
   Multilingual Matters: 173 | Includes bibliographical references and
   index. | Summary: "This book offers a fresh perspective on the social
   life of multilingualism through the lens of linguistic citizenship. Each
   chapter illuminates how multilingualism (in both theory and practice)
   should be, or could be, thought of as inclusive when we recognize what
   multilingual speakers do with language for voice and agency"— Provided
   by publisher. Identifiers: LCCN 2022003120 (print) | LCCN 2022003121 (ebook) | ISBN
   9781800415300 (paperback) | ISBN 9781800415317 (hardback) | ISBN
   9781800415324 (pdf) | ISBN 9781800415331 (epub)
Subjects: LCSH: Multilingualism—Social aspects. | Cultural pluralism. |
   Language policy. | LCGFT: Essays.
Classification: LCC P115.45 .S87 2022 (print) | LCC P115.45 (ebook) | DDC
   306.44/6—dc23/eng/20220218 LC record available at https://lccn.loc.gov/2022003120
LC ebook record available at https://lccn.loc.gov/2022003121

British Library Cataloguing in Publication Data
A catalogue entry for this book is available from the British Library.

ISBN-13: 978-1-80041-531-7 (hbk)
ISBN-13: 978-1-80041-530-0 (pbk)

Multilingual Matters
UK: St Nicholas House, 31–34 High Street, Bristol, BS1 2AW, UK.
USA: Ingram, Jackson, TN, USA.

Website: www.multilingual-matters.com
Twitter: Multi_Ling_Mat
Facebook: https://www.facebook.com/multilingualmatters
Blog: www.channelviewpublications.wordpress.com

The policy of Multilingual Matters/Channel View Publications is to use papers that
are natural, renewable and recyclable products, made from wood grown in
sustainable forests. In the manufacturing process of our books, and to further
support our policy, preference is given to printers that have FSC and PEFC Chain of
Custody certification. The FSC and/or PEFC logos will appear on those books
where full certification has been granted to the printer concerned.

Typeset by Nova Techset Private Limited, Bengaluru and Chennai, India.

For Christopher Stroud

Teacher. Supervisor. Mentor. Colleague. Friend.
Thank you for all your guidance, wisdom and support.

Contents

Contributors

Zannie Bock is an Associate Professor in the Linguistics Department and current Deputy Dean of Teaching and Learning in the Faculty of Arts and Humanities at the University of the Western Cape, South Africa. Her recent publications are in the fields of narrative and discourse analysis, with a focus on racializing discourses among university students, and decolonial pedagogies. She has a long-standing interest in adult literacy, curriculum and materials development, and is the project co-ordinator and co-editor of the first southern African textbook in Linguistics, *Language, Society and Communication: An Introduction* (Van Schaik Publishers). She co-edited *Language and Decoloniality in Higher Education: Reclaiming Voices from the South* (Bloomsbury, 2021, with Christopher Stroud). She also recently co-ordinated (with a student editorial team) a special issue of the journal, *Multilingual Margins*, titled *The Cat's Cradle of Multilingualism*.

Emanuel Bylund (Stellenbosch University and Stockholm University) studies the relationship between language and cognition, and the role of age in language acquisition and loss. His work has appeared in journals such as *Applied Linguistics, Bilingualism: Language and Cognition, Cognition* and *Psychological Science*.

Melanie Cooke is currently a Lecturer in ESOL Education at King's College, London. Her books include *Brokering Britain, Educating Citizens: Exploring ESOL and Citizenship* (2019, with Rob Peutrell), *The Routledge Handbook of Language and Superdiversity* (Routledge, 2019, section editor with James Simpson) and *ESOL: A Critical Guide* (2008, with James Simpson). She has published in *TESOL Quarterly, Language and Education, Linguistics and Education, Language Assessment Quarterly, Journal of Language, Identity and Education* and *Gender and Language*. She was a co-organizer of the ESRC seminar series *Queering ESOL* (with John Gray and Mike Baynham) and has collaborated with Dermot Bryers and Becky Winstanley on several participatory ESOL projects, the most recent being the Leverhulme funded *Our Languages*.

Ana Deumert is Professor of Linguistics at the University of Cape Town. Her research is located in the broad field of African sociolinguistics and has a strong transdisciplinary focus. She has worked on the history of Afrikaans (*The Dynamics of Cape Dutch*, 2004); co-authored *Introducing Sociolinguistics* (2009, with Rajend Mesthrie, Joan Swann and William Leap); and the *Dictionary of Sociolinguistics* (2004, with Joan Swann, Rajend Mesthrie and Theresa Lillis). She has also published extensively on mobile communication from a southern perspective (*Sociolinguistics and Mobile Communication*, 2014). Her current work focuses on decoloniality and southern theory in sociolinguistics and applied linguistics. She also explores the use of language in insurgent political movements, focusing, in particular, on the anti-colonial struggle. She was Editor of *IMPACT – Studies in Language and Society* until 2018); is currently Co-Editor of *Cambridge Approaches to Language Contact* (with Salikoko Mufwene); and Co-Editor of *Edinburgh Sociolinguistics* (with Paul Kerswill). She is a member of the scientific committee of GLOCAL (SOAS) and serves on several editorial boards. She received the Neville Alexander Award for the Promotion of Multilingualism in 2014 and the Humboldt Research Award in 2016.

Kathleen Heugh is a socio-applied linguist whose work has focussed on language policy and planning and multilingual education in sub-Saharan Africa, particularly South Africa. She has led several small, medium and large-scale (country-wide and multi-country) studies of literacy, mother-tongue and multilingual education, and large-scale assessments of multilingual students. She uses multilingual pedagogy and theory in her teaching of English to international students at the University of South Australia.

Amy Hiss is a Linguistics doctoral student at the University of the Western Cape at the Centre for Multilingualism and Diversities Research. Her research focuses on learner agency and African language(s) within the academic space of a former whites only high school in Cape Town and centres on decolonized education within the South African context. Her research forms part of a larger decolonial project led by Christopher Stroud and funded by the NRF. Her recent journal articles are: '"Good schooling" in a race, gender, and class perspective: The reproduction of inequality at a former Model C school in South Africa' (co-authored with Amiena Peck) and forthcoming, 'Turbulent Twitter and the semiotics of protest at an ex-Model C school' (co-authored with Amiena Peck). In 2018, Amy presented the research she did for her Master's degree at a Psycholinguistics workshop hosted by the University of Oslo in Norway and at a Virtual Linguistic Workshop hosted by Amiena Peck at the University of the Western Cape. In 2019, she presented at the Language in Media conference hosted by the University of Rio de Janeiro in Brazil and chaired a workshop hosted by Professor Feliciano Chimbutane in Maputo,

Mozambique. This focused on the processes and practices of community engagement in rural schools in Maputo Province.

Sam Holmes is a teacher and consultant specializing in English as an Additional Language. He has a PhD from King's College London looking at ethnic and linguistic monitoring in schools and is a member of the Hub for Education and Linguistic Diversity based at KCL. Sam has delivered training on catering to the needs of pupils with EAL within mainstream lessons for London Challenge, Teach First, Teach for All and Teach for India, and worked with London Gifted and Talented to help develop a toolkit of strategies for stretching able bilingual students. His work with arts organizations includes developing a series of mother tongue creative writing courses for teenagers on behalf of the Gulbenkian Foundation, curating Translation Nation's film subtitling workshops for Eastside Education, creating the Portuguese language course for Arsenal FC's Double Club scheme, and training professional translators to deliver workshops to children as part of Translators in Schools. He is co-founder and CEO of Causeway Education.

Kenneth Hyltenstam is Professor Emeritus of Bilingualism at Stockholm University. He has published extensively in the area of second language acquisition, specifically on topics such as age and ultimate L2 attainment, markedness, developmental sequences and variability, but his research also covers other topics within the area of bilingualism such as polyglottism and bilingualism and dementia. Edited volumes covering these areas are *Modelling and Assessing Second Language Acquisition* (Multilingual Matters, with Manfred Pienemann); *Bilingualism Across the Lifespan* (Cambridge University Press, 1989, with Loraine K. Obler); *Progression and Regression in Language* (Cambridge University Press, 1993, with Åke Viberg); *Advanced Proficiency and Exceptional Ability in Second Languages* (Mouton de Gruyter, 2016); *High-Level Language Proficiency in Second Language and Multilingual Contexts* (Cambridge University Press, 2018, with Inge Bartning and Lars Fant). In addition, he has contributed to multilingualism in the sociolinguistic and educational fields, as in *Entangled Discourses* (Routledge, 2017, with Caroline Kerfoot). Issues dealt with here include language policy, as well as language maintenance, shift and revitalization with respect to minority languages in Sweden and Norway. He has published widely on language and education issues in the Nordic context, as well as in the global South (Bolivia, Mozambique). He was the Director of the Centre for Research on Bilingualism at Stockholm University (1981–2007 and 2012–2013).

Keshia Jansen is a Master's student and tutor in Department of Linguistics at the University of Western Cape. Her research interests include multilingualism and decoloniality. Her current project focuses on how the members of a local choir draw on their multilingual (and musical) resources in the re-imagining of both new musical styles and participant identities and trajectories. She believes exploring alternative views of multilingualism may offer opportunities for a more cohesive sense of belonging and social justice in a South African society. Keshia has worked with a panel of guest editors to publish a special issue of *Multilingual Margins*, a scholarly journal founded by the Centre for Multilingualism and Diversities Research.

David Karlander is a Society of Fellows postdoctoral fellow in the School of English at the University of Hong Kong. He has held doctoral, research and teaching positions at the Centre for Research for Bilingualism, Stockholm University, and visiting fellowships at the University of the Western Cape and HKU. His research spans linguistics, intellectual history and the sociology of knowledge. Karlander currently investigates the use of international auxiliary languages in workers' movements from 1900 to 1945. He has previously published on Övdalsk language advocacy, graffiti, European language politics and the history of modern linguistic thought.

Caroline Kerfoot is Professor in Bilingualism at the Centre for Research on Bilingualism, Stockholm University. Her research theorizes the entanglements of language, race and social inequities in urban contexts, with a particular focus on southern theory, decolonial pedagogies and epistemic justice. She also has extensive experience of education policy work with trade unions and community-based organizations in South Africa. Her latest book *Towards Epistemic Justice: Language, Identity, and Relations of Knowing in Postcolonial Schools* will be published by Bloomsbury, 2023. Her work has appeared in journals such as *Applied Linguistics, Language and Education, Linguistics and Education, International Multilingual Research Journal, TESOL Quarterly,* and in a variety of edited volumes – most recently, *Reclaiming Voice: Languages and Decoloniality in Higher Education* (Bloomsbury, 2021); *The Multilingual Citizen*, Multilingual Matters, 2018; and *Entangled Discourses: South–North Orders of Visibility* (Routledge, 2017, lead editor with Kenneth Hyltenstam).

Don Kulick is Distinguished University Professor of Anthropology at Uppsala University, Sweden, where he directs the Engaging Vulnerability research programme (www.engagingvulnerability.se), and Chair Professor of Anthropology at Hong Kong University. His most recent books are *A Death in the Rainforest: How a Language and a Way of Life came to an End in Papua New Guinea* (Algonquin Books, 2019) and *A Grammar and Dictionary of Tayap: The Life and Death of a Papuan Language* (de Gruyter Mouton, 2019, with Angela Terrill).

Tommaso M. Milani is Professor of Multilingualism at the University of Gothenburg and Visiting Professor of Linguistics at the University of the Witwatersrand, Johannesburg. His research interests include sociolinguistics, language politics, language ideologies, language, gender and sexuality (with a focus on masculinities), Critical Discourse Analysis, multimodality and performativity theory. He is co-editor of the journal *Language in Society*. He also edits the Bloomsbury book series *Advances in Sociolinguistics* (founded by Sally Johnson).

Marcelyn Oostendorp is a Senior Lecturer in the Department of General Linguistics at Stellenbosch University, South Africa. Her research is primarily concerned with multilingual and multimodal forms of meaning-making in contexts such as education, the media and the workplace.

Amiena Peck is a Senior Lecturer in the Linguistics Department at the University of the Western Cape. She has a keen interest in post-apartheid realities, identity construction and linguistic landscapes. A frequent contributor to the field of linguistic landscapes, she is in the field of gender, sexuality and virtual landscapes.

Ben Rampton is Professor of Applied & Sociolinguistics at King's College London (www.kcl.ac.uk/ldc). His main research focus is interactional sociolinguistics, and his interests cover urban multilingualism, youth, ethnicity and social class, conflict and (in)securitization, and language education policy and practice. He is the author of *Crossing: Language & Ethnicity among Adolescents* (Longman, 1995/Routledge, 2018); *Language in Late Modernity: Interaction in an Urban School* (Cambridge University Press, 2006); and *Linguistic Practice in Changing Conditions* (Multilingual Matters, 2021). He co-authored *Researching Language: Issues of Power and Method* (Routledge, 1992), and co-edited *The Language, Ethnicity & Race Reader* (Routledge, 2003) and *Language & Superdiversity* (Routledge, 2015). He also edits *Working Papers in Urban Language and Literacies*. He was founding convener of the UK Linguistic Ethnography Forum, directed the King's ESRC Interdisciplinary Social Science Doctoral Training Centre from 2011 to 2014 and is regularly involved in adult ESOL teaching.

Linus Salö holds a PhD in Bilingualism and is currently an Associate Professor at the Centre for Research on Bilingualism, Stockholm University, where he teaches and supervises at all levels. Through the Division of History of Science, Technology and Environment, KTH Royal Institute of Technology, he is also active in the knowledge platform Making Universities Matter, funded by Sweden's innovation agency Vinnova. Within this context, he is editing a volume on the societal value and knowledge effects of the human sciences in Sweden. More broadly, his research interests include multilingualism, sociolinguistics of science, sociology of knowledge, linguistic minority education and science–society interaction. His work has featured in many leading journals, as well as in volumes produced by renowned publishers. He is the author of the book *The Sociolinguistics of Academic Publishing: Language and the Practices of Homo Academicus* (Palgrave Macmillan, 2017).

Christopher Stroud is Emeritus Professor of Linguistics at the University of the Western Cape and Professor of Transnational Bilingualism at Stockholm University. His current research focuses on practices and ideologies of multilingualism in Southern Africa, specifically *Linguistic Citizenship,* as a way of rethinking the role of language in brokering diversity in a decolonial framework. He has published in English, Swedish and Portuguese in journals such as *Language Policy, Journal of Sociolinguistics, Journal of Linguistic Anthropology, Sociolinguistic Studies, Semiotics, International Journal of Bilingualism and Bilingual Education, Journal of Multilingual and Multicultural Development, MAN* and *Multilingual Margins* (which he co-founded). He has edited and authored a number of volumes, most recently: *The Multilingual Citizen: Towards a Politics of Language for Agency and Change,* (Multilingual Matters, 2018, co-edited with Lisa Lim and Lionel Wee); *The Sociolinguistics of the South* (Routledge, 2021, co-edited with Kathleen Heugh, Peter da Costa and Kerry Taylor Leech); Critical Studies in Multilingualism; and *Language and Decoloniality in Higher Education: Reclaiming Voices from the South* (Bloomsbury, 2021, co-edited with Zannie Bock). He co-edits a series for Bloomsbury Press together with Kathleen Heugh and Piet van Avermaet titled *Multilingualisms and Diversities in Education.* He is a Fellow of the Academy of Science in South Africa (ASSAf), a Member of the UNESCO Chair *Multilingualism and Language Planning*; Scientific Board Member: The Centre for Multilingualism across the Lifespan (MultiLing), Oslo University.

Lauren van Niekerk is a Master's student and tutor in the Linguistic Department at University of the Western Cape. In July 2019, she presented her honours research, titled *The Role of Small Stories in the Racial Positioning of UWC Students in a Focus Group Interview,* at the Language in Media Conference (LiM19) hosted in Brazil. Her current research focus considers the lived experiences of colouredness through the lens of narratives and language, and how this is navigated by participants in both online and offline contexts.

Lionel Wee is a Provost's Chair Professor in the Department of English Language & Literature and Vice-Dean of the Research Division, Faculty of Arts and Social Sciences, National University of Singapore. His research interests include language policy, World Englishes and general issues in sociolinguistics and pragmatics. His recent books include *The Singlish*

Controversy (Cambridge University Press, 2018) and *Language, Space and Cultural Play: Theorizing Affect in the Semiotic Landscape* (Cambridge University Press, 2019, with Robbie Goh). He is currently working on *The Communicative Linguistic Landscape* (contracted, Routledge, 2021).

Quentin Williams is the Director of the Centre for Multilingualism and Diversities Research (CMDR) as well as an Associate Professor of Sociolinguistics in the Linguistics Department at the University of the Western Cape and a Ghent Visiting Professor (*Leerstoel Houer*) at the Centre for Afrikaans and the study of South Africa at Ghent University (2020/2021). His most recent books are *Making Sense of People and Place in Linguistic Landscapes* (Bloomsbury, 2018, with Amiena Peck and Christopher Stroud); and *Neva Again: Hip Hop Art, Activism and Education in Post-apartheid South Africa* (HSRC Press, 2019, with Adam Haupt, H. Samy Alim and Emile Jansen). He is the Co-Editor of *Multilingual Margins: A Journal of Multilingualism from the Periphery*.

Foreword: Linguistic Citizenship – Unlabelled Forerunners and Recent Trajectories

Kenneth Hyltenstam and Caroline Kerfoot

Introduced at the turn of the millennium, the term 'Linguistic Citizenship' (Stroud, 2001) now has a history of almost 20 years. The thinking behind the term, however, has a much longer record. There were many forerunners in Christopher Stroud's work, which, when viewed in retrospect, all reveal the kernel of concern with the role of language – and representations of language – in the production of marginalized, vulnerable and silenced voices that is at the centre of Linguistic Citizenship.

The thinking and research focus building up to the final coinage of the term emerged and were developed successively over an extended time in a seemingly heterogeneous medley of applied research areas. This can be seen in several of Christopher Stroud's diverse contributions to linguistics over the decades before 2000. They include themes, topics and agents as varied as those implicated by the following list of issues: a conceptual critique of the notion of semilingualism (Stroud, 1978); communicative practices in schizophrenia (Stroud, ms., nd.); communicative agency in bilingual dementia (Hyltenstam & Stroud, 1989); the intention and meaning of Taiap/Tok Pisin code-switching in Gapun, an isolated small village in Papua New Guinea (Stroud, 1992); patterns of literacy in Gapun (Kulick & Stroud, 1990); language shift and maintenance in the Swedish-Saami context (Hyltenstam & Stroud, 1991; Hyltenstam et al., 1999); the use of African languages in education in Mozambique (Stroud & Tuzine, 1998), a large-scale sociolinguistic review of oral Portuguese in Maputo, Mozambique (Gonçalves & Stroud, 1999, 2002; Stroud & Gonçalves, 1997a, 1997b, 2000); the ideology and political rhetoric about Portuguese in Mozambican language policy and planning (Stroud, 1999); English in Singapore (summarized later in Stroud & Wee, 2012). This seemingly heterogeneity of topics, spanning linguistic/communicative pathologies and Melanesian sociolinguistics to Nordic language politics, Singaporean multilingualism and Southern African educational linguistics is linked by aspects that are inherent components in the idea of Linguistic Citizenship: they all address linguistic manifestations of vulnerability, and they are all concerned with various degrees of lack of agency, with unheard voices, with the dominated constituency in unbalanced power relationships. Although the contexts are spread around the world, they illustrate the North–South relationship, many of them long before this distinction had entered the academic discourse. The diverse observations made and analyses undertaken in these heterogeneous areas have in different ways contributed to dense theorization through the introduction of the notion of Linguistic Citizenship. Trying to be more concrete, we will briefly review how some of these themes, which, together with the choice and variety of data on which they are based, can be seen as forerunners of Linguistic Citizenship theory development.

The first example is one of Christopher Stroud's earliest publications, if not the first one. Stroud (1978) was one of the early critics of the notion of semilingualism, which had gained wide currency in Scandinavian academia and beyond only 10 years after its introduction to a wider audience in a book with the title *Tvåspråkighet eller halvspråkighet?* [*Bilingualism or semilingualism?*] (Hansegård, 1968). Hansegård defined semilingualism as the unfavourable linguistic (and psychological) consequences of an early deprivation of the native language, and he used the term double semilingualism for 'a semi-command of Swedish [the second language] and a semi-command of the mother tongue [the first language]' (Hansegård, 1968: 128). In a multilayered analysis of the concept from both cognitive and sociolinguistic perspectives, Stroud notes that the concept lacks reliable empirical evidence. However, the main point of the analysis deals with the widespread use of the term semilingual in society at large and the stigma it attaches to individuals labelled as semilinguals. Similar critiques were aired a few years later when the notion of semilingualism had gone global via its spread to Canada and the US (see e.g. Martin-Jones & Romaine, 1986; see also Salö & Karlander, this volume). As a typical concept of deficit with an unclear definition and inadequate empirical basis, it created harmful consequences in terms of low expectations of academic success, high expectations of psychological difficulties, and even criminality. Revealing such serious consequences of a linguistic label is, indeed, compatible with a Linguistic Citizenship perspective.

A second example is that of Taiap/Tok Pisin code-switching in Gapun, as noted above, a small village in Papua New Guinea (Stroud, 1992). Taiap is the traditionally spoken language of Gapun, at the time of analysis actively used by fewer than the approximately 100 inhabitants of the village; as of 1987, no child under the age of 10 actively spoke Taiap (Kulick, 1992: 7). It is classified as an isolate Papuan language, probably belonging to the Sepic-Ramu phylum. Tok Pisin is the most widely spoken language in Papua New Guinea and also the official language of the country together with English and Hiri Motu. Stroud (1992) presents an analysis of a long talk given by a male villager to an audience in one of the 'men's houses', where the 'orator' throughout the talk intricately switches between the two languages. It can be understood that the speaker needs some help in organizing a burial ceremony, but this request is expressed extremely implicitly and indirectly, among other things, with many seeming contradictions. Parts of the talk are verbatim repetitions in each language of the same content. The context for this is the fact that in a Melanesian egalitarian society like the one under study, 'no relationship, not even that between adult and child, is understood by villagers to involve the legitimate power to order another person to do something against his or her will' (Stroud, 1992: 9). So why is it that the speaker uses all his linguistic repertoires in this instance? The study highlights a context where language is not primarily seen as a reflection of a person's individual thoughts or intentions, where meaning is constructed collectively, where some meanings are hidden, and where consensus is the overriding principle. It concludes that 'Western' perspectives where meaning is attached to individual code-switches cannot be applied to this context. The analysis further underscores the implausibility that sociolinguistic accounts of code-switching prevalent at the time which assumed that 'members of a bilingual speech community attach different identities, rights and obligations to each of their languages' (Stroud, 1992: 5) would give a reasonable insight into why Taiap/Tok Pisin code-switching occurs in this talk. The analysis is an example of the tenet held in a Linguistic Citizenship perspective that southern realities become invisible and deformed when analyzed with northern tools, an early example of identifying the effects of 'research through imperial eyes' (Smith, 1999: 42). It also contributes to challenging the adequacy of these very tools even for northern contexts.

The final example comes from a set of studies of communication disorders in bilinguals diagnosed with Alzheimer's dementia carried out in Stockholm in the 1980s. People suffering from dementia constitute a communicatively marginalized group generally, but aging migrants in this category, increasing in number along with the ever-growing migration flows, are especially defenseless because they are often dependent on interlocutors of their second language, a language that has been shown to be more vulnerable in dementia than a first language, even in cases where the second language has dominated their communicative interaction during most of their adult lives. For example, in Hyltenstam and Stroud (1989), which is a detailed case study, it was shown that GM, a German L1/Swedish L2 bilingual, had more topic-focused contributions, had fewer lexical search problems, used more relevant second-pair turns and more often complied with communicative task demands in conversations with a German-speaking interlocutor than in conversations with a Swedish-speaking interlocutor. Particularly interesting was the fact that GM never slipped into the other language (Swedish) in interaction with his German interlocutor. With the Swedish interlocutor this happened frequently. This is an obvious case where the potential agency of this category of speakers is systematically stronger in conversations with speakers of their first language, a condition to which they are in many cases denied access. Revealing such patterns is, again, an example of demonstrating obvious contextual requirements necessary for empowering marginalized groups and individuals, clearly a forerunner to Linguistic Citizenship.

The first explicit mention of Linguistic Citizenship, uniting a complex set of ideas as it does, came out of work in the late 1990s that attempted to delve into the factors behind the differential successes of bilingual and mother-tongue programmes in countries of the South (Stroud, 2001, 2003). This work showed contradictory results: programmes that operated under seemingly comparable conditions 'resulted in very dissimilar outcomes in different contexts' (Stroud, 2018: 18). A closer look, however, revealed that the failure of many programmes in reaching their goals 'could be traced to the more or less complete absence of indigenous and local participation in areas of curriculum design, materials development etc.' (Stroud, 2002: 82) and that solutions developed with strong parental participation by Western elites, such as Canadian immersion or European Union bilingual school models, were not considered viable in 'developing' contexts. This strong support for grassroots points of view is embedded in Linguistic Citizenship and has been presented as paradigmatically opposed to the Linguistic Human Rights perspective. The differences between the two have been discussed in terms of agency, language vs. repertoires, recognized vs. non-recognized varieties, etc. (Stroud, 2001, 2009; Stroud & Heugh, 2004). The links between multilingualism, marginalization and vulnerability were further developed in the early 2000s, emphasizing that a lack of recognition for local linguistic resources has a direct bearing on political, economic and social participation, along with other dimensions of well-being such as health (Hyltenstam & Stroud, 2016 [2002]).

It was this encounter with the realities of the global and metaphorical South which came to have – and continues to have – a catalytic influence on the subsequent development of the notion of Linguistic Citizenship as a contribution to a theory of critical multilingualism and to a decolonial sociolinguistics. From its early formulation, with a significant contribution from Kathleen Heugh's work on South African language politics and practices (see Heugh, 2003), Linguistic Citizenship carried a critique of the legitimacy of 'majority speaking, official-language society's validation of language practices solely in terms of the formal, public sphere and a systemic construct of language' (Stroud & Heugh, 2004: 214). An illustrative example is an analysis of how Mozambican women street vendors used multilingual repertoires to negotiate a political position in the first general elections (Stroud, 2004). Increasingly, attention has focused on how encounters across difference are mediated linguistically to offer a space for interrupting colonial relationships (e.g. Stroud & Williams, 2017). This work focuses on the manifold ways in which alternative voices can be inserted into processes and structures, especially those dominated by the 'zombie discourses' (Bock & Stroud, 2018) of a racialized past. Stroud and Guissemo (2017: 42) illustrate how the lingering effects of colonial social logics on postcolonial realities dictates that African languages in Mozambique 'dwell either in the past or in the future, but never in the present', an observation that applies to many other Southern sites. Linguistic Citizenship, however, highlights the importance of practices where speakers exercise control over the languages in their repertoires, however fleetingly, seizing the opportunity to forge decolonial subjectivities and articulate claims for justice from new spaces (Peck & Stroud, 2015; Stroud, 2016; Stroud & Jegels, 2014; Stroud & Mpendukana, 2009; Williams & Stroud, 2014). Where liberal perspectives on multilingualism allow other languages a space within existing frameworks of experience, Linguistic Citizenship seeks to rupture colonial regimes of language by building 'an inclusiveness of voice in ways that repair and rejuvenate relationships to self and others' (Stroud, 2018: 36), thus opening the possibility of a restorative mutuality.

Alongside this focus on non-institutionalized sites of activity, the potential of Linguistic Citizenship for the formal sphere of education in both Southern and Northern contexts has also been explored. Here multilingualism is seen as a transformative epistemology and methodology of diversity while the challenges involved in implementing such a vision are acutely perceived (Chimbutane & Stroud, 2012; Stroud & Heugh, 2011; Stroud & Kerfoot, 2013, 2021; Stroud & Wee, 2010). In this regard, Linguistic Citizenship emphasizes that linguistic diversity is generally entangled with the sociopolitics of inequality and therefore that remedies directed to language alone can seldom provide adequate solutions to supposed language problems (and *vice versa*).

Linguistic Citizenship is thus seen as a geopolitical Southern and decolonial concept (Stroud, 2018: 18). It is important to keep in mind, though, that south and north should not be seen as geographical locations *per se*, but as metaphors: 'a South [...] also exists in the global North, in the form of excluded, silenced and marginalized populations' (Santos, 2012: 51).

The theorizing of Linguistic Citizenship is clearly anchored in the millennium shifts in sociolinguistics, social anthropology and political theory. As noted by Rampton *et al.* (2018, and this volume) in their review of the notion of Linguistic Citizenship, Stroud repeatedly refers to two political theorists, Nancy Fraser (see e.g. Fraser, 1995) for her notion of 'transformative remedies' of inequalities (as opposed to 'affirmative remedies') and Engin Isin (see e.g. Isin, 2017) for his notion 'acts of citizenship': 'citizenship is not a status, but an act ... acts of citizenship are the practices whereby new actors, seeking recognition in the public space in order to determine a new course of events, shift the location of agency and voice' (Stroud, 2018: 21, italics in original).

Engaging with scholars as diverse as Agamben, Bloch, Fanon, Glissant, Levinas, Mbembe and Santos, to name but a few, Linguistic Citizenship offers to sociolinguistics a remarkable, pluriversal depth and rigour, solidifying its often-tenuous connections with philosophy, sociology and political theory. Its 'politics through/of language for the present' (Stroud, 2018: 10) simultaneously holds the seeds of transformative, linguistically mediated futures.

As outlined above, the theoretical implications of sociolinguistic analyses based on a Linguistic Citizenship perspective are far-reaching. Resonating with, and often prefiguring, recent developments in sociolinguistics such as raciolinguistics (Alim *et al.*, 2016; Rosa & Flores, 2017), decoloniality, embodiment and temporality, Linguistic Citizenship provides a means of enlarging knowledge of agents, practices and processes which could lay the basis for what Papadoupolous (2011) calls 'alter-ontologies', critiquing and replacing destructive institutional structures, classifications, and the technologies that sustain them.

The fundamental focus of Linguistic Citizenship has come to be on the role of voice, linguistic repertoire, communicative practices, agency and societal transformation of previously invisibilized constituencies. In other words, it focuses on the involvement of local communities and often silenced individuals in matters affecting the inequalities they suffer and, generally, their life trajectories and living conditions. At whatever point power imbalances exist in societies, the perspective behind Linguistic Citizenship is that of the dominated, the unheard. However, given the complexity of multiple, intersecting power relationships in any society, Linguistic Citizenship can have liberating and emancipating value for everyone.

The framework can typically be applied to multilingual sites with unequal status for different languages (which is more or less universal) as in the case of having a say in the planning and implementation of bilingual programmes, but more generally, to all kinds of situations where negotiations and other linguistic struggles occur, aiming at the transformation and elimination of inequalities between groups along multiple, intersectional axes of difference.

This book has an important role to play in pursuing the key questions that underpin Stroud's scholarship: What theorization of language and politics best allows for an understanding of multilingualism as a transformative technology for social change? What sort of questions should we be asking of language if we wish to become truly ethical, democratic subjects?

References

Alim, H.S., Rickford, J.R. and Ball, A.F. (eds) (2016) *Raciolinguistics: How Language Shapes Our Ideas about Race*. New York: Oxford University Press.

Bock, Z. and Stroud, C. (2018) Zombie landscapes: Apartheid traces in the discourses of young South Africans. In A. Peck, Q. Williams and C. Stroud (eds) *Making Sense of People, Place and Linguistic Landscapes* (pp. 11–28). London: Bloomsbury Press.

Chimbutane, F. and Stroud, C. (eds) (2012) *Educação bilingue em Moçambique: Reflectindo criticamente sobre políticas e práticas*. Maputo: Texto Editores.

Fraser, N. (1995) From redistribution to recognition? Dilemmas of justice in a 'post-socialist' age. *New Left Review* 212, 68–93.

Gonçalves, P. and Stroud, C. (eds) (1999) *Panorama do Português oral de Maputo. Vol. III, Struturas gramaticais do Português: Problemas e exercicios. Cadernos de Pesquisa* 27. Maputo: Instituto National do Desenvolvimiento da Educação.

Gonçalves, P. and Stroud, C. (eds) (2002) *Panorama do Português oral de Maputo. Vol. V, Vocabulário básico do Português. Dicionário de regências. Cadernos de Pesquisa* 41. Maputo: Instituto National do Desenvolvimiento da Educação.

Hansegård, N.E. (1968) *Tvåspråkighet eller halvspråkighet?[Bilingualism or Semilingualism?]*. Stockholm: Aldus/Bonniers.

Heugh, K. (2003) A re-take on bilingual education in and for South Africa. In K. Fraurud and K. Hyltenstam (eds) *Multilingualism in Global and Local Perspectives. Selected Papers from the 8th Nordic Conference on Bilingualism, November 1–3, 2001, Stockholm-Rinkeby* (pp. 47–70). Stockholm: Centre for Research on Bilingualism and Rinkeby Institute of Multilingual Research.

Hyltenstam, K. and Stroud, C. (1989) Bilingualism in Alzheimer's dementia: Two case studies. In K. Hyltenstam and L.K. Obler (eds) *Bilingualism Across the Lifespan. Aspects of Acquisition, Maturity, and Loss* (pp. 202–226). Cambridge: Cambridge University Press.

Hyltenstam, K. and Stroud, C. (1991) *Språkbyte och språkbevarande. Om samiskan och andra minoritetsspråk [Language Shift and Language Maintenance. On Saami and other Minority Languages]*. Lund: Studentlitteratur.

Hyltenstam, K. and Stroud, C. (2016 [2002]) At the nexus of vulnerability: Multilingualism in development. Paper 200, *Working Papers in Urban Language & Literacies* (at www.academia.edu).

Hyltenstam, K., Stroud, C. and Svonni, M. (1999) Språkbyte, språkbevarande, revitalisering. Samiskans ställning i svenska Sápmi. [Language shift, language maintenance and revitalization. The status of Saami in Swedish Sápmi]. In K. Hyltenstam (ed.) *Sveriges sju inhemska språk – ett minoritetsspråksperspektiv* (pp. 41–97). Lund: Studentlitteratur.

Isin, E. (2017) Performative citizenship. In A. Shadhar, R. Bauboeck, I. Bloemraad and M. Vink (eds) *The Handbook of Citizenship* (pp. 500–523). Oxford: Oxford University Press.

Kulick, D. (1992) *Language Shift and Cultural Reproduction. Socialization, Self, and Syncretism in a Papua New Guinean Village*. Cambridge: Cambridge University Press.

Kulick, D. and Stroud, C. (1990) Christianity, cargo and ideas of self: Patterns of literacy in a Papua New Guinean village. *Man* 25, 286–304.

Martin-Jones, M. and Romaine, S. (1986) Semilingualism: A half-baked theory of communicative competence. *Applied Linguistics* 7 (1), 26–38.

Papadopoulos, D. (2011) Alter-ontologies: Towards a constituent politics in technoscience. *Social Studies of Science* 41 (2), 177–201.

Peck, A. and Stroud, C. (2015) Skinscapes. *Linguistic Landscape* 1 (1–2), 133–151.

Rampton, B., Cooke, M. and Holmes, S. (2018) Sociolinguistic Citizenship. *Journal of Social Science Education* 17 (4), 70–83.

Rosa, J. and Flores, N. (2017) Unsettling race and language: Toward a raciolinguistic perspective. *Language in Society* 46 (5), 621–647.

Santos, B. de S. (2012) Public sphere and epistemologies of the South. *Africa Development* 37 (1), 43–67.

Smith, L.T. (1999) *Decolonizing Methodologies: Research and Indigenous Peoples*. London: Zed Books.

Stroud, C. (1978) The concept of semilingualism. *Studies in General Linguistics Dedicated to Bertil Malmberg by Students and Colleagues on the Occasion of his 65th Birthday*

22nd April 1978. Working Papers 16 (pp. 153–172). Lund: Phonetic Laboratory, Department of General Linguistics, Lund University.

Stroud, C. (1992) The problem of intention and meaning in code-switching. *Text* 12, 127–155.

Stroud, C. (1999) Portuguese as ideology and politics in Mozambique: Semiotic (re)constructions of a postcolony. In J. Blommaert (ed.) *Language Ideological Debates* (pp. 343–380). Berlin: Mouton de Gruyter.

Stroud, C. (2001) African mother-tongue programmes and the politics of language: Linguistic citizenship versus linguistic human rights. *Journal of Multilingual and Multicultural Development* 22 (4), 339–355.

Stroud, C. (2002) Framing Bourdieu socioculturally: Alternative forms of linguistic legitimacy in postcolonial Mozambique. *Multilingua* 21 (2–3), 247–273.

Stroud, C. (2003) Retheorising a politics of language for development and education. In K. Fraurud and K. Hyltenstam (eds) *Multilingualism in Global and Local Perspectives. Selected Papers from the 8th Nordic Conference on Bilingualism, November 1–3, 2001, Stockholm-Rinkeby* (pp. 17–29). Stockholm: Centre for Research on Bilingualism and Rinkeby Institute of Multilingual Research.

Stroud, C. (2004) The performativity of codeswitching. *International Journal of Bilingualism* 8 (2), 145–166.

Stroud, C. (2009) A postliberal critique of language rights: Toward a politics of language for a linguistics of contact. In J.E. Petrovic (ed.) *International Perspectives on Bilingual Education: Policy, Practice and Controversy* (pp. 191–218). Charlotte, NC: Information Age Publishing.

Stroud, C. (2015) Linguistic citizenship as utopia. *Multilingual Margins* 2 (2), 20–37.

Stroud, C. (2016) Turbulent linguistic landscapes and the semiotics of citizenship. In R. Blackwood, E. Lanza and H. Woldemariam (eds) *Negotiating and Contesting Identities in Linguistic Landscapes* (pp. 3–18). London: Bloomsbury Academic.

Stroud, C. (2018) Linguistic Citizenship. In L. Lim, C. Stroud and L. Wee (eds) *The Multilingual Citizen: Towards a Politics of Language for Agency and Change* (pp. 17–39). Bristol: Multilingual Matters.

Stroud, C. (ms., nd.) Language in schizophrenia.

Stroud, C. and Gonçalves, P. (eds) (1997a) *Panorama do Português oral de Maputo. Vol. I: Objectivos e métodos. Cadernos de Pesquisa* 22. Maputo: Instituto National do Desenvolvimiento da Educação.

Stroud, C. and Gonçalves, P. (eds) (1997b) *Panorama do Português oral de Maputo.* (Vol. II). *A constução du um banco de 'erros'. Cadernos de Pesquisa* 24. Maputo: Instituto National do Desenvolvimiento da Educação.

Stroud, C. and Gonçalves, P. (eds) (2000) *Panorama do Português oral de Maputo. Vol. I". Vocabulário básico do Português (espaço, tempo e quantidade): Contextos e prática pedagógica. Cadernos de Pesquisa* 36. Maputo: Instituto National do Desenvolvimiento da Educação.

Stroud, C. and Guissemo, M. (2017) Linguistic messianism: Multilingualism in Mozambique. In A.E. Ebongue, and E. Hurst (eds) *Sociolinguistics in African Contexts* (pp. 35–51). Cham: Springer International.

Stroud, C. and Heugh, C. (2004) Linguistic human rights and linguistic citizenship. In D. Patrick and J. Freedland (eds) *Language Rights and Language Survival: A Sociolinguistic Exploration* (pp. 191–218). Manchester: St Jerome.

Stroud, C. and Heugh, K. (2011) Language in education. In R. Mesthrie (ed.) *The Cambridge Handbook of Sociolinguistics* (pp. 413–439). Cambridge: Cambridge University Press.

Stroud, C. and Jegels, D. (2014) Semiotic landscapes and mobile narrations of place: Performing the local. *International Journal of the Sociology of Language* 228, 179–199.

Stroud, C. and Kerfoot, C. (2013) Towards rethinking multilingualism and language policy for academic literacies. *Linguistics and Education* 24 (4), 396–405.

Stroud, C. and Kerfoot, C. (2021) Decolonizing higher education: Multilingualism, linguistic citizenship and epistemic justice. In Z. Bock and C. Stroud (eds) *Languages and Literacies in Higher Education: Reclaiming Voices from the South* (pp. 21–51). London: Bloomsbury.

Stroud, C. and Mpendukana, S. (2009) Towards a material ethnography of linguistic landscape: Multilingualism, mobility and space in a South African township. *Journal of Sociolinguistics* 13 (3), 363–386.

Stroud, C. and Tuzine, A. (eds) (1998) *Uso de linguas africanas no ensino. Problemas e perspectivas. Cadernos de Pesquisa* 26. Maputo: Instituto National do Desenvolvimiento da Educação.

Stroud, C. and Wee, L. (2010) Language policy and planning in Singaporean late modernity. In L. Lim, A. Pakir and L. Wee (eds) *English in Singapore: Modernity and Management* (pp. 181–204). Hong Kong: Hong Kong University Press.

Stroud, C. and Wee, L. (2012) *Style, Identity and Literacy: English in Singapore*. Bristol: Multilingual Matters.

Stroud, C. and Williams, Q. (2017) Multilingualism as utopia: Meaning making in the periphery. *AILA Review* 30 (1), 167–188.

Williams, Q. E. and Stroud, C. (2014) Battling the race: Stylizing language and coproducing whiteness and colouredness in a freestyle rap performance. *Journal of Linguistic Anthropology* 24 (3), 277–293.

1 Introduction

Quentin Williams, Ana Deumert and
Tommaso M. Milani

Introduction

The world, from the global south to the global north, remains an unequal place, with language and multilingual practices involved in these inequalities in a myriad of ways. However, historically marginalized communities and individuals are redefining what it means to express one's agency and voice through multilingualism to enjoy the benefit of full citizenship. In the struggle to redress the current fragmentation of ethics (see Stroud & Williams, 2017), economic and ecological meltdown and linguistic discrimination brought about by colonialism, capitalism, racism and globalization, one challenge, in particular, remains. This challenge is how to transform the institutions and instruments of power that designed colonial governmentality while, at the same time, building a decolonial, anti-sexist, anti-racist, anti-homophobic and anti-capitalist society to provide access, equity and success for all. Key to this project is understanding the transformative power of multilingualism; its unequal uptake and distribution; and the intended and unintended consequences of liberating and constraining linguistic agency and voice as the realization of Linguistic Citizenship.

In 2019, Rhodes University (South Africa) issued a call for applications for its newly established MA Creative Writing degree (see Figure 1.1). This one-year degree programme comprises 16 weeks of intensive course work and assessments and a final creative writing project. It invites prospective writers to pen poetry, prose, graphic novels and hybrid genres in English, isiXhosa, Afrikaans and – notably – Kaaps. It is now in its second year.

The advertisement shown in Figure 1.1 is in English and Kaaps. A close study of its visual grammar reveals that although the name of the university and motto is in English (on top) as well as the search and contact details (at the bottom), and named languages such as English, isiXhosa and Afrikaans are mentioned, it is the explicit use of Kaaps which is significant for several reasons. Firstly, the statuses of English, isiXhosa and Afrikaans are enshrined in the constitution. As official languages, they are entitled to legal parity, even though isiXhosa, like other African languages, remains marginalized. Language communities and individuals

MA in Kreatiewe Skryfwêk 2021

CALL VI APPLICATIONS

Voltydse study oo een jaa, Februarie- November.

Engels, isiXhosa, Afrikaans, Kaaps

Intensive coursework oo 16 wieke, gevolg dee 'n kreatiewe projek

Poetry, Prose, Graphic Novels, Hybrid Genres.

Afslytingsdatum vi applications is 28 Augustus 2020

www.ru.ac.za/schooloflanguages/creativewriting/
www.facebook.com/RhodesUniversityMACW/

Figure 1.1 Rhodes University's MA Creative Writing advertisement in Kaaps

who primarily use English as a first language have long enjoyed full access to all levels of education and the economy. This has also held true for those who primarily use Afrikaans as a first language. This is not the case for speakers of Kaaps. This advertisement challenges the presumption that the constitutional status of Afrikaans includes Kaaps, and demonstrates that Kaaps is not coextensive with Afrikaans, but distinct from it. The use of Kaaps can be interpreted as an act of Linguistic Citizenship that asserts the presence of Kaaps as a medium of artistic expression as well as of teaching and learning. The language choice in the advertisements shifts the politics of language in significant ways, by empowering a thus far marginalized 'home language'.

The recognition, use and inclusion of Kaaps as a creative form at the level of higher education is supported by the current decolonial *zeitgeist*. It is a critical decolonial manoeuvre against apartheid Afrikaans literary knowledge systems and coloniality narratives of Afrikaans *sui generis*. Its emplacement in the advertisement of a historically white university is significant given that universities in South Africa are attempting to decolonize. Institutions such as Rhodes University are discovering that the recognition of historically marginalized varieties such as Kaaps challenges entrenched and complex matrices of power and resources that white supremacist *knowledging* continues to enjoy. The inclusion of Kaaps is but a small step towards the transformation of university curricula (Jansen, 2019). In addition, the promotion of Kaaps provides not only a vision to its speakers of what is to come in terms of how Kaaps is recast as a 'language' of power in the academy, but also helps them to take one more step away from mainstream, standard, academic and white Afrikaans creative writing cultures in university classrooms, which had previously refused the cultural and socioeconomic experiences of Kaaps speakers, as well as their voices, agency and futures in literary texts.

Crucial to understanding the Linguistic Citizenship of speakers of Kaaps, the advertisement speaks to the long struggle of bringing Kaaps as a peripheral 'language' into the centre of knowledge creation. This struggle is bookended by an initial attempt to capture space at the university level under apartheid (Carstens & Le Cordeur, 2016), and the intellectualization and institutionalization of participatory spaces for Kaaps writers in literary, basic education and university spaces; spaces that have always privileged white varieties of English and Afrikaans at the expense of so-called 'coloured' speakers of those varieties.[1]

The struggle for the recognition and institutionalization of Kaaps and the empowerment of speakers of Kaaps to live out fully their (linguistic) citizenship is a long and protracted one. Kaaps has always been a language variety without an army and a navy and, since colonialization at the Cape and preceding the standardization of Afrikaans, it was first heard coming out of the mouths of the indentured Indigenous as well as enslaved populations. The ways of speaking that developed in the high-contact scenario of the Cape included a wide range of languages: local Khoe and San languages, languages from across Africa, South East Asia and Madagascar. In addition, colonial trade languages were used, namely, Creole Portuguese and Bazaar Malay. From the late 18th century onwards Arabic was increasingly used among the growing Muslim population (Davids, 2011). In colonial times, the communicative space was complex: it included a well-crystalized pidgin (basilectal varieties), creolized forms of speech (mesolectal varieties) as well as acrolectal varieties which represented locally inflected forms of Dutch (often referred to as Kaaps-Hollands) (Den Besten, 2012; Deumert, 2004). Regional dialects emerged in the 19th century, as well as social and racialized dialects. Kaaps Vernacular Afrikaans is a form of Afrikaans that emerged under the influence of English and was spoken mainly by the working classes. Cape Afrikaans is also known as Southwestern Afrikaans; it includes the dialects of the Boland, Swartland and the Overberg region, as well as those spoken in the north-east of the country. Heavily creolized varieties continued in particular regions such as along the Orange River (*Oranje Rivier* Afrikaans).

This linguistic diversity *within* Afrikaans was erased by the standardization of Afrikaans during the late 19th and early 20th centuries which was a heavily racialized project, closely linked to white Afrikaner nationalism. As a result, Kaaps became racialized to the same degree as the identity and citizenship of its speakers: the (mainly) so-called 'coloured' speakers with wretched, uncouth tongues of Afrikaans, who were often referred to in derogatory racist ways. They were positioned as speakers of 'Kitchen Afrikaans,' coloured people's parlance or patois, 'coloured language,' 'coloured Afrikaans', 'Capey', 'Gammat-taal' (Blignaut, 2014: 2;

Small, 1972) and 'Gamtaal', the latter Cape Flats dialect of Afrikaans that 'has stereotypically been associated with notions of the "authentic" working-class coloured' (Haupt, 2001: 173).

But in spite of erasure, racial suppression, Kaaps became a resistant language (see Hendricks, 2012; Small, 1987). Increasingly, Kaaps activists began to ask for recognition of their way of speaking and demanded sociolinguistic agency. As Dyers cogently puts it, the realization of the restoration of dignity and humanity in Kaaps 'are indicative of the fact that its users are finding their voice ... [and] ... a growing self-confidence' (Cloete, 2012: 122; Dyers, 2015: 62).

Yet, in post-apartheid South Africa, speakers of Kaaps still do not enjoy full Linguistic Citizenship: Kaaps is not recognized in the Constitution. It is not seen consistently across the linguistic landscape nor is it a language of power, used in government institutions and the education system. Informally, speakers of Kaaps act out and practise their use of it as a language across modalities that matter to them, where they share in the cultural, spatial and interactional power, with the hope it will be included in the school curriculum, used as a language of communication in the economy, despite prevailing negative attitudes and a political discourse narrated for them in *suiwer* (pure) Afrikaans.

Linguistic Citizenship by and for Multilingual Speakers

We chose the above example as an entry point that illustrates the issues that speakers of Kaaps face at all levels of society and institutions, ultimately affecting their voice and agency. This is not unique to Kaaps, or South Africa, but similar – yet also different – for speakers of other historically marginalized languages across the world. Most importantly for the purpose of this volume, the example raises a question that is at the heart of Linguistic Citizenship: what benefits would historically marginalized speakers, living in a country with a long history of racism, gain if they enjoyed all the benefits of their Linguistic Citizenship?

As Stroud put it two decades ago, Linguistic Citizenship seeks to capture:

> the situation where speakers themselves exercise control over their language, deciding *what* languages are, and what they *mean*, and where language issues ... are discursively tied to a range of social issues – policy issues of questions of equity. (Stroud, 2001: 353)

It is a concept that:

> permits multiple (democratic, participatory) approaches to citizenship issues based on an idea of languages as a political and economic 'site of struggle', on respect for language diversity and difference and on the deconstruction of essentialist understanding of language and identity. (Stroud, 2001: 353)

Although a nation-state understanding of citizenship – the reception of it or the naturalization to it – is still dominant (not least in academic circles), current theorizing in the social sciences and the humanities has encouraged us to move away from a static conceptualization of citizenship as *status* (e.g. the wielding of a passport tied to a particular nation-state), and from too much focus on the *state*. As Magnette points out, 'Citizenship confined to the nation-state seems insufficient, or, to be more precise, out of focus with the real places of power' (Magnette, 2005: 168). The 'real places of power' Magnette refers to are those subnational and supra-regional locations, places that pose innumerable challenges for historically marginalized speakers who find themselves at the crossroads between discourses of multiculturalism and those of 'subject' and 'other' (see Kymlicka, 1996; Mamdani, 2017). It is precisely with a view to offering a more dynamic understanding of citizenship in the context of 'real places of power' that the notion of Linguistic Citizenship seeks to grasp those *practices* through which speakers – no matter what legal status they have – 'position themselves agentively' and 'craft new, emergent, subjectivities of political speakerhood, often outside those prescribed or legitimated in institutional frameworks of the state' (Stroud, 2018: 4). A variety of meaning-making resources, which include multilingualism, multimodality and the body are the building blocks of such acts of political claimstaking. The reason why a dynamic understanding of citizenship is necessary can be explained with the help of examples of activism that question the limit of legal rights discourses. While the recognition of, say, linguistic or sexual rights is seen as a key milestone in the pursuit of sociopolitical enfranchisement, history has taught us that the legal enshrinement of certain rights does not necessarily benefit all the members of the linguistic or sexual constituencies in question. This is something that was made patent by the feminist group One in Nine in 2012 when they performed a so-called 'die-in' (that is, a performance of death) in order to stop the yearly Jo'burg Pride Parade. By stopping a parade organized by a mainly white and middle-class gay and lesbian constituency in the wealthy suburb of Rosebank in Johannesburg, the One in Nine sought to bring attention to the very different lived experiences of black queer individuals living in townships. Put bluntly, white middle-class and black working-class queers might have the same rights on paper, but their lived realities are very different in South Africa.[2]

Linguistic Citizenship helps us to study and understand how, through different semiotic resources (multilingualism, the body, space, etc.), speakers not only negotiate 'new discourses of citizenship' in social contexts bookended by globalization, racial capitalism and nation-state ideologies, but also the symbolic and embodied tensions brought about by discourses of neoliberalism and democracy. Linguistic Citizenship is thus a concept that 'recognizes the manifold challenges posed by late-modern contexts of migration and multilingualism and voice, and that takes as its central point of departure the desirability of constructing and maintaining voice across media, modalities and contexts' (Stroud, 2010: 208). In other words, it describes democratic participation by emphasizing cultural and political voice rather than just language. It describes how multilingualism can be 'both a facilitative and constraining factor in the exercise of democratic citizenship and voice' (Stroud, 2010: 208). It sees all sorts of linguistic practices – including practices that are subversive or transgressive – as potentially relevant to social and economic well-being, and it accepts that it is very hard to predict any of this if you're watching from the centre, positioned in notions of normativity and normalcy. Linguistic Citizenship, therefore, stresses the importance of grassroots activities; that is, activities that exist on the margins of state control, and outside formal institutions.

Linguistic Citizenship is important to the sociolinguistic and linguistic-anthropological description of languages, varieties and registers that are used by multilingual speakers across a range of modalities and contexts. It is the freedom of such usage, or the struggle for this freedom, that can create inclusive and participatory spaces for citizens to interact (see Kerfoot, 2009). Linguistic Citizenship is a notion that combines the tenets or practices of cosmopolitan citizenship and deliberative democracy, and that opens up modalities and contexts where voice is contested; where modernist and exclusionary forms of citizenship are enforced and resisted; and where language and multilingualism are used as a political resource in transitioning and changing diverse societies. Thus, Linguistic Citizenship is an approach to multilingualism that highlights how marginalized speakers, or speakers of marginalized languages, mediate agency, and voice in manifold ways. It reads multilingualism in a way that helps us to understand how symbolic power can become entrenched in 'structures of feeling' (Williams, 1977), creating hierarchies that are experienced as naturalized. According to Milani and Shaikjee (2013), it is a notion that 'can be usefully employed in order to understand the many ephemeral and apparently banal "micro-occurrences" of agency *on grounds of language* that unfold in daily interactions – whether private or public' (2013: 75, emphasis in original).

Linguistic Citizenship with Multilingualism: A Global Conversation

Kaaps speakers, in the way they act out their Linguistic Citizenship in the various modalities and contexts we alluded to above, provide nuanced and radical insight into the complex matrices of power and resources, as well as the politics of agency and voice that historically marginalized and racialized speakers have to navigate generally across the world. Their Linguistic Citizenship wants and desires purposely privilege a political agenda focused on local knowledge and the realization of alternative futures of language, away from the injurious politics of Afrikaans, and the cultivation of new relationalities.

Albeit very specific to the context of South Africa, the acts of Linguistic Citizenship by Kaaps speakers offer important tread marks through which to gauge the pathways of connected marginalities and lived liberatory practices of historically marginalized multilingual speakers in other countries. As a consequence of globalization, technological transformations, the ongoing migration of people from one continent to another as a result of *forces majeures*, the present anthropocene crises, persistent economic inequalities, devolving carnal regimes and the emergence of new affective economies, we have had to rethink the various ways and means in which multilingual speakers struggle to (re)claim ownership and authority over their right to speak (to have voice) and to bring about change (that is, exercise their agency; Ramanathan, 2013). Undoubtedly, multilingual speakers situated in Euro-American (Khan, 2020; Oakes & Peled, 2018), Asian (Wee, 2011) and Middle Eastern (Paz, 2018; Suleiman, 2017) countries also struggle against centrist and neoliberal/colonial replications of languages and selves, akin to speakers of Kaaps, and at the same time are moving towards shared schemata and frames that rearticulate the conditions of dignity in diversity. They are also thinking and doing language 'otherwise' and what it means to be a speaker in contexts either defined as home, away, foreign, new and turbulent (Stroud, 2010).

In this book, authors take stock implicitly and explicitly of conservative, liberal, progressive and radical social transformations in democracies in the north and south, and consider the implications for multilingualism as a resource, as a way of life, and as a feature of identity politics and the potential for and realization of Linguistic Citizenship. Each chapter builds on earlier research on Linguistic Citizenship by illuminating how multilingualism (in theory and practice) should be, or could be, thought of as inclusive when we recognize what multilingual speakers do with language for voice and agency. More importantly, this book builds on the path-opening anthology by Lim *et al.* (2018) by centring the important conceptual contributions Christopher Stroud has made in enriching our understanding, description and analysis of the relationship between multilingualism and Linguistic Citizenship. More than a celebration of his academic legacy and scholarship, this book, *Struggles for Multilingualism and Linguistic Citizenship*, is an anthology that aims to offer a fresh perspective on the social life of multilingualism through the lens of the notion of Linguistic Citizenship. The common denominator underpinning all the contributions to this volume is a theoretical and methodological engagement with Linguistic Citizenship as a useful theory through which to understand sociolinguistic processes in late modernity, focusing in particular on linguistic agency and voices on the margins of our societies.

In this volume we spotlight the manifold ways that Linguistic Citizenship as a theoretical notion and everyday practice recuperates the lost semiotics of historically marginalized linguistic agency and voices in multilingual societies under transformation. We use Linguistic Citizenship as a term that highlights how linguistic agency often takes place in non-institutionalized and relational networks of association, and in ways that cannot be fully captured by models of rational, deliberative debate in institutionalized public spheres. Rather, as each contribution illustrates, the exercise of agency, voice and participation comprises modes of speaking/writing/signing that cannot always be accounted for in terms of conventional and fixed linguistic structures, but in practices and textualities that are effervescent, momentary and fleeting (following Stroud, 2001). Perhaps significantly, the chapters in this volume trace the emergence of agency and voice at local points of production in a variety of semiotic forms, and the material affordances for this, as well as the insertion of meaning across chains of artefacts and spaces of circulation. And all underline the importance of Linguistic Citizenship as a notion that emphasizes features of multilingual choices and uses on the margins and how both the former and latter open up the potential for understanding the rhetorical foundations of radically different types of speaker agency that go 'against the grain' of a conventional politics of language.

As we will illustrate in more detail below, the notion of Linguistic Citizenship as an approach to multilingualism allows the contributors in this volume to offer new insights into a variety of old and new topics in sociolinguistics: the linguistic workings of the nation-state; discursive performances of culture; usage of small languages in small places (Pennycook, 2012); small stories in the contexts of racialization; pedagogical challenges and transformation within higher education language curricula; the semiosis of the body, mind and multilingual being; and mobilities. Linguistic Citizenship is also helpful in conceptualizing the historically fraught relations between north and south in the production of sociolinguistic knowledge. For this purpose, this volume consists of contributors who come from, and are based in, both northern and southern contexts, and are self-reflexive about their 'historical bodies' (Scollon & Scollon, 2004) and positionalities in epistemological production. They thus bring different histories and research traditions to bear on the analysis of multilingualism and diversity in their application of the notion of Linguistic Citizenship. The authors focus not only on English, but also on other languages such as Afrikaans, isiXhosa, Cockney English, Singaporean English and Singlish, as well as Swedish and its varieties. Across chapters, authors demonstrate how the notion of Linguistic Citizenship helps to anchor the analysis of multilingualism and diversity. Needless to say, while Linguistic Citizenship provides the overarching perspective that runs across the volume, the chapters also draw on and contribute to a plethora of other theoretical and analytical notions: namely, sociolinguistic consumption, remixing multilingualism, sociolinguistic citizenship, narrative theory of 'small stories', silence, dystopia, utopia, art-based narrative theory, decoloniality, semilingualism, entextualization, turbulence, WEIRD bias analysis and bare life.

We see this theoretical diversity as an asset rather than as a drawback; it is an indicator of the impossibility of settling into monistic positions for the study of multilingualism and, indeed, future analysis of multilingual practices in both northern and southern contexts. Overall, the book seeks to offer a global twist to our understanding of the struggles *for* and *with* multilingualism, agency and voice on the margins.

Organization of the Book

This book is organized into four parts. Each part draws on Linguistic Citizenship in order to re-imagine well-established notions and topics in sociolinguistic inquiry, which include, but are not limited to, agency, education, narration and mobility, body and ontology, as well as sociolinguistic categories and epistemology.

Linguistic Citizenship as Theory and Practice of Multilingualism

The three chapters in this section introduce the reader to Linguistic Citizenship as both *theory* and *practice* of multilingualism, focusing in particular on the speaker's agency. This is done through an exploration of (1) the consumption of language and what it means to 'consume' multilingual repertoires, (2) the semiotic activities multilingual speakers are engaged in when they put forward their voices in contexts of transformation, without losing sight of (3) how multilingual speakers are regimented by national language models. Each chapter aims at charting multilingual trajectories through often highly regimented spaces.

In an attempt to deconstruct the myth of orderly multilingualism, Wee develops earlier research he conducted with Christopher Stroud on sociolinguistic consumption (Stroud & Wee, 2007) by revisiting the notions of official and unofficial multilingualism in Singapore. Wee puts forward the argument that the need to order multilingualism, either by compartmentalizing languages to control the use of language, or even by separating languages and reassigning them for use in different domains or contexts, sustains the myth of orderly multilingualism. In order not only to critique but do away with such a false notion and practice, Linguistic Citizenship plays an important role in advancing a sociolinguistics that emphasizes 'resilience' in the face of orderly multilingual onslaughts. It is a notion that helps us to better describe the fluidity of codes, languages and, of course, multilingualism, or reminds us to be aware that language is not to be thought of outside individuals and communities, as autonomous. Importantly, Linguistic Citizenship challenges the durability of orderly multilingualism by highlighting the variability of language contact situations where new forms of speech and registers emerge that undo the supposed foreverness of named languages.

The second chapter by Heugh challenges some of sociolinguistics' deeply entrenched ideas about language and multilingualism. She argues that southern multilingualisms (in the plural) cannot be understood adequately through theories formulated in the global north. Rather, southern and decolonial theories offer new vocabularies and theories for the study of linguistic diversity. Focusing on 'multilingualisms in contexts of conflict-induced mobilities', Heugh presents an argument for 'mestizo consciousness' through which to advance sociolinguistics research in the south. At the same time, she demonstrates how Linguistic Citizenship became the anchoring to advance the latter argument as originally proposed by Stroud (2001), for not only understanding linguistic heterogeneity but also decoloniality and the formation of new epistemologies. For Heugh, Linguistic Citizenship presents an opportunity to revisit and rethink the dynamics of language use by those citizens living in postcolonial societies; to recognize their agency and voice. Thus, Linguistic Citizenship in Heugh's contribution interrogates the ethics for reflecting on how language is rooted and routed in southern contexts. In particular, Heugh shows how a conception of Linguistic Citizenship is able to help us understand how multilingual speakers advance decolonial perspectives on languages and knowledge systems in the global south.

The final chapter in this section looks at an example of multilingualism and Linguistic Citizenship 'from below'. Rampton, Cooke and Holmes explore a national language model that seeks to homogenize heteroglot language practices by multilingual speakers in urban spaces in the UK. The authors demonstrate how an insistence on national language models by government institutions is at odds with everyday practices and experiences of multilingualism. Rampton and colleagues establish a clear distinction between a rights-based perspective that remains rooted within monolingual models, on the one hand, and citizenship approaches that encourage heteroglot mixing, on the other hand. By bringing the research on Linguistic Citizenship in conversation with Hymesian ethnographic sociolinguistics, the authors unpack 'problems associated with the national-language perspective dominating education in England' to illustrate 'forms of pedagogy which are much more consistent with the [linguistic] citizenship approach'. And with a strong emphasis on the social too, Rampton *et al.* uniquely suggest that we also consider that in the UK the expanded Linguistic Citizenship notion – that is, 'Sociolinguistic Citizenship' – is equally useful to understand the politics and educational changes that centralize language. Sociolinguistic citizenship, according to Rampton *et al.*, is a local version of linguistic citizenship that 'adds the need to strengthen democratic participation with political and educational efforts tuned to the significance of language' in the UK.

The chapters in Part 1 bring together a focus on multilingualism from below in contexts of social transformation and the role of multilingual diversity therein.

Multilingual Narratives and Linguistic Citizenship

Multilingual narratives, master or small, are often formed in contexts of social transformation (Bamberg & Georgakopolou, 2008). They are defined by metaphors and discourses of harmony, utopia and interruptions, and can give a glimpse of new political futures. Taking South Africa as a case in point, the two chapters in this section, offer insights into the ways in which multilingual speakers talk about the changing sociolinguistic landscape of the country.

Van Niekerk, Jansen and Bock's chapter discusses how students at the University of the Western Cape narrate, through small stories, their experiences of racialized discourses (past and the present). Van Niekerk and colleagues argue that small stories counter powerful master narratives, particularly where it concerns racializations in post-apartheid South Africa. In this regard, Linguistic Citizenship becomes a useful lens that allows the authors to explore how small stories reveal the narrators wanton desire to 'disinhibit' and need to 'step out', or away, from 'inherited ethnolinguistic subjectivities'. Linguistic Citizenship enriches van Niekerk *et al.*'s analysis by linking micro discourses of race, linguistically marked in the small story narratives, to larger macro hegemonic discourses of race and vulnerability that is defined by the social remains of apartheid and the ambivalent racial discourses surrounding colouredness experiences by the narrators. In this regard, Linguistic Citizenship as a theoretical framework is important to the authors in understanding how race and racial discourse continually reinforce 'exclusion, rejection and shame' but also provide the indicators for how to disrupt and destabilize the former, in the least reflections on spaces of vulnerability experienced by the narrators in the study.

Oostendorp's chapter deals with migrants living and working in South Africa. By employing an arts-based approach to narratives, the author demonstrates how African migrants construct nostalgia for their home country while wrestling with their current precarious situation. The migrants narratives reveal gaps and silences, a structured incompleteness that is representative of the fact that they do not, or maybe cannot, fully belong to South Africa. The narratives also index a dystopia of experience that is thought about differently, but in conversation with what the notion of Linguistic Citizenship can offer in understanding further the use of linguistic resources by migrants coming from outside and into South Africa. Oostendorp argues in this regard that a deeper dialectical interconnection between the notions of utopia and dystopia could further enrich the notion of Linguistic Citizenship and provide a better understanding of how migrants use their linguistic repertoires.

Together, the chapters in this section unveil spaces within South Africa's democracy where multilingual citizens desire and wish for 'social improvements' and a more equal multilingual future.

Linguistic Citizenship for Linguistic Knowledge, Digital Activism and Popular Culture

Linguistic Citizenship is a helpful analytic lens for understanding contexts across the world where the struggle for multilingual education continues around linguistic labels, activism against institutional (read: educational) racism, and the practice of popular culture. In this section, the contributions by Salö and Karlander, Hiss and Peck and Williams provide a window on the politics of language inside and outside institutional settings. Salö and Karlander explore processes of knowledge production about language in the far north of Europe. Taking the notion of 'semilingualism' as a case in point, they trace how this notion circulated and became entextualized and authoritative. They also illustrate how this very entextualization produced the condition for the critique of this notion. Here we can see once again an example of Linguistic Citizenship in action, in which knowledge about language is created and contested.

Hiss and Peck use Linguistic Citizenship to foreground the activism of high school students against anti-black racism at Winterberry Girls' High School (WBGHS), a middle-class, historically white, all-girls school in Cape Town. The unit of analysis is the 2016 Twitter campaign that documented the protest against alleged institutionalized racism at the school and as a result of social, institutional, media and political pressure led to rapid transformation in the language policy and processes of the school. The authors demonstrate how the 2016 Twitter campaign was created by members of the Fallists movement (that began with the Rhodes Must Fall uprising), which subsequently established an online forum that was multilingual and multimodal, and read by Twitter users from across the world. Linguistic Citizenship, for Hiss and Peck, is a useful theoretical anchor to unpack how institutional affirmative politics brush institutional racism and anti-black racism under the rug, using various material artefacts as media of cultural and social discipline at the school, but at the same time for understanding how semiotic processes, from school to Twitter and back to the school, are interlinked to discourses of decoloniality, the body and language.

In the final chapter of this section, Williams reflects on conceptual efforts to link Linguistic Citizenship to popular culture research in South Africa. In that chapter, Williams describes how a 'remixing' of Linguistic Citizenship led to understanding not only the importance of multilingualism for greater agency and voice in the nooks and crannies of popular cultural contexts found outside institutional ones, but how young multilingual speakers are the drivers behind popular culture today where language and acts of Linguistic Citizenship feature importantly. Furthermore, Williams describes how the term 'remixing' is underwritten by the rhetoric and language political discourse of Linguistic Citizenship, in particular, the emphasis of new forms of human mutuality and the creative practices we discover in everyday multilingual practices, often exported in popular culture performances such as hip hop and stand-up comedy. The remixing of Linguistic Citizenship, Williams argues, from within the context of popular culture, has led to an emphasis on new forms of relationality in our understanding of citizenship as we struggle against powers that seek to erase, silence and invisibilize multilingual speakers. It has also led to the argument that agency and voice in the context of popular culture is defined by a linguistics of transgression and entanglement, often a key aspect of acts of Linguistic Citizenship.

Postscripts: Taking Linguistic Citizenship towards New Directions

While the previous three parts dealt with multilingualism as discursive practice, the chapters in this section focus on the ontology of multilingualism and its relations to the mind and on the body. Bylund's chapter analyses the controversies surrounding concepts in psycholinguistics by focusing on a number of dogmas that have come to define the study of language acquisition of multilingual speakers. The author argues for what he calls an egalitarian approach to the study of second/foreign language acquisition. In order to do so, Bylund suggests, we need to give due regard to multilingual diversity to enrich the cognitive sciences.

While Bylund is concerned with overturning old dogmas that have come to define psycholinguistics and the cognitive sciences, Kulick's chapter deals with multilingual being, more specifically (multilingual) ontology and the importance of the philosophical work of Agamben and Levinas, and what they may offer the field of sociolinguistics – more specifically the study of multilingualism. Kulick suggests in his chapter that Agamben and Levinas could teach us much about the ontological dimensions that emerge in multilingual interactions. On the one hand, Agamben offers us his theories of 'bare life', particularly his biopolitical notion of *homo sacer* that could help us understand subjectivity under governmentality. On the other hand, Levinasian ethics of the self and the other may assist us with that which is elusive in our analysis of shared responsibility and politeness in cross-cultural communication. Together, these two chapters tackle turbulent disciplinary debates about language that either shape dogmas or seek to transform the field of sociolinguistics and multilingualism, while at the same time advancing the importance of Linguistic Citizenship for such a transformation.

This edited collection closes with an Afterword in which Christopher Stroud engages with all the contributions, highlighting the ordinariness of acts of linguistic citizenship across a variety of contexts, the affective nature of such acts, as well as their complex and unpredictable ambivalences. Ultimately, as Stroud puts it, a linguistic citizenship perspective forces us to move towards a political ontology of language based on the primacy of ethics, relationality and responsibility. It is through such a view of language that alternative futures can be crafted.

Notes

(1) The term 'coloured' is a racial epithet created in colonial times, the use of which continues in the apartheid era to describe someone as not quite white nor strictly black or African.
(2) Critical race scholars do not agree about the capitalization (or not) of labels for racial constructs. In this book, we follow Kessi *et al.* using 'lower case "black" to signify that it is a social construct and political identity. In the South African context, "black" (lower case) invokes black consciousness and can be used to describe people of African, Indian and mixed heritage and descent' (Kessi *et al.*, 2020: 4). However, we acknowledge that in other contexts such as the US, capitalized forms may be used for the same purpose.

References

Bamberg, M. and Georgakopoulou, A. (2008) Small stories as a new perspective in narrative and identity analysis. *Text and Talk* 28 (3), 377–396.

Blignaut, J. (2014) 'n Ondersoek na die taalgebruik in die *Son* as verteenwoordigend van Kaapse Afrikaans. Unpublished master's thesis, Stellenbosch University.

Carstens, W.A.M. and Le Cordeur, M. (eds) (2016) *Ons Kom van Vêr: Bydraes oor Bruin Afrikaanssprekendes se Rol in die Ontwikkeling van Afrikaans.* Tyger Valley: Naledi.

Cloete, M. (2012) Language and politics in the philosophy of Adam Small: some personal reflections. *Tydskrif vir Letterkunde* 49 (1), 115–130.

Davids, A. (2011) In H. Willemse and S.E. Danger (eds) *The Afrikaans of the Cape Muslims.* Pretoria: Protea Book House.

Den Besten, H. (2012) In T. van der Wouden (ed.) *Roots of Afrikaans. Selected Writings of Hans den Besten.* Amsterdam: John Benjamins.

Deumert A. (2004) *The Dynamics of Cape Dutch. Language Standardization and Language Change.* Amsterdam: John Benjamins.

Dyers, C. (2015) The conceptual evolution in linguistics: Implications for the study of Kaaps. *Multilingual Margins* 2 (2), 55–64.

Haupt, A. (2001) Black thing: Hip hop nationalism, race and gender in Prophets of da City and Brasse Vannie Kaap. In Z. Erasmus (ed.) *Coloured by History, Shaped by Place: New Perspectives on Coloured Identities in Cape Town* (pp. 172–194). Cape Town: Kwela Books.

Hendricks, F. (2012) Illuminating the neglected: A view on Adam Small's literary integration of Kaaps. *Tydskrif vir Letterkunde* 49 (1), 95–114.

Jansen, J. (ed.) (2019) *Decolonisation in Universities: The Politics of Knowledge.* Johannesburg: Wits University Press.

Kerfoot, C. (2009) *Changing Conceptions of Literacies, Language and Development.* PhD thesis in Bilingualism Nr. 18. Stockholm: Stockholm University.

Kessi, S., Marks, Z. and Ramugondo, E. (2020) Decolonizing African Studies. *Critical African Studies* 12 (3), 271–282.

Khan, K. (2020) *Becoming a Citizen: Linguistic Trials and Negotiations in the UK.* London: Bloomsbury Press.

Kymlicka, W. (1996) *Multicultural Citizenship: A Liberal Theory of Minority Rights.* New York: Oxford University Press.

Lim, L., Stroud, C. and Wee, L. (eds) (2018) *The Multilingual Citizen: Towards a Politics of Language for Agency and Change.* Bristol: Multilingual Matters.

Magnette, P. (2005) *Citizenship: The History of an Idea.* Colchester: ECPR.

Mamdani, M. (2017) *Citizen and Subject: Contemporary Africa and the Legacy of Late Colonialism.* Johanneburg: Wits University Press.

Milani, T. and Shaikjee, M. (2013) Afrikaans is bobaas: Linguistic citizenship on the BBC *Voices* website. In C. Upton and B.L Davies (eds) *Analysing Twenty-first Century British English: Conceptual and Methodological Aspects of the Voices Project* (pp. 71–90). London: Routledge.

Paz, A.L. (2018) *Latinos in Israel: Language and Unexpected Citizenship.* Bloomington, IND: Indiana University Press.

Pennycook, A. (2012) *Language and Mobility: Unexpected Places.* Bristol: Multilingual Matters.

Ramanathan, V. (ed.) (2013) *Language Policies and (Dis)Citizenship: Rights, Access, Pedagogies.* Bristol: Multilingual Matters.

Scollon, R. and Scollon, S.W. (2004) *Nexus Analysis: Discourse and the Emerging internet.* London: Routledge.

Small, A. (1972) Adam Small in gesprek met Ronnie Belcher. In A.H. Aucamp, J.P. Smuts, C. Barnard and A.J. Coetzee (eds) *Gesprekke met Skrywers 2* (pp. 93–105). Cape Town: Tafelberg.

Small, A. (1987) *Kitaar My Kruis* (3rd revised edn). Pretoria: HAUM-Literêr.

Stroud, C. (2001) African mother tongue programs and the politics of language: linguistic citizenship versus linguistic human rights. *Journal of Multilingual and Multicultural Development* 22 (4), 339–355.

Stroud, C. (2010) Towards a postliberal theory of citizenship. In J.E. Petrovic (ed.) *International Perspectives on Bilingual Education: Policy, Practice and Controversy* (pp. 191–218). New York: Information Age Publishing.

Stroud, C. (2018) Linguistic Citizenship. In L. Lim, C. Stroud and L. Wee (eds) *The Multilingual Citizen: Towards a Politics of Language for Agency and Change* (pp. 17–39). Bristol: Multilingual Matters.

Stroud, C. and Wee, L. (2007) Consuming identities. Language planning and policy in Singaporean late modernity. *Language Policy* 6, 253–279.

Stroud, C. and Williams, Q. (2017) Multilingualism as Utopia: Fashioning Non-racial selves. *AILA Review* 30, 165–186.

Suleiman, C. (2017) *The Politics of Arabic in Israel: A Sociolinguistic Analysis.* Edinburgh: Edinburgh University Press.

Wee, L. (2011) *Language without Rights.* Oxford: Oxford University Press.

Williams, R. (1977) *Marxism and Literature.* Oxford: Oxford University Press.

Part 1

Linguistic Citizenship as Theory and Practice of Multilingualism

2 The Myth of Orderly Multilingualism

Lionel Wee

Introduction

In an earlier work on sociolinguistic consumption (Stroud & Wee, 2007), Christopher Stroud and I made a number of points. One, it is important to distinguish between the direct consumption of languages as denotational codes (e.g. 'I want to learn the French language') and the indirect consumption of linguistic repertoires to engage in various activities such as listening to K-pop, being conscripted into the army for National Service (e.g. 'I picked up some Singlish phrases during my time as an infantryman') or having an interest in wine (e.g. 'I picked up some French words because I enjoy tasting different kinds of wine').

Two, official views of multilingualism usually emphasize the direct consumption of languages. However, direct consumption does not necessarily lead to official multilingualism. Direct consumption simply treats languages as denotational codes, and not all such codes are given official status, which is why some groups may feel the need to fight for their codes to be recognized (Wee, 2011). But official multilingualism does tend to rely on viewing languages as denotational codes. That is, insofar as official multilingualism is concerned with the kinds of languages that ought to be taught in schools, used in the media, or allowed in society, it typically approaches these issues by trying to encourage or prohibit the use of specific denotational codes. Of course, indirect consumption does not necessarily lead to unofficial multilingualism. Indirect consumption simply shows that linguistic resources may be acquired in various ways. Whether or not such resources happen to correlate with unofficially (or even officially) recognized multilingualism is a separate matter. For example, in Singapore, a person may pick up some Malay and some Singlish phrases while serving National Service. However, it is only in the case of Malay, which is an officially recognized language, that indirect consumption can be said to lead to official multilingualism. In the case of Singlish, which the government has denounced as 'bad English' (Wee, 2018a), indirect consumption only leads to unofficial multilingualism.

Three, as consumption becomes an increasingly significant aspect of how identities are constructed and even legitimized in late modernity, it is important to give greater acknowledgement to the value of unofficial multilingual repertoires and relatedly, the indirect consumption activities by which such repertoires are acquired.

In this chapter, I argue that the distinction between the direct consumption of languages as denotational codes and the indirect consumption of repertoires via being involved in activities that may have little or no direct association with language learning is based on the notion of *orderliness*. Official multilingualism, with its tendency to emphasize on the direct acquisition of languages as denotational codes, presumes that there can be an orderliness to the learning and use of different languages. Concomitantly, this leads to the view that disorder, contingency and unpredictability in multilingualism are problems or obstacles that need to be managed, if not altogether eliminated.

However, there are serious questions surrounding the ontological viability of treating languages as fully formed autonomous systems, which is what the idea of learning a language as a denotational code rests on. And this suggests that disorder, contingency and unpredictability need to be recognized as being ever-present in multilingualism. It is orderliness, albeit only temporary. Greater space and attention then need to be given to the indirect consumption of linguistic repertoires that come about as a result of persons being engaged in various activities which may not have any ostensible connection to language learning. The implications and affordances of such a move also need to be better appreciated. But first the shackles of the myth of orderly multilingualism have to be broken.

The aim of this chapter, then, is to provide a critique of the myth of orderly multilingualism, explain why there is an urgent need for this critique, and suggest how a shift away from the myth might be achieved. Therefore, in what follows, I emphasize how this myth relies on conceptually problematic assumptions regarding both the nature of language and how it is acquired. I show how the myth of orderly multilingualism is predicated on the presumption that disorder and messiness are temporary and removable nuisances that can and should be eradicated by careful planning and rational action. I also make the point that whereas the relative stability of various social and political conditions may have made it easier to sustain this myth, increasing social complexity makes the retention of this myth costly, not least because of the roles that unofficial multilingual repertoires play in identity construction.

Getting rid of the myth of orderly multilingualism need not mean being resigned to accepting chaos. Nevertheless, it has to be acknowledged that the deeply entrenched status of the myth means that shifting away from it can result in turmoil for communities and institutions that are built on the notion of orderly multilingualism. I then suggest ways in which such turmoil can be minimized (but never eliminated). In this regard, I emphasize the important role that linguistic citizenship can play in cultivating social resilience *vis-à-vis* the changing relationships between language and society.

Understanding the Myth of Orderly Multilingualism

There are many different situations where the myth of orderly multilingualism prevails. For example, Weber and Horner (2012) observe that many educational systems insist on compartmentalizing school languages and home languages, for fear that the latter can contaminate or compromise students' abilities to learn the former properly. Thus, they (Weber & Horner, 2012: 116) critique the multilingual educational systems in Singapore, Brunei and Luxembourg as being 'strongly based on monolingual standards and compartmentalization of languages'. An insistence on standard language ideology means that children's home languages are usually ignored. This insistence of compartmentalizing school and home languages fails to recognize that the latter can and should be used as linguistic resources that could help scaffold learners towards gaining proficiency in the former. The result, regrettably, is a punitive situation for students. When the home language is denigrated as useless or irrelevant, as is the case for the migrant students in Luxembourg (Weber & Horner, 2012: 115), these students fail to 'achieve the language skills necessary for classroom interaction and study' (Davis, 1994: 188).

Such policing of languages boundaries extends beyond educational systems. For example, Rappa and Wee (2006: 5) describe how a proposal to allow the use of English in the Malaysian Parliament led to angry responses, including newspaper editorials that called the proposal 'shameful', and a senator who worried that such a move would 'belittle our own national language'. In this example, the issue is not about compartmentalizing languages in an attempt to facilitate language learning. Rather, the concern is that an appropriate 'status' relationship be maintained so that the prestige of a language such as Malay is not undermined by the intrusion of some other language, such as English. The feeling in Malaysia is that, as far as the political domain of parliamentary proceedings is concerned, the only suitable language is Malay. The presence and use of any other language is seen as undermining the prestige and nationalism that should accompany such political debates.

And, finally, it has been pointed out that in Thailand, media regulations insist that:

> ... all advertisement and commercial features must be broadcast in the Thai language. Only brand names, names of manufacturers, and names of the countries which produce the goods can be in foreign languages. Newscasts between 20:00 and 20:40 on Channel 9 (belonging to the Mass Communications Organization of Thailand) are translated into English and broadcast through FM Radio of Thailand. (Masavisut *et al.*, 1986: 203)

Unlike the first two examples, strict compartmentalization at the level of named languages (whether on the grounds of enhancing language learning or maintaining national pride) is not the only focus. The media regulations do allow for some forms of English. But these must only be proper nouns, specifically, product and country names. No other English lexical items are allowed. Thus, it is obvious that some attempt at order and control still prevails, albeit at the level of a class of lexical items, in this case, proper nouns.

The concept of orderly multilingualism thus covers a range of language policy and planning enterprises, all of which share the belief that language exposure can and should be neatly and methodically controlled. In the educational systems described by Weber and Horner (2012). This involves attempts to strictly separate the home language from the school language, so that the former does not encroach on the latter. In the case of the Malaysian Parliament (Rappa & Wee, 2006), the separation is about ensuring that the Malay language does not have to share the domain of parliamentary discussions with English. And finally, the issue in the Thai case involves both compartmentalization as well as controlled porosity. Compartmentalization is evidenced in the case of newscasts. English news is to be transmitted by a recognized institution (Channel 9 of the Mass Communications Organization of Thailand) and only at specific times of the day. Controlled porosity can be seen in the stipulation that only English lexical items of a particular type – the names of brands, manufacturers and countries – are acceptable in the case of advertising.

Orderly multilingualism is a language policy and planning enterprise that attempts to control the specific languages (or parts of them, in the case of controlled porosity) that can or should co-exist as part of a speaker's repertoire. The notion of orderly multilingualism encapsulates the belief that multilingualism can and should be neatly planned. Moreover, if the planning is done properly and the targets of the planning are being rational and cooperative (e.g. learners and teachers are serious about language education; politicians are patriotic and sincere about maintaining national pride; newscasters and advertisers understand that communicative and commercial goals have to be balanced against one another), then the result will be a multilingualism that is methodical and disciplined.

There are reasons why orderly multilingualism has to be recognized as a myth. Firstly, the conceptual assumption that underlies it – that is, the idea that language exists as a 'whole, bounded system' (Heller, 2008: 505; see also Blommaert, 2005: 11; Jaspers & Madsen, 2018; Rampton, 2006: 16) – is problematic. The illusion of such systems arises because of the failure to look beyond language names (e.g. 'English', 'French', etc.) to recognize the variation and changeability in language practices, as well as the ideological influences that lead some speakers and institutions to accept certain practices as, say, 'Standard English' while rejecting others. As Schneider (2011: 155) rightly cautions in his discussion of English in

Asia, a label like 'Chinese English', 'unless understood very loosely and non-technically, implies more homogeneity than is warranted'. From this problematic conceptual foundation, then, orderly multilingualism is really an attempt to manage whole, bounded linguistic systems – or demarcated sub-systems such as the lexicon of names (see above) or even 'bad words' (Allan & Burridge, 2006) – and to assign these systems/sub-systems to properly demarcated functions or banning them altogether. The problem is that such ordered and bounded linguistic systems/sub-systems do not in fact exist (Heller, 2008; Pennycook, 2016; see also discussion below). One implication that follows from rejecting such bounded systems is that there is no sharp distinction between multilingualism and multi-dialectalism, and so the myth of orderly multilingualism applies just as relevantly to attempts that separating varieties of, say, English as it does to conventionally distinguished language names (see below).

Secondly, the idea that exposure to specific languages or sets of lexical items can be tightly controlled is also problematic. For example, in attempting to discourage the use of Singlish in Singapore, the Media Development Authority issued the following advisory (MDA Free-To-Air Television Programme Code):

> Singlish, which is ungrammatical local English, and includes dialect terms and sentence structures based on dialect, should not be encouraged and can only be permitted in interviews, where the interviewee speaks only Singlish. The interviewer himself, however, should not use Singlish. (Wee, 2018a: 55)

The Media Development Authority's attempt to engage in orderly multi-lingualism makes the by now all too familiar, problematic assumption that both Singlish and Standard English are completely autonomous systems. This assumption leads to the view that there will be cases 'where the interviewee speaks only Singlish' and consequently, it should be possible to enforce a demarcation between the two varieties. This problematic assumption creates different difficulties for the Media Development Authority as it tries to exert control over the use of Singlish. Unsurprisingly, it has not been easy to implement the advisory for the simple reason that most Singlish usage involves switching between Singlish and Standard English. There are few, if any, movies or television serials that are *totally* in Singlish. As pointed out in Wee (2010: 107), 'Singlish is usually interspersed with other lexicogrammatical constructions that are, to varying degrees, more or less standard'. This is a point also noted by Alsagoff (2007: 26), who observes that 'fluidity and movement between Standard English and Singlish is not the exception but the rule in modern Singapore'.

And of course, it should come as no surprise that attempts to enforce orderly multilingualism also face difficulties in language education. For example, even a language that is acquired initially via formal instruction in classroom situations cannot escape the wider and more informal social influences of exposure to media, peer interaction and contact with local languages (Stroud & Wee, 2012). Thus, quite aside from the issue of language ontology, the idea that a domain of language use can be somehow hermetically sealed off from other domains is highly questionable.

Moreover, there are studies showing that the type of language that learners end up acquiring is not simply modelled on the speech of their teachers or that found in textbooks.[1] Rather, learners take their own social identity into account in the course of their learning attempts. Thus, students in the same study-abroad programme in France were found to acquire different patterns of French variation depending on whether they identified as middle-class or working-class, with middle-class learners tending to use more formal features (Regan *et al.*, 2009). This suggests that individuals approach the learning of a language not simply as rote learners, but from the perspective of a particular social identity. This finding has concrete implications for language education: we cannot present the same material to children of different social classes and expect the outcomes to be the same.

Matras (2009: 144) provides a useful summary of how the cognitive and individual perspective on language acquisition cannot be dissociated from the dynamic and ever-changing social environment, noting that 'communicative interaction does not involve the activation or disengagement of "systems", but rather constant choices among components of the full repertoire of linguistic structures (word-forms, constructions, phonetic realizations and so on)'. Matras's (2009) focus is on second language acquisition rather than first language acquisition. But his points are nevertheless relevant because they are concerned with language acquisition in contexts where multiple codes are present. A child learning a second language will learn to organize her linguistic repertoire (of words, phrases, sounds) into different sets as a result of various social cues, such as addressee, setting, individual interlocutors, purpose of interaction. Matras (2009: 68) then goes on to call for the abandonment of any reliance on 'linguistic systems' in trying to understand the nature of language learning, suggesting instead that it may be more useful to focus on 'the development of the child's linguistic repertoire'.

We have seen that the myth of orderly multilingualism rests on the ontologically problematic view that languages exist (whether as sociocultural constructs or cognitive knowledge) as neatly organized bounded units. The direct consumption of languages as denotational codes relies on this problematic view of language.

From such a perspective, it is no wonder that there can be no place for any sense of disorder or ambiguity. Disorder and ambiguity – in the form of mixing language resources across the boundaries that language names are supposed to represent, in the appropriation of a language that has been designated for one purpose for some other purpose instead, or simply the apparent lack of regard for prescribed rules of grammar – is seen as upsetting the social order and opening the door to chaos (Cameron, 1995: 85). As Milroy and Milroy (1999: 2–3) point out, such attempts at policing linguistic practices are more often than not proxies for racial, religious, gender and class discrimination. In a similar vein, Stroud (2004) describes how in Sweden, immigrants are stereotypically characterized as speaking Rinkeby Swedish (Rinkeby is the name of suburb outside Stockholm where many immigrants have settled). This is a variety that is considered by both native Swedes and even some immigrants themselves to be inauthentic, improper Swedish as compared to the 'authentic/proper' variety supposedly spoken by 'real' Swedes. The irony here is that native Swedes have been known to appropriate some Rinkeby Swedish constructions in order to come across as 'trendy' or 'hip', while at the same time, these constructions when spoken by their original speakers, i.e. the immigrants, continue to be stigmatized (Stroud, 2004: 204–206).

As I now show, while the myth of orderly multilingualism may have been easier to sustain in the past, there is an increasingly urgent need to critique the myth. This is because increasing social and linguistic diversity makes it highly problematic if the mythical nature of orderly multilingualism is not recognized.

Increased Disorder and Complexity

In recent years, Vertovec (2007: 3; see also Arnaut *et al.*, 2016: 2) has argued, with particular respect to the issue of migration, that the tendency to treat migration as a relatively predictable or patterned phenomenon (e.g. migrants to country X tend to come from country Y, or migrants tend to move mainly because of political persecution or in search of better economic prospects) has to be reconsidered because of what he calls 'superdiversity'. Thus, Blommaert and Rampton (2016: 22) suggest that 'Superdiversity is characterized by a tremendous increase in the categories of migrants, not only in terms of nationality, ethnicity, language, and religion, but also in terms of motives, patterns, and itineraries of migration, processes of insertion into the labor and housing markets of the host societies, and so on' (see Vertovec, 2010).

Separate from the arguments about superdiversity, but nonetheless making the related observation that families, individuals and groups are increasingly characterized by transnational connections, Jacquemet (2005) calls for greater attention to be given to what he calls 'transidiomatic practices' to 'describe the communicative practices of transnational groups that interact using different languages and communicative codes simultaneously present in a range of communicative channels, both local and distant' (2005: 264–5). Jacquemet (2005: 262–263) gives examples of making of videotapes by Moroccan families to send to relatives based in Italy (Jacquemet, 1996), and Pakistani taxi-drivers in Chicago listening to sermons recorded in mosques in Kabul or Teheran (Appadurai, 1996), suggesting that these point to identities that find expression 'in the creolized, mixed idioms of polyglottism'.

In a similar vein, Otsuji and Pennycook (2010) highlight the mixed use of Japanese and English in an Australian workplace, where none of the interlocutors are Japanese, and note that 'such instances of English/Japanese mixed code use derive not so much from the use of different first and second languages but rather as the result of a mixed Japanese/English code becoming the lingua franca of the workplace' (Otsuji & Pennycook, 2010: 241).

Finally, Canagarajah (2015: 41) points to the 'hybrid form of literacy activity' found in a Facebook page created by students from a South African township school, where 'the participants use the conventions of text messaging (featuring abbreviations and icons) in addition to mixing English and Xhosa'.

These are all examples that point to increased sociolinguistic turbulence – at least from the perspective of orderly multilingualism. As Park and Wee (2017: 4) point out in their discussion of language and transnationalism:

> Transnationalism, then, presents an interesting complication for the nation-state because it problematizes the essentialist ties between territory, language and national identity that form the very foundation of the nation-state. The imagination of multiple belongings and flexible sense of moorings mean that the need to rely on the territorial boundedness and security of the nation-state is, arguably, lessened.

These examples serve to highlight the fact that identity construction in the form of communicative practices and the communal, as well as professional activities, that they help support and constitute is difficult to pigeonhole into the neat demarcations prescribed by the myth of orderly multilingualism. It is via the engagement in various kinds of activities that linguistic resources come into play as serving to reflect, as well as to construct, the relevant identities of the individuals or groups involved. Thus, there is a need to better acknowledge the role of the indirect consumption of linguistic repertoires, which can be expected to play ever greater roles in facilitating the negotiation of increasing social complexity.

Whether labels such as superdiversity, hybridity, transidiomaticity or even the terms that are part of the 'trans-super-poly-metro movement' (Pennycook, 2016) are adopted or not, the main issue is to move away from the myth of orderly multilingualism. Stubborn adherence to this myth is costly because it prioritizes an ontologically suspect view of language that is also fundamentally at odds with the ways in which communication is conducted.

The reason that the myth is so difficult to dislodge is because much of language policy and planning continues to operate on the assumption that 'civil society is definable, relatively organised, homogeneous and actively consensus-seeking ...' (Watson, 2009: 2264). This assumption, Connell (2014: 210) argues, is a result of inherited epistemologies and ontologies that are reflective of 'north–south globalities', and it has led to managerial projects – from education to urban planning – that presume the homogeneity of knowledge, including the nature of language and multilingualism. This underestimates the degree of societal complexity and conflict that is endemic to the urban experience.

Urban struggles and disturbances, however, are not 'problems' to be solved away if only the optimal (i.e. most rational) management model could be envisaged and implemented. Rather, these struggles and disturbances have to be recognized as inescapable constituents of urban life because they arise from the diverse nature of the city itself. Conflict, ambiguity and indeterminacy are always present:

> ... a central concern for planning is how to locate itself relative to conflicting rationalities – between, on the one hand, organisations, institutions and individuals shaped by the rationality of governing (and, in market economies, modernisation, marketisation and liberalisation), within a global context shaped by historical inequalities and power relations (such as colonialism and imperialism) and, on the other hand, organisations, institutions and individuals shaped by (the rationality of) the need and desire to survive and thrive (broadly the 'poors' and the 'informals'). (Watson, 2009: 2269)

Consider, as an example, the case of Singapore (Wee, 2014), which has been keen to re-invent itself as a global/cosmopolitan city, where talented individuals of diverse backgrounds from all over the world are encouraged to work hard, play hard and even settle down permanently. This global city aspiration has also resulted in an emphasis on Singapore being perceived as a place that is fun, vibrant, and, exciting, making it attractive to global talent. Consequently, the state has adopted a more tolerant attitude towards homosexuality (*Elegant*, 2003) and it has also approved the controversial construction of casinos as part of 'integrated resorts' (Wee, 2012).

But the shift into a global city narrative also requires a re-evaluation of the country's language policy. The language policy, however, creates greater problems than the legalization of casinos for the global city narrative because entrenched ideologies about language are much harder to displace, and re-evaluating these ideologies may even be perceived as undermining Singapore's commitment to interethnic equality. This commitment to interethnic equality is reflected in the recognition of Mandarin, Malay and Tamil as the official mother tongues of the major ethnic communities: Mandarin for the Chinese, Malay for the Malays and Tamil for the Indians. The state's attempts at fostering a sense of nationalism have also relied heavily on distinguishing (Asian) Singapore from 'the West' (Vasil, 1995). This 'Asian-ness' is reflected in the fact that while English is recognized as an official language, it is denied mother tongue status.

Instead, the status of English as an official language is justified on the basis of its perceived global economic value. As Bokhorst-Heng (1998) explains, Singapore encourages bilingualism in English and an officially approved mother tongue, but they are expected to be learnt for very different reasons: the former for the pragmatic goal of being economically competitive and accessing Western technology and scientific knowledge, the latter for the cultural purpose of maintaining a connection with one's ethnic heritage.

There is clearly in Singapore's language policy a strong commitment to the myth of orderly multilingualism. Language is treated as a stable entity with clear boundaries, one that has a historically continuous relationship to its speakers (Gal, 1989). The language is consequently also viewed as an inalienable aspect of their shared cultural (in this case, ethnic) identity, serving in the transmission of traditional knowledge and values. The emphasis, then, is on language as a homogeneous entity that has a stable relationship with a well-defined community of speakers. And the policy is grounded in attempts to regulate language and identity by assigning different functions to different languages. Thus, in his 1984 Speak Mandarin Campaign Speech, Lee Kuan Yew, then prime minister, explained why it is not possible for English to be officially treated as a mother tongue:

> One abiding reason why we have to persist in bilingualism is that English will not be emotionally acceptable as our mother tongue. To have no emotionally acceptable language as our mother tongue is to be emotionally crippled ... Mandarin is emotionally acceptable as our mother tongue ... It reminds us that we are part of an ancient civilization with an unbroken history of over 5000 years. This is a deep and strong psychic force, one that gives confidence to a people to face up to and overcome great changes and challenges.

Two years later, the then Minister for Education Tony Tan (1986), stated in more general terms the rationale behind Singapore's bilingual policy:

> Our policy of bilingualism that each child should learn English and his mother tongue, I regard as a fundamental feature of our education system ... Children must learn English so that they will have a window to the knowledge, technology and expertise of the modern world. They must know their mother tongues to enable them to know what makes us what we are.

The ethnic mother tongues are supposed to assume the function of establishing cultural heritage, to ensure that Singaporeans remain rooted in their Asian heritage even as they compete globally. And although the state recognizes English as an official language, it does not wish to accord it the status of an official mother tongue because it is 'emotionally unacceptable'. But as Singapore aims to be a global city, modernist assumptions about language, community and identity will need to be revisited. For example, the economic development of China has led the state to emphasize Mandarin–English bilingualism as part of Singapore' s strategy of cosmopolitanism: it allows Singapore to serve as a middleman, connecting China to West, and vice versa (Lee Kuan Yew, 2009). This has obligated the state to highlight the economic value of Mandarin alongside its cultural value. As a consequence, Mandarin is increasingly popular among non-Chinese Singaporeans, even though it is not their officially assigned mother tongue (Wee, 2003). Mandarin' s position as a language that Chinese Singaporeans need to learn for heritage reasons becomes harder to sustain.

But the government's success in the Speak Mandarin Campaign should not be taken to mean that the other Chinese dialects have been completely eradicated. Dialects can still be found in Singapore, albeit not as commonly as in the days prior to the Campaign's launch. More relevantly, they have also been gaining some measure of increased popularity, so much so that several Singaporeans have even asked for the government to relax the rules prohibiting the use of Chinese dialects in the media (Ong & Goy, 2013: np):

> Several participants, who were Zaobao [a Chinese newspaper] readers ranging in age from 20 to 47, also asked for a relaxation of the rules on the use of Chinese dialects in media. They also said the utilitarian approach to teaching Chinese would strip away the beauty of the language.

> Mr Heng noted that the gradual decrease in dialect speakers can be seen even in Chinese cities like Shanghai. Singapore already has a 'complicated language environment' with its current focus on English and the mother tongue 'first and foremost', he said. Those keen to learn dialects can do so at a later age, he added.

Heng Swee Keat, Education Minister at the time (and now Deputy Prime Minister but also touted as a strong candidate to be the next Prime Minister of Singapore), responded by reiterating Singapore's language policy, specifically, its view concerning the Chinese dialects *vis-à-vis* Mandarin (Ong & Goy, 2013). Heng's reference to Shanghai is obviously intended to suggest that if the appeal of the dialects is already waning even in China, then it is not clear why Singaporeans should wish to learn them. Singaporeans wishing to learn the dialects, therefore, have to do so on their own accord. The government therefore is standing firm regarding the status of Mandarin as the official mother tongue of Chinese Singaporeans and its related view that the other Chinese dialects should not be encouraged. Nevertheless, as far as the notion of orderly multilingualism is concerned, this demonstrates that even after decades of sustained government efforts at eliminating the dialects, these linguistic weeds persist.

The state's positioning of English as an unacceptable mother tongue is also problematic. While the presence of English contributes to

Singapore's attempt to cultivate an image of being a cosmopolitan city, its wide usage has also meant that many Singaporeans are taking pride in the local variety Singlish, despite the state's own misgivings (Wee, 2018a; also see above). For many Singaporeans also, the language of the home is English rather than one of the official mother tongues.

Finally, Singapore's attempt to attract foreign talent is needed not only to replace emigrating Singaporeans. Singapore, like many other modern Asian societies such as South Korea and Japan, is struggling with low fertility rates. Consequently, the state views foreign talent as potential new citizens who might marry and have children. All this raises the likelihood of hybrid identities emerging, especially if more Singaporeans marry foreigners.

Singapore's attempt to attract foreign talent will eventually also impact upon the current approach to mother tongue education (Stroud & Wee, 2012: 200–201). This is because the foreign talent policy aims to persuade such talent to take up Singaporean citizenship, and the success of this policy could well change the nation's demographics. Japanese, Korean, French or American foreign talent who become citizens obviously cannot be expected to embrace Mandarin, Malay or Tamil as their official mother tongues. The insistence on mother tongue education has also had to be more flexible because the children of Singaporean expatriates returning to Singapore would probably not have been studying their official mother tongue while studying abroad. This has led the Ministry of Education to acknowledge that these children might need to be exempted from the mother tongue requirement (1998), thus further problematizing the notion that English-mother tongue bilingualism is the key to building a Singaporean national identity.

Linguistic Citizenship and the Cultivation of Sociolinguistic Resilience

The problems associated with the myth of orderly multilingualism indicate that we need to be better prepared to treat the mixing of language resources as the norm. However, as the myth of orderly multilingualism is one that is deeply entrenched in both institutions, as well as in public expectations about what languages 'are', there can be little doubt that trying to shift away from the myth can result in societal turmoil and anxiety about whether languages are indeed 'properly' used and/or learned (see Cameron, 1995; Milroy & Milroy, 1999). I, therefore, now turn to the issue of how the notion of Linguistic Citizenship can help cultivate sociolinguistic resilience as to minimize such turmoil. Hall and Lamont (2013: 13) point out that:

> We see resilience in dynamic terms, not as the capacity to return to a prior state but as the achievement of well-being even when that entails significant modifications to behavior or to the social frameworks that structure

and give meaning to behavior. At issue is the capacity of individuals or groups to secure favorable outcomes (material, symbolic, emotional) under new circumstances and, if need be, by new means.

The comments from Hall and Lamont emphasize the dynamic nature of resilience. It is about maintaining a sense of well-being even when there are potentially disruptive changes to social expectations, and this involves responding to such disruptions in ways that maximize the possibility of influencing the resulting consequences.

This is where Stroud's (2001, 2015, 2018a, 2018b) notion of Linguistic Citizenship constitutes a useful construct. 'Linguistic Citizenship is fundamentally an invitation to rethink our understanding of language through the lens of citizenship and participatory democracy' and it does this by interrogating 'the historical, sociopolitical and economic determinants of how languages are constructed, at the same time as it pinpoints the linguistic, structural and institutional conditions necessary for change' (Stroud, 2018b: 20). The notion of citizenship here is not restricted to formal status of being a citizen that is accorded by the state.

The notion of Linguistic Citizenship may involve speakers exercising agency through a rights' framework, as well as through institutionalized means of recognizing political participation. However, it also acknowledges and indeed gives equal if not more emphasis to 'the use of language (registers etc.) or other multimodal means in circumstances that may be orthogonal, alongside, embedded in, or outside of, institutionalized democratic frameworks for transformative purposes ... It refers to what people do with and around language(s) in order to position themselves agentively, and to craft new, emergent subjectivities of political speakerhood, often outside of those prescribed or legitimated in institutional frameworks of the state' (Stroud, 2018a: 4). Here are two examples (Stroud, 2018a: 4–5):

- So-called 'service delivery protests' on the streets of South Africa, with their highly multilingual and multimodal articulation in chants, placards, songs – and violence – comprise examples of how forms of semiosis are creatively deployed to create a disruptive space for 'citizen' engagement for those whose voices are habitually silenced ...
- Likewise, Somali refugees in Ugandan camps are also exercising Linguistic Citizenship when they use the resources – teaching spaces under trees, chalk and boards, etc. – provided by a foreign NGO to teach English literacy for their own purposes of learning to read the Quran (Kathleen Heugh, personal communication, August 2015). They are exercising their agency, and pursuing a goal that is important to *them*, but likely not to the 'keepers' of the programme. They are doing so on the sidelines and margins of the formally structured literacy programme, taking part in 'informal' networks of learning at the same time as they create the conditions for participating in new roles in alternative communities of practice.

Linguistic Citizenship is relevant in developing sociolinguistic resilience because it does not presume a stable notion of language, much less one that is construed as an autonomous well-demarcated system. It emphasizes instead that notions of what constitutes a language are varied and changeable, and as well, that a properly sophisticated approach to language politics has to be concerned with a commitment to multimodality beyond a focus on named varieties.[2]

By insisting that constructions of language cannot be separated from sociopolitical agency, Linguistic Citizenship is at its very core a dynamic understanding of the relationships between language and society. This is an understanding that links the goals of individuals and communities – and their achievable outcomes –to their willingness to actively participate in monitoring social, political and linguistic changes and, where necessary, adapting. There is, therefore, an emphasis on sustained sociolinguistic engagement in face of indeterminacy, ambiguity and power differentials so as to achieve transformative effects in institutional structures as well as in communicative practices. Precisely because of this, there are clear resonances between Linguistic Citizenship's construal of language and society, on the one hand, and the framing of social resilience offered by Hall and Lamont (2013).

Conclusion

The myth of orderly multilingualism remains powerful and persuasive. The attraction it holds – for policymakers as well as many ordinary citizens – is that it offers clarity on how to think about the otherwise highly complex relationship between language society. But this clarity comes at a price: it oversimplifies, misleads and penalizes. Ridding ourselves of the myth is therefore no easy task. But it is, nevertheless, a sociolinguistic imperative.

The basic precepts underlying the myth are inherited from northern perspectives on language planning and the desire for order. These need to be countered by southern views that are more accommodating of ambiguity and conflict, understanding that these cannot be eliminated if only everyone were properly rational but, rather, that these are endemic to the diverse and ever-changing nature of social life. Combined with the notion of Linguistic Citizenship, a shift away from the myth of orderly multilingualism need not mean chaos. Instead, it opens the way towards better appreciating the dynamic relationship between language and society.

Notes

(1) My thanks to Rebecca Starr for this example.
(2) This perspective contrasts significantly with that of, say, linguistic human rights (Phillipson & Skutnabb-Kangas, 1995; Skutnabb-Kangas, 2000), which, unfortunately, presumes an ontologically naïve (Wee, 2018b) notion of what language is, and furthermore, by adopting a rights discourse, tends to foster a sense of entitlement rather than encouraging resilience and adaptability.

References

Allan, K. and Burridge, K. (2006) *Forbidden Words: Taboo and the Censoring of Language.* Cambridge: Cambridge University Press.

Alsagoff, L. (2007) Singlish: Negotiating culture, capital and identity. In V. Vaish, S. Gopinathan and Y. Liu (eds) *Language, Capital, Culture* (pp. 25–46). Rotterdam: Sense Publishers.

Appadurai, A. (1996) *Modernity at Large.* Minneapolis: Minnesota University Press.

Arnaut, K., Blommaert, J., Rampton, B. and Spotti, M. (2016) In K. Arnaut, J. Blommaert, B. Rampton and M. Spotti (eds) *Language and Superdiversity* (pp. 1–17). New York: Routledge.

Blommaert, J. (2005) *Discourse: A Critical Introduction.* Cambridge: Cambridge University Press.

Blommaert, J. and Rampton, B. (2016) Language and superdiversity. In K. Arnaut, J. Blommaert, B. Rampton and M. Spotti (eds) *Language and Superdiversity* (pp. 21–48). New York: Routledge.

Bokhorst-Heng, W. (1998) Language and imagining the nation in Singapore. PhD dissertation, University of Toronto.

Cameron, D. (1995) *Verbal Hygiene.* London: Routledge.

Canagarajah, S. (2015) Negotiating mobile codes and literacies at the contact zone. In C. Stroud and M. Prinsloo (eds) *Language, Literacy and Diversity* (pp. 34–54). London: Routledge.

Connell, R. (2014) Using Southern theory: Decolonizing social thought in theory, research and application. *Planning Theory* 13 (2), 210–223.

Davis, K. (1994) *Language Planning in Multilingual Contexts: Policies, Communities and Schools in Luxembourg.* Amsterdam: John Benjamins.

Elegant, S. (2003) The Lion in Winter. *Time,* 7 July, 2003.

Gal, S. (1989) Lexical innovation and loss: The use and value of restricted Hungarian. In N. Dorian (ed.) *Investigating Obsolescence: Studies in Language Contraction and Death* (pp. 313–331). Cambridge: Cambridge University Press.

Hall, P. and Lamont, M. (2013) Introduction. In P. Hall and M. Lamont (eds) *Social Resilience in the Neoliberal Era* (pp. 1–34). Cambridge: Cambridge University Press.

Heller, M. (2008) Language and the nation-state: Challenges to sociolinguistic theory. *Journal of Sociolinguistics* 12 (4), 504–524.

Jacquemet, M. (1996) From the Atlas to the Alps. *Public Culture* 8 (2), 377–388.

Jacquemet, M. (2005) Transidiomatic practices: Language and power in the age of globalization. *Language and Communication* 25, 257–277.

Jaspers, J. and Madsen, L. (eds) (2018) *Critical Perspectives on Linguistic Fixity and Fluidity.* London: Routledge.

Lee Kuan Yew (2009) Speak Mandarin Campaign 30th anniversary launch, 17 March.

Masavisut, N., Sukwiwat, M. and Wongmontha, S. (1986) The power of the English language in Thai media. *World Englishes* 5 (2–3), 197–207.

Matras, Y. (2009) *Language Contact.* Cambridge: Cambridge University Press.

Milroy, J. and Milroy, L. (1999) *Authority in Language: Investigating Standard English* (3rd edn). London: Routledge.

Ministry of Education (1998) *The Straits Times,* 20 March 1998.

Ong, A. and Goy, P. (2013) Calls to rethink 'sacred cows' in nation-building. *The Straits Times,* 22 April 2013. See http://www.straitstimes.com/singapore/calls-to-rethink-sacred-cows-in-nation-building (accessed October 2021).

Otsuji, E. and Pennycook, A. (2010) Metrolingualism: fixity, fluidity and language in flux. *International Journal of Multilingualism* 7, 240–254.

Park, J. and Wee, L. (2017) Nation-state, transnationalism, and language. In S. Canagarajah (ed.) *The Routledge Handbook of Language and Migration* (pp. 47–62). London: Routledge.

Pennycook, A. (2016) Mobile times, mobile terms: The trans-super-poly-metro move-ment. In N. Coupland (ed.) *Sociolinguistics: Theoretical Debates* (pp. 201–216). Cambridge: Cambridge University Press.

Phillipson, R. and Skutnabb-Kangas, T. (1995) Linguistic rights and wrongs. *Applied Linguistics* 16, 483–504.

Rampton, B. (2006) *Language in Late Modernity*. Cambridge: Cambridge University Press.

Rappa, A. and Wee, L. (2006) *Language Policy and Modernity in Southeast Asia: Malaysia, the Philippines, Singapore and Thailand*. New York: Springer.

Regan, V., Howard, M. and Lemée, I. (2009) *The Acquisition of Sociolinguistic Competence in a Study Abroad Context*. Bristol: Multilingual Matters.

Schneider, E. (2011) English into Asia: From Singaporean ubiquity to Chinese learners' features. In M. Adams and A. Curzan (eds) *Contours of English and English Language Studies* (pp. 135–156). Ann Arbor, MI: University of Michigan Press.

Skutnabb-Kangas, T. (2000) *Linguistic Genocide in Education – Or Worldwide Diversity and Human Rights*. Mahwah, NJ: Lawrence Erlbaum.

Stroud, C. (2001) African mother-tongue programmes and the politics of language: Linguistic citizenship versus linguistic human rights. *Journal of Multilingual and Multicultural Development* 22 (4), 339–355.

Stroud, C. (2004) Rinkeby Swedish and semilingualism in language ideological debates: A Bourdieuean perspective. *Journal of Sociolinguistics* 8, 196–214.

Stroud, C. (2015) Linguistic citizenship as utopia. *Multilingual Margins* 2, 20–37.

Stroud, C. (2018a) Introduction. In L. Lim, C. Stroud and L. Wee (eds) *The Multilingual Citizen: Towards a Politics of Language for Agency and Change* (pp. 1–14). Bristol: Multilingual Matters.

Stroud, C. (2018b) Linguistic citizenship. In L. Lim, C. Stroud and L. Wee (eds) *The Multilingual Citizen: Towards a Politics of Language for Agency and Change* (pp. 17–39). Bristol: Multilingual Matters.

Stroud, C. and Wee, L. (2007) Consuming identities: Language policy and planning in Singaporean late modernity. *Language Policy* 6 (2), 253–279.

Stroud, C. and Wee, L. (2012) *Style, Identity and Literacy: English in Singapore*. Bristol: Multilingual Matters.

Tony Tan Keng Yam (1986) Parliamentary speech, March 1986.

Vasil, R. (1995) *Asianising Singapore*. Singapore: Heinemann Asia.

Vertovec, S. (2007a) *New Complexities of Cohesion in Britain: Superdiversity, Transnationalism and Civil-Integration*. Oxford: COMPAS, Oxford University Press.

Vertovec, S. (2010) Towards post-multiculturalism? Changing communities, contexts and conditions of diversity. *International Social Science Journal* 199, 83–95.

Watson, V. (2009) Seeing from the South: Refocusing urban planning on the globe's central urban issues. *Urban Studies* 46 (11), 2259–2275.

Weber, J. and Horner, K. (2012) *Introducing Multilingualism: A Social Approach*. London: Routledge.

Wee, L. (2003) Linguistic instrumentalism in Singapore. *Journal of Multilingual and Multicultural Development* 24 (3), 211–224.

Wee, L. (2010) 'Burdens' and 'handicaps' in Singapore's language policy: On the limits of language management. *Language Policy* 9 (2), 97–114.

Wee, L. (2011) *Language without Rights*. Oxford: Oxford University Press.

Wee, L. (2012) Neoliberalism and the regulation of consumers: Legalizing casinos in Singapore. *Critical Discourse Studies* 9 (1), 15–27.

Wee, L. (2014) Language politics and global city. *Discourse: Studies in the Cultural Politics of Education*. DOI: 10.1080/01596306.2014.922740.

Wee, L. (2018a) *The Singlish Controversy: Language, Culture and Identity in a Globalizing World*. Cambridge: Cambridge University Press.

Wee, L. (2018b) Standards in English. In P. Seargeant, A. Hewings and S. Pihlaja (eds) *The Routledge Handbook of English Language Studies*. London: Routledge.

3 Linguistic Citizenship as a Decolonial Lens on Southern Multilingualisms and Epistemologies

Kathleen Heugh

Introduction

The challenges of understanding the historical, geographical and multi-dimensional complexity of multilingualism(s) bring epistemological and ethical cleavages increasingly to the fore. At first glance, these cleavages may appear to be cast as south–north or decolonial–colonial antagonisms. At a second glance, these are reflections of dynamic 'entanglements' (Kerfoot & Hyltenstam, 2017) of both interdependencies (Heugh, 2017; Heugh & Stroud, 2019) and cleavages (e.g. Santos, 2012, 2018). Stroud's (2001) proposal of 'Linguistic Citizenship' was an invitation to pause and reflect on the circulation of competing and divisive narratives of whose views matter in discussions of linguistic heterogeneity. It was also an opportunity to provide a lens through which participants in opposing narratives among linguists might recognize conversations of decoloniality that had been circulating in Africa and South America for some decades (e.g. Achebe, 1958; Fanon, 1963 [1961]; Ngũgĩ wa Thiong'o, 1986). Stroud (2001) carried several voices, including some filtered through conversations between Stroud and me, in which habituated practices of social division were recognized in ill-conceived interpretations of post-apartheid language policy. Linguistic Citizenship signals an opportunity to listen, with respect, to what it is that people in the post-colonies have to say about the languages they use, how they use them and their views of how best to use them for different purposes as they go about their lives and livelihoods across time and place.

The purpose here is to offer an historical account that situates Linguistic Citizenship alongside a long vein of preceding decolonial, African and southern discussions of language (see also Heugh & Stroud, 2020). It also offers a contextual background for understanding how participants from various disciplines and spaces of power in the rapidly changing political circumstances in southern Africa during the 1990s failed to listen to and/or hear how people in 'southern' post-colonies revealed their views of language. It is in the process of uncovering some of these voices that Linguistic Citizenship can be understood as a phenomenon of *longue durée*.

There had been a moment of possibility for reimagining a decolonial language policy for South Africa, influenced by the literary works and analyses of Achebe, Fanon and Ngũgĩ wa Thiong'o, and encouraged by discussions of language planning from below (Bamgbose, 1987; Chumbow, 1987). Some of these appeared through attempts to identify the multiple ways in which people make use of their linguistic heterogeneity in Africa. Two examples include a recognition that 'multilingualism is the lingua franca in Africa' (Fardon & Furniss, 1994); and that people make use of 'functional multilingualism' as a fluid resource for horizontal purposes and also as carefully curated for vertical purposes (Heugh, 1995). By the late 1990s, however, it had become clear that the moment of decolonial possibility had begun to recede. The inept interpretations in the Constitution of the Republic of South Africa (1996) and compromised arrangements in the amendments to the legislation affecting the Pan South African Language Board (PANSALB) had reproduced colonial language regimes (Heugh, 2003). Stroud's witnessing of a reproduction of coloniality in language regimes of Mozambique and South Africa led him to propose 'Linguistic Citizenship' (Stroud, 2001) as a lens and stance consistent with decoloniality. While the phenomenon itself was not new, it was one that had gone largely unnoticed in literature that focuses on (mis)perceptions, mishearings and assumptions of how people make decisions about their languages and language practices. It is the naming of and illustrating of this phenomenon that contributed then, and continues now, to decolonial and southern ways of thinking about language.

Erasure as Coloniality Reproduced

Historical practices of erasure, including well-rehearsed use of labelling and stigma in revisionist spoken and written recollections have occluded ideologies, scholarship and African agency in research and linguistic endeavour for much of the 20th century. Partly, this may be ascribed to different practices of knowledge circulation between people who have placed greater weight on practices of orature in what some would argue are more than two thousand languages of the continent and those who have placed and continue to place greater weight on published literature. This is literature in one of what Kusch (1970, 2010) refers to as the (six) 'imperial languages'. Very little of the knowledge embedded in the languages of Africa travels into English, French, German, Italian, Portuguese, Spanish[1]; and that which does is often misunderstood and distorted (e.g. Owino, 2002). Partly, as Ngũgĩ wa Thiong'o points out, this may be accounted for in an ideological and sociopolitical cleavage between knowledge systems that accord greater significance to orature and those that accord this to literature, particularly when published by 'the academy' in English (Ngũgĩ wa Thiong'o, 1986, 1993).[2] Partly, this erasure arises from the arrogance of northern perceptions of a universal view of theory (Connell, 2019) that circulates in written documents in a few languages (Kusch, 2010 [1970]; see also Medina, 2014).

For the most part, the persons whose voices are included in this chapter have either not been recognized in the mainstream academic press or they have undergone processes of erasure, misinterpretation and predation. Here, attention is drawn to speakers of African languages who have been active contributors to discussions of the nature of linguistic diversity and contradictory practices of linguists, yet their identities and participatory roles have been invisibilized, not so much by their contemporaries, but by critics at a later stage keen to offer simplistic accounts of the past. An attempt is also made to bring from the shadows glimpses of 'forgotten people' (Johnson, 1997) whose linguistic and epistemological-rich voices have with wanton disregard been ignored. In these, discussions, which include contemporary sociolinguists, are caught within the webbing of coloniality, Christian evangelism and European crafted policies of segregation through much of the 20th century. They continue in revisionist texts of the last four decades, where 'scholars' of history, sociology and sociolinguists have found it difficult to disentangle misreadings and misperceptions in the absence of close examination of archival texts and records.

Routes and Re-rooting[3] Linguistic Epistemes

In this chapter, there is an attempt to respond to what seems to be ongoing myopia about who gets to decide the hierarchies of knowledge, the basis of such knowledge, the source or ownership of knowledge and the context from which these emerge. It is a response to claims of knowledge about language practices and multilingualisms in Africa that continue to filter through a lens that mutes and invisibilizes the views of, and even the presence of, linguistic minorities. It is a lens that filters and refracts but, nevertheless, retains the structure of a northern or 'North Atlantic' (e.g. Connell, 2007, 2014) frame of reference. It is one that may also take on new life across an 'abyssal line' (Santos, 2018) of epistemological divide. Although sociolinguistics as a discipline has affiliations with anthropology and historical linguistics, and despite having apparently embraced critical postcolonial discourses of Gramsci (Gramsci et al., 1971), Foucault (e.g. 1972), Bourdieu (e.g. 1989, 1990), and even Fanon (1963 [1961]), it has, with few exceptions, been unable to sever its taproot shared with disciplines nourished by philosophical and scientific discourses of 'Reason' and 'Enlightenment'. Ironically, it is from this rootstock that we can trace the unscientific notion of race in the work of Kant (e.g. Mikkelsen, 2013), Hegel (2001) and Macaulay (1835) as this filtered through 18th- and 19th-century colonial appropriation. The legacy of Kant and Hegel, associated with early racist discounting of knowledge and scholarship in Africa[4] was extended by Thomas Babington Macaulay (1835) in his infamous 'Minute on Education' in India:

> ... the dialects commonly spoken among the natives of this part of India contain neither literary nor scientific information, and are moreover so poor and rude that, until they are enriched from some other quarter, it will not be easy to translate any valuable work into them....

> I have no knowledge of either Sanscrit or Arabi .... I have conversed ... with men distinguished by their proficiency in the Eastern tongues. I am quite ready to take the oriental learning at the valuation of the orientalists themselves. I have never found one among them who could deny that a single shelf of a good European library was worth the whole native literature of India and Arabia. (Macaulay, 1835)

A dual pattern of speaking about 'the natives' in ways that excluded their voice and agency, was coupled with revisionist and racist 19th-century narratives that dismissed long histories of scholarship and literary practices beyond Europe. This continued in overt narratives of race and European hegemony in the rise of 20th-century fascism in Europe, recycled in southern Africa, continuing even in Oxford historian Hugh Trevor Roper's astonishing dismissal of pre-colonial history of Africa (Trevor-Roper, 1965). This lineage of thinking predisposes a habitus, in which erasure of voice, agency, scholarship and, ultimately, the citizenship of people previously subjected to European colonialism continues, albeit reshaped by linguists, other scholars and administrative agents who have since continued to speak on behalf of, or about, people in the post-colonies. It is perhaps, as suggested by Pavlenko (2019), a sociolinguistics more concerned with positioning authors within a northern, often narcissistic, academy than one closely attuned or attentive to voices beyond an increasingly unstable and unpredictable 'centre' of assumed authority.

While the late 20th century has certainly taken a critical cue from Gramsci (Gramsci et al., 1971), Foucault (1972) and even Fanon (1963[1961]), several southern thinkers, e.g. Connell (2007), Kusch (1970, 2010), Mignolo (2011a, 2011b), Nakata (2007) and Smith (1999), argue that they may not have ventured far enough. Proponents of critical thinking and linguistics have found it difficult to step out of (or rip out) deep-rooted assumptions of southern epistemic inferiorities and northern authority in the academy. Instead, northern 'authority' is reproduced through urgent (often lexical) prescriptivism immune to history, context and linguistic realities of many, if not most people, whose systems and experiences of belief, knowledge and being occur in the borderlands beyond the academy (e.g. Heugh, 2017).

This chapter builds on the swelling of southern and decolonial thinking across the humanities, and particularly in sociolinguistics (e.g. Bock & Stroud, 2021; Heugh & Stroud, 2019; Kerfoot, 2009; Kerfoot & Hyltenstam, 2017; Macías *et al.*, 1971; Mignolo, 1996; Ndhlovu, 2018a, 2018b; Stroud & Mpendukana, 2009; Williams, 2017; Williams & Stroud, 2015). It continues an exploration of how it is that sociolinguistics may be enriched through a lens of Linguistic Citizenship as this intersects with 'mestizo consciousness' (Kusch, 2010 [1970]), and 'epistemic reflexivity' (Bourdieu, 1989, 1990; Salö, 2017, 2018) and thus advances sociolinguistics beyond what appears to be an 'abyssal line' (Santos, 2012, 2018) being drawn between a northern hegemony of sociolinguistics and southern agents and resistances.

Heugh (2017), following Mignolo (2010), reflects on 'mestizo consciousness' as a conscious awareness and perhaps capacity to hear, see and understand that there is no singular, universal, knowledge system or system of knowledge production. There are perhaps only pluriversalities of knowledge systems, ways of being and ways of doing (see also Connell, 2007, 2014; Nakata, 2007; Smith, 1999). Kusch, whose parents migrated to Argentina, recognized that his own epistemology was shaped from the northern cannon, and that he recognized the presence of alternative, Indigenous systems of South America. He further recognized that while Indigeneity(ies) may be distinct from it, they were also entangled with a European/northern, essentialist and universalist view of knowledge production. It is the reflexive capacity to recognize epistemic pluralities and their entanglements that is central to mestizo consciousness. Writing from an Australian context in which plurality of knowledge systems are both deeply rooted and veiled through a coloniality of myopia, Connell (2019) argues in a related vein:

> As well as recognizing indigenous knowledge formations and alternative universalisms, we need to pay attention to knowledge generated from the colonial encounter, and from colonial and postcolonial social dynamics. This is what I have called 'Southern Theory'. (2019: 92)

In a recent essay that revisits Bourdieu's notion of 'epistemic reflexivity', 'Seeing the point from which you see what you see', Salö (2018) reminds researchers to set aside hubris and the arrogance of certainty. The purpose here, drawing upon linguistic citizenship, mestizo consciousness, southern theory and epistemic reflexivity, is an attempt to navigate towards and perhaps re-root or re-route[5] an ethics of sociolinguistic scholarship that is sensitive to the relationship among communities, place, being and knowledges. It is thus part of a much broader quest for a way of thinking that might restore balance among ethos, pathos and logos. It involves a journey that revisits multiple voices and recognition of 'linguistic citizenship' as preceding and continuing beyond our inclination, as linguists, to default to linguistic prescriptivism, however much we try to resist this.

Below, several southern voices that may not circulate as widely as others are brought to the fore. Three small examples of the erasure of voices of speakers of languages of Southern Africa are offered. In the first, a historical example illustrates how this has bled across revisionist linguistics of Africa in ways that occlude contributions of African scholars in populist revisionist accounts of linguistic endeavour. In the second, the early years of the 'new' South Africa reproduced an apartheid-style disposition of exclusion of minority communities through a re-layering of marginality and invisibilization. Ironically, this occurred under the guise of 'democracy', social transformation and a human rights-based constitution. The third example illustrates the processes of invisibilizing data collected for PANSALB's first sociolinguistic survey of the country in 2000. In my conclusion, I return to Stroud's concept of Linguistic Citizenship as an ethical frame for re-placing and re-rooting southern voice, agency and consciousness in narratives that circulate within the academy.

Southern Discourses of Decoloniality

Neither decolonial nor southern thinking is new. There are several strands of discussions that have been travelling and criss-crossing Africa, the Americas, Asia and the Pacific for decades if not longer. These include interest in Chicana/o studies from the 1960s (Macías, 1977, 2005; Macías et al., 1971); literary figures (Fanon, [1961] 1963; Ngũgĩ wa Thiong'o, 1983, 1986); and Indigenous Knowledge Systems in the 1990s (e.g. Goula, 1995; Hoppers, 2001, 2002; Odora Hoppers, 1999; Smith, 1999). In each of these, the voice and agency of most people in southern contexts, obscured through centuries of European conquest surface with narratives that have either not been heard or they have been misunderstood when translated into more powerful texts of a northern-metropolitan academy. This is one fixated on theoretical frames generated among people of the north, often about, but not with, people of the south.

One hundred and seventy years after the 'Macaulay Minute', Martin Nakata captures how such frames continue in the introduction to his volume, *Disciplining the Savages, Savaging the Disciplines*:

> To me, they [cross-cultural and Australian Indigenous university course components] seemed to be less about 'me', 'us' or 'our' situation and more about what people with academic knowledge – the 'experts' – thought about things ... Our perspective ... was mostly obscured from view and, it would seem, irrelevant as it could always be explained away by theoretical knowledge. Yet, I felt, this large body of theoretical knowledge was only able to chart the surface level of our historical experience; it could never penetrate within and illuminate the shadowy corners. (Nakata, 2007: 2)

In this, Nakata, and others before him, take issue with the historical misrepresentations and revisionism that perhaps began with Hegel (2001 [1822–1830]), Kant (Mikkelsen, 2013) and Macaulay (1835).

Uncomfortable Erasure

I turn now to three cases in which I hope to illustrate that African voices, languages and knowledges are often erased or occluded by those who through misguided patriarchies of practice, attempt to speak for others or who claim authoritative understanding of historical narratives, realities and scholarship of linguistic diversity in Southern Africa.

Languages and linguists in 20th-century South Africa

For various reasons, including the tightening grip of apartheid segregationist language policy from the mid-1950s to the student revolt in SOWETO in 1976, the debates about African Languages have been overlaid with racism and political ideologies. By the early 1980s, the spotlight turned towards the role of linguists, often conflated as a homogenous entity of European missionaries, with questions of their legitimacy, past and then present collaboration or complicity with colonial administrations (see e.g. Errington, 2001; Hirson, 1981; Makoni, 1998; Ranger, 1984). This has led to some 'legitimate' critiques, but also a process in which the voice, agency and scholarship of many 20th-century African linguists have, however unintentionally, been cast aside or occluded. It has also led to essentialist assumptions about both native and non-native speakers of African languages, issues of authenticity and questions of legitimacy in relation to voice and agency. In effect, an abyssal line has been drawn between linguists who have legitimacy and those who do not. An interesting aspect of this apparent divide is 'who call the shots' and 'whose voices are absent'.

There are and have been layers of invisibilization or silencing of the voices of African participants in language debates, both prior to the 1980s and since this time. In the discussions since the early 1980s of the activities of early 20th-century linguists at least two shifts in thinking about linguistics in Southern Africa have become evident. The first is a shift from 'speaking with' to 'speaking about' or 'speaking for' communities of people whose histories predate European colonization in Africa. The second is an argument that associates linguists from the late 19th and through much of the 20th centuries in Southern Africa with one or more of the following characteristics or dispositions: colonial, neocolonial,'white', 'missionary', or 'collaborator' – in a manner that is accusatory or stigmatizing. The intention appears to delegitimize the work of all 'white' and or 'missionary' linguists prior to the late-1980s. African linguists, scholars, writers and commentators have either been 'written out', or their voice and agency 'stripped out' of revised accounts of debates and participation within what has been framed as 'colonial' or 'missionary linguistics' of the 20th century (e.g. Errington, 2001). In cases where African scholars were appointed to or served on language committees, language boards and writers' guilds, they were labelled 'collaborators' by prominent critics in the 'resistance' movements and university employed academics. It became almost impossible to express one's resistance to the blanket stigma cast over all white missionary linguists and/or African linguists who worked with African languages if one wished to avoid being labelled 'apartheid collaborator' in the tumultuous late 1980s and early 1990s.[6]

There would be few, if any, who would dispute the apartheid regime's intention to invisibilize and hence 'de-legitimize' speakers of African languages in many ways, especially minority communities of people who identified as speakers of languages that were not accorded 'officially recognized' status between 1948 and 1994. Ironically, however, precisely the same process of rendering inaudible the voices of minority or 'oppressed' communities, as had occurred during apartheid, was attempted and replicated in the most persuasive of the debates during the terminal stages of apartheid and in the new post-apartheid structures (noted in Heugh, 2003, 2016; Sotashe, 1992, 2017; Stroud, 2001; Stroud & Heugh, 2004).

The concern here is to attempt to disentangle how northern and southern discourses of linguistic heterogeneity and (in)visible patriarchies anchored in pervasive racism cross abyssal lines and are sometimes turned upside down. This, as illuminated in Kerfoot and Hyltenstam (2017), is an attempt to illustrate how easily well-meaning linguists in search of social justice, or opportunistic public sector officials, may risk speaking for or about, rather than with, those they hope or claim to liberate from oppression. This is a weakness in literature and language policy framed in language rights' arguments that both Heugh and Stroud (Heugh, 1995, 2003; Stroud, 2001; Stroud & Heugh, 2004) have noted in postcolonial language policy in Southern Africa. A similar weakness appears in postcolonial literature that relies on redacted secondary rather than primary archival documents (discussed below). The point here is to argue that advisers to, and administrators in, the apparently transformed post-apartheid South Africa have clung to essentialist and racist perceptions of linguists from African and European backgrounds that allow de facto *laissez-faire* language policy to continue rather than disrupt practices of exclusion (Heugh, 1995, 2004; Sotashe, 2017).

Example 1: Invisibilization and muting of African linguists and debates

In the first illustrative example, attention is drawn to the debates about processes of transcribing African languages and development of orthographies through the 20th century, and how the participation of first-language speakers in these processes has been erased from accounts of the debates. This erasure permits the risk of a neo-colonial habitus to entrap scholars who use and recycle secondary, sometimes ill-founded, sources that are often not authored by linguists or specialist scholars in the field. Debates about transcription, orthography, standardization and harmonization of languages in Africa led to and gained prominence at the Rejaf Conference in Sudan in 1928, and appear, subsequently, to have become misreported, at least in part. Archival research undertaken by August Cluver (1992, 1996) has revealed that as early as 1906, missionary linguists had realized that owing to their different conventions for transcription and orthographic endeavour, the processes of selection and codification of African languages were inconsistent. They recognized that these had led to the separation and divergence of closely related languages and artificial 'territorialization' of language communities. The inconsistencies and practices of divergence occupied the attention of linguists from across Africa who gathered at the Rejaf Conference in 1928 to discuss the possibilities of convergence through a process they named 'harmonizing' of African orthographies. This was captured in a proposal for a 'The Practical Orthography of African Languages' (James, 1928). The issue of how to approach convergence continued in discussions among several linguists over the next few years (e.g. Cluver, 1996: 71–73, 76–77; Lestrade, 1929; Tucker, 1929).

The debates were taken up by additional stakeholders in the 1940s in South Africa, when Jacob Nhlapo, a journalist and educator, shifted attention away from the linguists, and argued for the convergence of languages within the Nguni and within the Sotho clusters of languages. Effectively, Nhlapo (1944: 5) argued this as a democratic process that would de-stigmatize urban practices of code-mixing and code-switching in which, 'a Tswana speaker ... uses some Sotho words' or someone else 'mixes Zulu with Xhosa' to strengthen each of the respective language clusters, and eventually to lead to the convergence of the two clusters themselves:

> To build Nguni, Zulu could easily use good Xhosa words, and Xhosa could use good Zulu words. Pedi, Tswana and Southern Sotho could also take good words from each other ... It is easy for Nguni to make a Sotho borrowed word take a Nguni shape, and it is easy for a Nguni borrowed word to take a Sotho shape ... [J]oining languages together is a good thing ... [I]t is really happening and it will go on happening wherever two or more languages are spoken in the same place. (Nhlapo, 1944: 7–9)[7]

In this, and later, Nhlapo (1944, 1945, 1953) continued discussions of linguistic convergence that had circulated in the language committees and at the Rejaf Conference and he pre-empted sociolinguistic debates on repertoires of language and linguistic fluidity that surfaced six decades later. It is highly likely that Nhlapo was aware of the debates among linguists, for example that Gladstone Llewellyn Letele had been investigating the influence of Nguni vocabulary on Southern Sotho (Letele, 1945). Letele's research certainly informed the work of Archibald Tucker (1949) who had been exploring the feasibility of a combined or unified Sotho-Nguni orthography subsequent to his participation in the Rejaf conference some 20 years earlier. While Tucker acknowledged Letele's research from which he was able to revise his own earlier work, only seven authors, including Heugh (2016), appear to have done likewise or linked this to Nhlapo's challenge.

As suggested earlier, critiques of missionary linguistics began to resurface in the 1980s from a variety of historians, linguists, political scientists and sociologists (e.g. Errington, 2001; Hirson, 1981; Makoni, 1998, 2003; Ranger, 1984). Among these, there has been a consistent line of argument suggesting that missionary linguists in collusion with colonial administrators were either negligent or deliberately engaged in artificial or illegitimate processes of selection, exclusion, fragmentation of African languages in southern Africa. For some reason, these critics stop short of acknowledging the linguists' internal debates, changes of direction and attempts to resolve their errors.

There are several troubling features in this literature. Most significant for this discussion is that it includes suggestions or implications that African authors who were active members of writers' guilds and scholars who were members of language boards or committees between the 1950s and mid-1990s were either incompetent or collaborators with a new generation of linguists believed to be servants of the apartheid government. The critics from the 1980s onwards were neither closely involved with nor close observers of how the contributors to literary, lexicographic, orthographic, terminological, translation and other language 'development' work went about their endeavours, usually *pro bono*. While the critics certainly identified inconsistencies and contradictory practices, they offer partial truths, stopping short of careful analysis of the archival records of continuing debates among the linguists. Prominent linguists, Cluver (1996), Msimang (1992, 1994, 2000), Satyo (2001, personal communication[8]) and Sotashe (1992), argued that at best the criticisms were exaggerated, at worst grossly unjust.[9] The omission of the contributions of and participation by African scholars to the processes of transcription, orthographic decision-making, harmonization and standardization, often as office-holders in 'language committees' and 'language boards' requires some reflexivity. All of the critics who were located within institutions of higher education in South Africa at the time of their writing and prior to April 1994, might equally have been accused of collaborating with the apartheid regime that paid their salaries and offered additional perks.[10]

Example 2: Post-apartheid administration reinventing instruments of erasure

In the reimagining of post-apartheid South Africa, new provincial administrative boundaries were drawn. The former Cape Province was divided into three provinces: Eastern, Northern and Western Cape. Here I attempt to show that in the context of apparent sociopolitical transformation, a provincial government authority commissioned two linguists to draft a language policy for the Northern Cape Government in 1997. The African National Congress had an overwhelming majority of political power in the province at the time, and one might have expected that there would be an interest in an inclusive language policy for the province, certainly one that would be inclusive of minority communities that had experienced the greatest degree of marginality under the apartheid regime. But this was not the case. The linguists, Dumisane Ntshangase and I, a 'white' English-speaking woman, neither of whom were home language speakers of the majority languages of the province (Afrikaans, Setswana and isiXhosa) were asked to take on this task. Very soon it became apparent that the task was intended to be superficial.[11] It had been assumed that Ntshangase would be observant of and ensure that the prevailing political preferences of the ANC would be upheld, and that together with Heugh, an assumed anglophile, would draft a language policy in which English would be placed in a triumphal position despite only 21% of people claiming to understand the language in the province at the time (PANSALB, 2000a: 180). Ntshangase, to the surprise of the administrators, had animated and enthusiastic discussions with the leader of the most conservative of the political parties in the province, Dr Carel Boshoff, an Afrikaans-speaking person with enviable knowledge and fluency in the most respectful register of several African languages, including Setswana, the most widely spoken of these in the province.

The government administration certainly did not intend the researchers to offer a granulated policy acknowledging heterogeneity, and particularly not one that would draw attention to minority communities, previously silenced or considered a hindrance, in a new vision of provincial unity. The terms of reference were that the linguists should consult government agencies in the capital, Kimberley, and no provision was made for travelling to communities that lived beyond the outskirts of the capital city. There was considerable dismay when I insisted on visiting Schmidtsdrift, 80 km from Kimberley, where approximately 3500 speakers of !Xun and 1200 speakers of Khwe were living in army tents.[12] The South African Defence Force had co-opted or coerced !Xun and Khwe men living close to the Anglolan and Namibian borders to serve as 'trackers' prior to the 1990 independence of Namibia. The trackers and their families had to be evacuated at Namibian independence as their lives were at risk of reprisals for 'collaboration' with the South Africans, however unwilling this had been. The Northern Cape Government was reluctant to accept responsibility for the educational needs of the children of these communities, because this would be inconvenient and because Schmidtsdrift was subject to a local land claim from the Bathlaping community at the time.

> During lengthy discussions … the elders insist they still possess a significant store of knowledge about field craft, traditional medicines and folklore. The problem is that much of this information is neither being documented nor passed on to the youngsters. The histories, cultures, languages of the communities are not taught at school … Most of the materials that women in the !Xu[13] and Khwe communities need for the traditional craft work are not available. (Johnson, 1997)

In addition to their failure to acknowledge responsibilities towards the communities that had been displaced from Angola and Namibia, the administrators had limited information about minority Khoe and San language communities elsewhere in the province. For example, they claimed that there were no remaining speakers of Gri (Griqua) in the province, despite informal reports to the contrary. There was further dismay in Kimberley when I insisted on remaining in the province for another two weeks to travel to remote areas to investigate informal reports that there were still speakers of Gri (Griqua) in and around two towns, Campbell and Douglas. Things got worse for the officials when Heugh indicated that even if the province did not provide transportation (and they did not), she would also travel to communities known to speak Nama to the west, and of Nama, /'Auni, and ǂKhomani in the northern reaches of the province. This was not what had been expected of a docile 'white' English-speaking woman. It also meant that the officials would have to send their own vehicle to monitor me and, one assumes, to ensure that I did not 'make up' (invent) or distort data relating to speakers of minority languages.

Shortly after arriving in Douglas and speaking with people in and around a community centre, a person identified as a community leader, Kaptein Isak Nel, volunteered to put the word out that there were people wanting to know if there were speakers of the Gri language near the town. Over a period of two hours approximately 200 people came to the community centre, each claiming to be speakers of Gri, or bilingual speakers of Gri and Afrikaans. Not only did it become evident that there were people who wished to identify as speakers of and who remained speakers of Gri, but that they offered clearly articulated views about the vitality of Gri. They expressed disappointment and regret that the use of the language had declined, attributing this partly to stigma experienced by the younger generation (youth) who experienced ridicule from peers for speaking a 'click' language.

> Ouma Kaatjie Elam complains about the [*elektroniese kinders*] 'electric children' who want little to do with the [*oudtydse*] 'outdated' language, cultural rituals and folklore of the older people.... Oupa Wessel van Vuuren ... says that unless the knowledge of the elders about traditional herbs and medicines, folklore and language is documented soon, [*die Griquas sal afgesny word van hul' kultuur en taal*] 'the Griquas will be cut away from both their language and their culture'. (Johnson, 1997)[14]

A matter of concern to older members of the community was the then recent death of a particular medical practitioner. The doctor, who although a 'white' Afrikaans-speaking member of the mainstream medical fraternity, had understood Griqua medicinal practices and had learned from traditional healers the art of gathering and preparing herbs from the 'veld', what is known as *veldkennis* (knowledge of the veld), for various ailments administered through *inspuitings* (injections). At the time, the

Griqua community were distrustful of 'western' medicine but had trusted this doctor because he had learned to serve the community's medical needs using Griqua knowledge practices. The death of this medical practitioner before he had been able to pass on his knowledge to another local doctor signalled to the community that knowledge of Griqua medicinal practices was either lost or at serious risk of loss (see also Crawhall, 1997). This was cause for anxiety and compromised both mental and physical health among community members.

The government officials who accompanied me found it difficult to understand the consequences of or empathise with the relationship between stigma and language loss or the loss of medicinal knowledge. However, they were able to confirm in a later meeting in the provincial government offices that they had indeed listened to, recognized and witnessed at least 200 people in one town claim to be speakers of Gri.

The government officials were not prepared to travel or work over weekends and so lost contact with me for several days, reappearing in the northern part of the province for only two days the following week. This was to make cursory connections with a small community of ‡Khomani speakers in the Mier district near Welkom. After this, they tired of the journey and returned once more to Kimberley. This was before contacting Elsie Vaalbooi, who at 95 years of age was thought to be the last remaining speaker of /'Auni, at Rietfontein on the Namibian border. Senior government officials sent a message to me insisting that I ask Elsie Vaalbooi to translate or interpret the motto of the province into her home language. It is telling that no official thought that this might be disrespectful, insensitive, predatory or that it should have been important for them to be present when Vaalbooi was asked to gift her language expertise to the province. Through her son, Petrus, we did ask Elsie to interpret the motto 'Ons strewe vir 'n beter lewe' (We strive for a better life) into her language. We recorded her several times saying, 'Sa ||a !aĩsi 'uĩsi', and her words are now included in the provincial motto. Linguist Nigel Crawhall (2004) was later to identify her language as N|u a dialect of the N||n‡e (‡Khomani) people. All that Elsie hoped for was to be able to return to the area from which she and her community were forcibly removed in 1930. This area was subsequently proclaimed a national park, the Kalahari Gemsbok Park (later the Kgalagadi Transfrontier Park bordering Namibia and Botswana). She wanted to collect some *tsamma tsamma* melons and prepare the seeds for nourishment – something she remembered doing with her mother before 1930. Owing to her family's language shift to Nama and Afrikaans, and her isolation from other remaining speakers of her language, she had never been able to pass on the knowledge of how to prepare the seeds (see also Crawhall, 1997).[15]

The Northern Cape was never to implement a granulated language policy, and except for Elsie Vaalbooi's gift, entirely ignored the voices and wishes of minority communities that both anticipated and feared the consequences of language, cultural and epistemic loss. Instead, the provincial authorities, as if they were 19th-century colonial predatory agents, preferred to adopt an English-mainly policy despite this language being less viable in the province than perhaps in any other part of the country (see also Heugh, 1997; Heugh & Ntshangase, 1997).

Example 3: The National Sociolinguistic Survey of South Africa

Elsewhere I have offered a documentary critique of the structural failure of the statutory body the PANSALB established in 1996 to monitor the implementation of constitutional clauses that support a multilingual society (e.g. Heugh, 2003). Here I refer to one of PANSALB's initiatives that offered potentially enabling data that government could use to implement the clauses of the constitution, *Language Use and Language Interaction in South Africa. A National Sociolinguistic Survey* (PANSALB, 2000a). A collaborative process for the development of the survey structure and each of the individual questions (items) was undertaken between the Language Policy sub-committee of the Board between 1999 and 2000[16] and MarkData, the agency contracted to undertake the survey. MarkData conducted the survey using a 'multi-stage stratified probability sample of 2160 households... using a randomised grid' from which one person over the age of 16 from each household was chosen to respond to the questions (PANSALB, 2000a: 2). Stratification of the survey comprised rural–urban distinctions such as: traditional vs. commercial farming areas, towns vs. metropolitan, low-cost housing vs. suburban, main households vs. domestic workers, hostels and collective residences, informal settlements. Data were collected through face-to-face interviews conducted by experienced fieldworkers, with appropriate local language matched expertise, and specialised training for this survey. Back-checks were conducted on 15% of the interviews (PANSALB, 2000a: 2).

There are multiple instances of findings from this survey that did not align with anecdotal accounts of language preferences and use that circulated in prominent circles and literature at the time. Here only three sets of findings are mentioned briefly. It had been widely expected that questions relating to the preferred language/s of instruction at schools and universities would return an overwhelming response showing a preference for English. This was not in fact the case. Only 12% of respondents recorded a preference for English medium only, whereas 88% of people returned responses that indicated a preference for both home language and English (i.e. bilingual medium of instruction) in both school and university education (PANSALB, 2000a: 121–139). A further surprising finding was that although it had been anticipated that most respondents would report household practices of bi-/multilingual and/or code-mixing or code-switching, the data did not match public perceptions or predictions (e.g. Makoni, 1998, 2003). Thirty-six percent of people overall (i.e. slightly more than one-third) identified as bilingual or multilingual, and acknowledged use of code-mixing and code-switching practices at home. Speakers of Siswati (62%) were most likely to engage in these practices because of their identity as minority language speakers in proximity to speakers of isiZulu and Xitsonga in Northern KwaZulu-Natal and Mpumalanga. Of the 36% of people that reported language mixing in homes, the following combinations of language mixing, (the first mentioned language being more dominant in the home) were reported (PANSALB, 2000a: 3–13) in descending order of prevalence as:

- Afrikaans and English
- Sesotho, Setswana and isiZulu
- Setswana, Afrikaans, Sepedi and Sesotho
- Sepedi and Xitsonga
- Siswati and isiZulu
- isiNdebele, isiZulu and Afrikaans
- isiXhosa, English, isiZulu and Afrikaans
- isiZulu and English
- Tshivenda, Xitsonga and Sepedi
- Xitsonga and Tshivenda
- European and Oriental languages and English.

The degree of assumed multilinguality or multilingualism, particularly in urban contexts was not borne out by these data. The prevalence of English as the language added into the main language of the home was reported more frequently among younger and more highly educated younger respondents. The findings also indicated that the home language was identified most frequently as the language of greatest fluency and thought. The media release of the survey, prepared by the Language Policy sub-committee (PANSALB, 2000b, 7 September) reported that the survey indicated that the four main languages of communication in South Africa at the time and the degree to which people understood messages from government as follows:

> English (35% of all South Africans understand English but only 25% of African language speakers understand English), Afrikaans (28%), isiZulu (29%) and Isicamtho (23%) .... This shows Tsotsitaal/Isicamtho as an emerging lingua franca ... It also challenges the widely held belief that 'everybody' understands English ....

> The survey revealed that 45% of South Africans are unable to understand (or understand very little of) the information that prominent leaders are trying to convey, when this is done in English only. (PANSALB, 2000b: 3)

Of these data, it is clear from the survey data that the roles of both isiZulu and isiCamtho (an urban hybrid language) were increasing in significance *vis à vis* Afrikaans and English.

The PANSALB data were not received with enthusiasm from government departments. The Board received censure from various government departments in relation to both the Press Release and the release of the Summary Findings and the Full Report on 7 September. Particularly irksome were the data that indicated dissatisfaction of most citizens regarding lack of access to services in their home languages and dissatisfaction with their ability to understand messages from government when delivered in English. Despite the comprehensive data available to government to contribute to language planning from 2000 onwards, there has been no discernible take-up of any of these. Although there have been some suggestions from government sources that these data may not be reliable since they rely on self-reporting by respondents, this is a disturbing reflection of the degree to which the voices of people have or have not been acknowledged in the post-apartheid years. Self-reporting of language proficiency and wishes is regarded as reliable elsewhere (e.g. Broeder & Extra, 1999).

Is it Possible to Move Beyond 21st century 'Missionaries' and 'Zealots'?

In this chapter an attempt has been made to illustrate that the voice and agency, i.e. the linguistic citizenship, of speakers of languages marginalized or minoritized during the colonial and apartheid years have been systematically elided from discourses of the centre in South Africa. It is argued that many of the criticisms of language policy and planning practices during the 20th century have occluded the agency and participation of speakers of African and minority languages, thus presenting, at best, partial truths in the history of debates and activities that have circulated over the last half century. Issue is taken with those who speak for rather than with speakers of African languages and who, therefore, occlude the linguistic citizenship of the speakers themselves. Mindful that similar criticism may be directed against the discussion in this chapter, one might ask whether this discussion is any different from those in which linguists speak for or about informants from minority communities. I suggest that this discussion does differ because voices of those who have been invisibilized are uncovered. This is done through a variety of processes which includes archival and historical research, field research in remote areas, initiation of the first national sociolinguistic survey of the country and participation of the author in language policy debates and structures over a 26-year period in South Africa (1982–2008), mostly from within alternative educational NGOs. During this time and in subsequent fieldtrips within the country, I have witnessed and engaged in conversations with people who have expressed clear views about language and how this relates to their participatory and linguistic citizenship. Often this is a process that takes time and is not something that can be hurried. I have learned through my own mistakes that there is a substantial body of published literature that relies on second, third or even fourth-hand reports of the views of people and their languages in Southern Africa and often beyond (e.g. as discussed in Mahlalela-Thusi & Heugh, 2002). These are often wrong; data are misinterpreted, or are redacted and repurposed to fit popular agendas.

As evidenced in the examples that I discuss above, residues of colonial discourses, including seeping racism, continue to demand adherence to a new universality or to deny heterogeneity (Heugh, 2017). Definitions and perspectives about people who engage in multilingual practices are often nourished by data collected in the former colonies and peripheries, and then carefully pruned, espaliered and reshaped for faux displays of sociolinguistic correctness or 'theory'.[17] Being able to distinguish prescriptivists from descriptivists; or authentic and legitimate voice from those that lack authenticity and legitimacy becomes challenging, particularly in contemporary times of academic narcissism (Heugh, 2017; Pavlenko, 2019).

Literature that speaks of (or for) multilingualism from recently gleaned perspectives formulated in contemporary Europe and urban North America appears in several enthusiastic texts to be cocooned from the layered histories and memories of displacement that accompany linguistic agility and mobility in metropolitan, urban, rural and remote 'borderlands' (Anzaldúa, 1987) of Africa, the Américas and Asia. It is a literature that despite laudable intentions of promoting social justice, defaults to a colonial habitus of 'speaking over' or denying the agency or linguistic citizenship of dissenting voices. An inability to hear, recognize and respond with comprehension reflects poorly on those from 'without'. It is a denial of the linguistic citizenship of people who retain expertise and memory of multilingualisms that cannot be reduced to a new universality of 'thought' control. It is a literature of reconfigured coloniality that seeks to pin down a new regime of homogeneity circumscribing what multilingualism is and what it is not.

This is not a literature that can legitimately claim social justice. It is one in which the resilience of colonial habitus exerts epistemic violence. Ironically, such literature suffers from the flaw or hubris often associated with successive generations of evangelists, missionaries and philanthropists who travelled to the 'colonies' to tell people what to do, how to abandon their 'ignorant ways', how to jettison not only their belief systems, but also their systems of knowledge (documented, in texts written for example in Ajami, Arabic, Ethiopic and Sanskrit scripts). There seem to be troubling parallels of co-dependent interest groups among colonial administrations of the past and contemporary interests of postcolonial administrators and sociolinguists in the present. In the case of the former, the colonial administrations became co-dependent with entrepreneurs and philanthropists that together found ways to finance their work through harvesting natural resources found in the colonies and re-selling these to the colonies in altered state. In the case of the latter, enthusiastic 21st-century sociolinguists accompanied by the missionary zeal of 'social justice' believe they need to redefine and take ownership of conceptual neologisms to explain linguistic heterogeneity and theory not only to themselves, but to those from whom linguistic resources have been harvested, pruned, and returned in an unrecognizable shape.

'Linguistic Citizenship' has been an invitation and opportunity to *vula iindlebe,* to open the ears (and eyes), to the way that southern people have been narrating accounts of their multilingualisms from decolonial stances and how their languages and knowledge systems have significance for themselves and others. The purpose of this chapter has been to offer a historical account of the circumstances and context from which a lens or instrument emerged through which to recognize linguistic heterogeneity alongside conversations of decoloniality. There are now two decades of rich discussions in which Linguistic Citizenship has become rooted in and entwined in decolonial literature. These include several more recent papers (e.g. Stroud & Mpendukana, 2009; Williams & Stroud, 2015), and edited volumes (Bock & Stroud, 2021; Kerfoot & Hyltenstam 2017; Lim *et al.*, 2018; and this volume).

In drawing to a conclusion, perhaps it may be worth considering a question posed by Phumzile Sotashe, a former member of the National Language Project based in Cape Town in the early 1990s, who asks some 25 years later: 'Why is it that we are faced with the situation where the diminishing use and status of [our] languages is even worse than it was before the advent of freedom and democracy? (Sotashe, 2017: 4). If there were potential to loosen the grip and hubris of the (neo)colonial enterprise for linguistics, then it is to understand that an ecology of southern multilingualisms cannot be refracted through a northern gaze that seeks to occlude the agency and voice of southern people and communities. Southern multilingualisms and their conjoined systems of knowledge are multidimensional and pluriversal experiences that need to be recognized through the inner and outer ears of mestizo consciousness, and attentiveness to the linguistic citizenship of those with whom these phenomena reside.

Acknowledgements

I should like to acknowledge with appreciation my colleagues who with patient guidance have taught me first how to listen and then how to learn a little, especially Pamela Maseko, Gerda de Klerk, Phumzile Sotashe, Nigel Crawhall, Collette February, Noxolo Mgudlwa, Somikazi Deyi, Naledi Mbude, Zola Wababa, Babazile Mahlalela-Thusi, Thabile Mbatha, Sizwe Satyo, Sydney Zotwana, Caroline Kerfoot, Amanda Siegrühn, Madeyandile Mbelani, Blasius Chiatoh, Francis Owino, Titi Ufomata, Hassana Alidou, Peter Plüddemann, Zubeida Desai, Vuyokazi Nomlomo, Matthews Makgamatha and Christopher Stroud.

Notes

(1) Durk Gorter and Marilyn Martin-Jones have both pointed out that Kusch forgot to include Dutch in his list of imperial languages.

(2) See also Connell (2019: 92).

(3) I borrow from Stroud's metaphors of 're-routing' and 'rooting' of multilingualism in Heugh *et al.* (2019).

(4) Discussed earlier in Heugh, 2017.

(5) See Stroud's metaphors of (re-)rooting and (re-)routing in Heugh *et al.* (2019).

(6) Having been a language and linguistics worker in two NGOs, preparing for new language policy, and having participated in both the constitutional negotiations about language policy, what is called the Language Plan Task Group for the Minister of Arts, Culture, Science and Technology, and in the background work of the establishment of the Pan South African Language Board for Ministers responsible for the finalization of the 1996 Constitution, Roelf Meyer and Cyril Ramaphosa, and as an ad hoc adviser to the Minister of Education, Kader Asmal in 1999, I write from my encounters with many colleagues across the country who have been 'forgotten' or elided from published documents.

(7) For a fuller discussion, see Heugh, 2016.

(8) Professor Sizwe Satyo, Head of the Department of African Languages at the University of Cape Town, had spent much of his life's work compiling the Dictionary of the isiXhosa Language. During an interview with him in 2001, he expressed dismay at how African linguists had experienced alienation from not only government agents during apartheid years, but also from those who had replaced them after 1994. This was a line of scholarship that criticized from 'without', and without the courtesy or academic rigour of examining the work of African linguists first-hand.

(9) During my term of office as a member of the first Pan South African Language Board, PANSALB (1996–2001), I found it disturbing to witness first-hand accounts of how authors and scholars, whose lifework had been invested as serving members of guilds and language boards, were summarily dismissed and language boards, without consultation, were shut down by a new 'democratic' government in 1996. These were people who had devoted their entire working lives to literary and linguistic contributions to their languages, and whose work was thoughtlessly and without evidence cast aside as irrelevant (see also Heugh, 2004). The PANSALB substructures never picked up or continued this work at the pace or degree of commitment exhibited by the language boards prior to 1996. (For a detailed discussion, see Sotashe, 2017).

(10) Archival and textual analysis undertaken by Mahlalela-Thusi and Heugh (2002), and cross-checked with officials of the post-apartheid South Africa, demonstrated that many of the pejorative assumptions regarding the production of dictionaries, glossaries and textbooks in African languages during the apartheid period lacked evidence or substance.

(11) The linguists were given two weeks to develop the draft language policy: 1 week on site in and around the capital, Kimberley; and 1 week of writing off-site. This is a sparsely populated province of 372,889 sq km, with an average of 3.1 persons per sq km, with only 20% of people living in or near Kimberley.

(12) Realizing that the Northern Cape government was not inclined to support an extensive or thorough investigation of the language needs of minority communities, the author had asked her partner, Anthony Johnson, political correspondent of the *Cape Times* newspaper, to accompany her and drive her to remote communities across the province. He provided valuable research assistance with translations, recording and documenting informants' contributions, some of which I cite in this chapter.

(13) At the time, !Xu was used more frequently as the spelling convention which is why it appeared thus in Johnson's article. Later, !Xun became the preferred convention.

(14) Because Johnson was writing in English for an English-medium newspaper, he translated the quotations into English for the publication. I have included the original quotations as offered in Afrikaans inside the editorial parentheses.

(15) Much of the work of drawing attention to and uncovering the voices of speakers of San and Khoe languages in South Africa in the 1990s and early 2000s occurred via the South African San Institute, based in Rondebosch, Cape Town. I should like to acknowledge the work of Nigel Crawhall who worked with members of the language communities to raise public and international awareness of the human, linguistic, knowledge and spiritual resources which were and continue to be endangered.

(16) Initiated by this author for the language policy sub-committee of the board in 1999.

(17) See Kitching, 2008 for a sober discussion of either over-egging, or engaging in misconstrued, theory.

References

Achebe, C. (1958) *Things Fall Apart*. London: Heinemann.

Anzaldúa, G. (1987) *Borderlands: La Frontera*. San Francisco: Aunt Lute.

Bamgbose, A. (1987) When is language planning not planning? *The Journal of West African Languages* 7 (1), 6–14.

Bock, Z. and Stroud, C. (2021) *Language and Decoloniality in Higher Education: Reclaiming Voices from the South*. London: Bloomsbury.

Bourdieu, P. (1989) Social space and symbolic power. *Sociological Theory* 7 (1), 14–25.

Bourdieu, P. (1990) *In Other Words: Essays Towards a Reflexive Sociology*. Stanford: Stanford University Press.

Broeder, P. and Extra, G. (1999) *Language, Ethnicity, and Education: Case Studies on Immigrant Minority Groups and Immigrant Minority Languages*. Clevedon: Multilingual Matters.

Chumbow, B.S. (1987) Towards a language planning model for Africa. *Journal of West African Languages* 17 (1), 15–22.

Cluver, A.D.V. (1992) Language planning models for a post-apartheid South Africa. *Language Problems and Language Planning* 16 (2), 105–136.

Cluver, A.D.V. (1996) *Language Development in South Africa: A LANGTAG Report*. Pretoria: Department of Arts, Culture, Science and Technology.

Connell, R. (2007) *Southern Theory: The Global Dynamics of Knowledge in Social Science*. Cambridge: Polity Press.

Connell, R. (2014) Using southern theory: Decolonizing social thought in theory, research and application. *Planning Theory* 13, 210–223.

Connell, R. (2019) *The Good University. What Universities Actually Do and Why It's Time for Radical Change*. Clayton: Monash University Press.

Crawhall, N. (1997) Results of Consultations with ‡Khomani, !Xu and Khwe Communities. South African San Institute (SASI) Second Submission to the Pan South African Language Board. Rondebosch: SASI.

Crawhall, N.T. (2004) !Ui-Taa language shift in Gordonia and Postmasburg districts, South Africa. Unpublished doctoral dissertation, University of Cape Town.

Errington, J. (2001) Colonial linguistics. *Annual Review of Anthropology* 30 (1), 19–39.

Fanon, F. (1963 [1961]) *The Wretched of the Earth*. Translated by C. Farrington. New York: Grove Press.

Fardon, R. and Furniss, G. (1994) Introduction: Frontiers and boundaries – African languages as political environment. In R. Fardon and G. Furniss (eds) *African Languages, Development and the State* (pp. 1–29). New York: Routledge.

Foucault, M. (1972) *The Archaeology of Knowledge and The Discourse on Language*. London: Pantheon Books.

Goula, M. (1995) Les états-nations postcoloniaux en Afrique de l'Ouest comme obstacles à des innovations dans la politique éducative à l'exemple du Burkina Faso: Analyses des aspects socio-politiques, économiques et culturels. Unpublished doctoral dissertation. Frankfurt am Main: Johann Wolfgang Goethe-Universität.

Gramsci, A., Hoare, Q. and Nowell-Smith, G. (1971) *Selections from the Prison Notebooks of Antonio Gramsci*. London: Lawrence & Wishart.

Hegel, G.W.F. (2001) [1822–1830]) *The Philosophy of History: Georg Wilhelm Friedrich Hegel*. Prefaced by C. Hegel and translated by J. Sibree. Kitchener, Ontario: Batoche Books.

Heugh, K. (1995) Disabling and enabling: Implications of language policy trends in South Africa. In R. Mesthrie (ed.) *Language and Social History: Studies in South African Sociolinguistics* (pp. 329–350). Cape Town: David Philip

Heugh, K. (1997) Considerations for and background to the Draft Language Policy for the Northern Cape Province. Kimberley (Report): Northern Cape Government.

Heugh, K. (2003) Can authoritarian separatism give way to linguistic rights? A South African case study. *Current Issues in Language Planning* 4, 126–145.

Heugh, K. (2016) Harmonisation and South African languages: Twentieth century debates of homogeneity and heterogeneity. *Language Policy* 15 (3), 235–255.

Heugh, K. (2017) Re-placing and re-centring Southern multilingualisms. A de-colonial project. In C. Kerfoot and K. Hyltenstam (eds) *Entangled Discourses. South-North Orders of Visibility* (pp. 209–229). Series: *Critical Studies in Multilingualism*. New York: Routledge.

Heugh, K. and Ntshangase, D.K. (1997) A draft language Policy for the Northern Cape Province. Kimberley: Department of Arts and Culture, Northern Cape Provincial Government.

Heugh, K. and Stroud, C. (2019) Diversities, affinities and diasporas: A southern lens and methodology for understanding multilingualisms. *Current Issues in Language Planning* 20 (1), 1–15.

Heugh, K. and Stroud, C. (2020) *Multilingualism in South African education: A southern perspective*. In R. Hickey (ed.) *English in Multilingual South Africa: The Linguistics of Contact and Change* (pp. 216–238). Cambridge: Cambridge University Press.

Heugh, K., Stroud, C. and Scarino, A. (2019) Spaces of exception: Southern multilingualisms as resource and risk. *Current Issues in Language Planning* 20 (1), 100–119.

Hirson, B. (1981) Language control and resistance in South Africa. *African Affairs* 80 (319), 219–237.

Hoppers, C.A. (2001) Indigenous knowledge systems and academic institutions in South Africa. *Perspectives in Education* 19 (1), 73–86.

Hoppers, C.A.O. (ed.) (2002) *Indigenous Knowledge and the Integration of Knowledge Systems: Towards a Philosophy of Articulation*. Cape Town: New Africa Books.

James, A.L. (1928) The practical orthography of African languages. *Africa: Journal of the International African Institute* 1 (1), 125–129.

Johnson, A. (1997) Forgotten people gather. SA's oldest cultures under threat. *Cape Times*, 14 July.

Kerfoot, C. (2009) *Changing Conceptions of Literacies, Language and Development: Implications for the Provision of Adult Basic Education in South Africa*. Stockholm: Centre for Bilingual Research, Stockholm University.

Kerfoot, C. and Hyltenstam, K. (2017) Introduction: Entanglement and orders of visibility. In C. Kerfoot and K. Hyltenstam (eds) *Entangled Discourses* (pp. 1–15). London: Routledge.

Kerfoot, C. and Hyltenstam, K. (eds) (2017) *Entangled Discourses: South-North Orders of Visibility*. New York: Routledge.

Kitching, G.N. (2008) *The Trouble with Theory: The Educational Costs of Postmodernism*. Philadelphia: Penn State University Press.

Kusch, R. (1970) *El Pensamiento Indígena y Popular en América*. Buenos Aires: Hachete.

Kusch, R. (2010 [1970]) *Indigenous and Popular Thinking in América*. Translated by J. Price and M. Lugones. Durham, NC: Duke University Press.

Lestrade, G.P. (1929) Some remarks on the practical orthography of the South African Bantu languages. *Bantu Studies*. 3, 261–273.

Letele, G.L. (1945) *A Preliminary Study of the Lexicological Influence of the Nguni Languages on Southern Sotho*. Lovedale: Lovedale Mission Press.

Lim, L., Stroud, C. and Wee, L. (eds) (2018) *The Multilingual Citizen: Towards a Politics of Language for Agency and Change*. Bristol: Multilingual Matters.

Macaulay, T.B. (1835) Minute by the Hon'ble T. B. Macaulay, dated the 2nd February 1835. See http://www.columbia.edu/itc/mealac/pritchett/00generallinks/macaulay/txt_minute_education_1835.html (accessed 2 June 2019).

Macías, R.F. (2005) El Grito en Aztlán: Voice and presence in Chicana/o Studies. *International Journal on Qualitative Studies in Education*. (*Special issue on Chicana and Chicano Studies*) 18 (2), 165–184.

Macías, R.F. (ed.) (1977) *Perspectivas en Chicano studies*. Los Angeles, CA: Aztlán Publications & NACCS.

Macías, R.F., Gómez-Quiñones, J. and Castro, R. (1971) Objectives of Chicano studies. *Epoca-The National Concilio for Chicano Studies Journal* 1 (2), 31–34.

Mahlalela-Thusi, B. and Heugh, K. (2002) Unravelling some of the historical threads of mother–tongue development and use during the first phase of Bantu education (1955–1975). *Perspectives in Education* 20 (1), 241–257.

Makoni, S. (1998) African languages as European scripts: The shaping of communal memory. In S. Nuttall and C. Coetzee (eds) *Negotiating the Past: The Making of Memory in South Africa* (pp. 242–248). Oxford: Oxford University Press.

Makoni, S. (2003) From misinvention to disinvention of language: Multilingualism and the South African Constitution. In S. Makoni, G. Smitherman, A. Ball and A.K. Spears (eds) *Black Linguistics: Language, Society and Politics in Africa and the Americas* (pp. 132–153). New York: Routledge.

Medina, L.R. (2014) *Centres and Peripheries in Knowledge Production*. Oxford: Oxford University Press.

Mignolo W. (2010) Introduction. Immigrant consciousness. Translated by M. Lugones and J.M. Price. In R. Kusch (ed.) *Indigenous and Popular Thinking in America* (pp. xiii–lxxiv). Durham, NC: Duke University Press.

Mignolo, W. (1996) Linguistic maps, literary geographies, and cultural landscapes: Languages, languaging, and (trans)nationalism. *Modern Language Quarterly* 57 (2), 181–197.

Mignolo, W. (2011a) *The Darker Side of Western Modernity: Global Futures, Decolonial Options*. Durham, NC: Duke University Press.

Mignolo, W. (2011b) Geopolitics of sensing and knowing: On (de) coloniality, border thinking and epistemic disobedience. *Postcolonial Studies* 14 (3), 273–283.

Mikkelsen, J.M. (2013) (ed., trans.) *Kant and the Concept of Race: Late Eighteenth-Century Writings*. Albany, NY: SUNY Press.

Msimang, C.T. (1992) *African Languages and Language Planning in South Africa. The Nhlapo-Alexander Notion of Harmonisation Revisited*. Pretoria: Bard Publishers.

Msimang, C.T. (1994) Language Attitudes and the harmonisation of Nguni and Sotho. *South African Journal of Linguistics, Supplement* 20, 147–167.

Msimang, C.T. (2000) Grammatical terminology for the teaching of African Languages at tertiary level. *Lexicos* (*AFRILEX-reeks/series* 10) 10, 225–233.

Nakata, M. (2007) *Disciplining the Savages: Savaging the Disciplines*. Canberra: Aboriginal Studies Press.

Ndhlovu, F. (2018a) Omphile and his soccer ball: Colonialism, methodology, translanguaging research. *Multilingual Margins: A Journal of Multilingualism from the Periphery* 5 (2), 2–19.

Ndhlovu, F. (2018b) Can the other be heard? Response to commentaries on 'Omphile and his soccer ball'. *Multilingual Margins: A Journal of Multilingualism from the Periphery* 5 (2), 42–49.

Ngũgĩ wa Thiong'o (1986) *Decolonising the Mind.* London: James Currey.

Ngũgĩ wa Thiong'o (1993) *Moving the Centre: The Struggle for Cultural Freedoms.* London: Heineman.

Nhlapo, J. (1944) *Bantu Babel: Will the Bantu languages live? The Sixpenny Library, No. 4.* Cape Town: The African Bookman.

Nhlapo, J. (1945) *Nguni and Sotho.* Cape Town: The African Bookman.

Nhlapo, J. (1953) The problem of many tongues. *Liberation* 4, 13–14.

Odora Hoppers, C. (1999) Indigenous knowledge and the integration of knowledge systems: Toward a conceptual and methodological framework. A comparative study of the development, integration and protection of knowledge systems in the Third World. A discussion document prepared for the HSRC. Pretoria: Human Sciences Research Council of South Africa.

Owino, F. (2002) Conquering the conqueror: The empowerment of the African languages casts a shadow over English in Africa. *Perspectives in Education* 20 (1), 197–212.

Pan South African Language Board. (2000a) *Language Use and Language Interaction in South Africa. A National Sociolinguistic Survey.* Pretoria: Pan South African Language Board.

Pan South African Language Board (2000b) Media Release. National survey on language use and language interaction in South Africa. 7 September. Pretoria: PANSALB.

Pavlenko, A. (2019) Superdiversity and why it isn't. In B. Schmenk, S. Breidbach and L. Küster (eds) *Sloganization in Language Education Discourse: Conceptual Thinking in the Age of Academic Marketization* (pp. 142–168). Bristol: Multilingual Matters.

Ranger, T. (1984) *Missionaries, Migrants and the Manyika: The Invention of Ethnicity in Zimbabwe.* Johannesburg: University of the Witwatersrand, African Studies Institute.

Salö, L. (2017) Sociolinguistics and epistemic reflexivity. *Working Papers in Urban Language & Literacies* 206, 1–20.

Salö, L. (2018) Seeing the point from which you see what you see: An essay on epistemic reflexivity in language research. *Multilingual Margins: A Journal of Multilingualism from the Periphery* 5 (1), 24–39.

Santos, B. de S. (2012) Public sphere and epistemologies of the south. *Africa Development* 37 (11), 43–69.

Santos, B. de S. (2018) *The End of the Cognitive Empire: The Coming of Age of Epistemologies of the South.* Durham, NC: Duke University Press.

Smith, L.T. (1999) *Decolonizing Methodologies. Research and Indigenous Peoples.* London: Zed Books, London.

Sotashe, P. (1992) Looking for language boards. *Language Projects' Review* 7 (4), 7–8.

Sotashe, P. (2017) *Challenges in Developing and Empowering Indigenous Languages. A Case of isiXhosa* (South Africa). Balti: Lambert Academic Publishing.

Stroud, C. (2001) African mother-tongue programmes and the politics of language: Linguistic citizenship versus linguistic human rights. *Journal of Multilingual and Multicultural Development* 22 (4), 339–355.

Stroud, C. and Heugh, K. (2004) Language rights and linguistic citizenship. In J. Freeland and D. Patrick (eds) *Language Rights and Language Survival: Sociolinguistic and Sociocultural Perspectives* (pp. 191–218). Manchester: St. Jerome Publishing.

Stroud, C. and Mpendukana, S. (2009) Towards a material ethnography of linguistic landscape: Multilingualism, mobility and space in a South African township. *Journal of Sociolinguistics* 13 (3), 363–386.

Trevor-Roper, H. (1965) *The Rise of Christian Europe*. New York: Harcourt Brace.

Tucker, A.N. (1929) *The Comparative Phonetics of the Suto-Chuana Group of Bantu Languages*. London: Longmans, Green and Co. (reproduced in 1969 by Gregg International Publishers, Westmead).

Tucker, A.N. (1949) Sotho-Nguni orthography and tone-marking. *Bulletin of the School of Oriental and African Studies, University of London* 13 (1), 200–224.

Williams, Q. (2017) *Remix Multilingualism: Hip Hop, Ethnography and Performing Marginalized Voices*. London: Bloomsbury Publishing.

Williams, Q.E. and Stroud, C. (2015) Linguistic citizenship: Language and politics in post-national modernities. *Journal of Language and Politics* 14 (3), 406–430.

4 Linguistic Citizenship and the Questions of Transformation and Marginality

Ben Rampton, Melanie Cooke and Sam Holmes

This chapter sets the notion of Linguistic Citizenship (LC) developed by Stroud and associates in dialogue with (a) ethnographic sociolinguistics of the kind shaped by Dell Hymes, and with (b) experiences of language and education over the last 50 to 60 years in England.[1] We see LC as a major contribution to research and practical intervention, but the first dialogue interrogates LC's emphasis on transformation, and the second qualifies its association with struggle at the margins.

LC is 'an attempt at a comprehensive *political* stance on language' (Stroud, 2008: 45), arguing that a subtle understanding of how language positions people in society can and should enhance democratic participation. This is similar to the view that motivated Hymes's work on language in society in the United States (e.g. 1996 [1975]: 63–106), and the strength of the LC argument partly derives from the way its central ideas are echoed elsewhere in the fields that Hymes influenced – in the deconstruction of named languages and the focus on communicative practice found in linguistic anthropology and linguistic ethnography as well as LC. But these links also point to productive complications. 'Voice' and the effective expression of one's views and perceptions are central to LC, but getting heard and influencing relations of power often requires linguistic and discursive negotiation and compromise, and if the influence is going to be more than fleeting, some kind of institutionalization or conventionalization will also be necessary. Both processes make it harder to speak of political and social transformation than the discussions of LC sometimes recognize.

Across a range of publications, Stroud and others conceive of LC as a concept from the global south, but how far and in what ways is the idea of LC relevant or achievable outside the African contexts they describe, and what modifications might be required in a place such as England? The sociolinguistic terrain flagged by the notion of superdiversity (Arnaut *et al.*, 2015) has actually generated a significant number of relatively small-scale projects promoting LC, and we describe two that rely on fund-raising from charities and other sources of short-term finance. But this does not mean that the promotion of LC can always only ever happen outside the state: from the 1960s to the 1980s, state schooling in England was strongly influenced by educationalists who accepted linguistic diversity, promoted a broadly sociolinguistic understanding of communication and sought to develop creatively independent voices among their students. This was ultimately closed down by the Conservative government in the 1990s, but this case shows that LC is not necessarily just an alternative in the margins. It can also be a mainstream objective, promoted, contested and defended in the corridors of power.

'Linguistic Citizenship' Rather than 'Linguistic Human Rights'

Stroud's notion of LC first emerged in his 2001 paper, which focused on the success and failure of educational programmes in Africa using local rather than ex-colonial metropolitan languages as media of instruction. It argued that although the idea of Linguistic Human Rights was widely invoked, it was inadequate as a framework for understanding and promoting mother-tongue programmes that actually worked. Stroud (2001: 349) characterized Language Human Rights as an approach to language education that involves:

(a) the selective provision for a specific group, usually designed to overcome historic disadvantage;
(b) the identification, description and introduction of the group's distinctive language as an entitlement in institutional activity – in schools, in law courts, in aspects of state bureaucracy;
(c) an expectation that the courts and other bodies overseeing the nation-state will grant and monitor all this.

The constitutional recognition given to 11 official languages after apartheid has meant that the Linguistic Human Rights perspective has been very influential in South Africa, where Stroud is based, but he pointed to a number of serious limitations (see also Makoni, 2003; Stroud & Heugh, 2004):

(a) the Linguistic Human Rights approach marginalizes people who use non-standard versions of the group's language, generating new sociolinguistic inequalities;
(b) it promotes an arbitrary and essentialist view of language and ethnicity – it creates artificial boundaries between ways of speaking that are actually continuous, and it overlooks mixing and hybridity; and
(c) it appeals to a rather top-down and managerial politics; it presupposes membership of a single state; and it neglects population mobility.

It isn't well adapted to the fact that 'individuals now find themselves participating in a variety of sites in competition for resources distributed along multiple levels of scale, such as the nation, the supranation, the local and the regional' (Stroud, 2010: 200).

To overcome these problems, Stroud proposed the notion of LC which differed from Linguistic Human Rights in:

(1) putting democratic participation first, emphasizing cultural and political 'voice' and agency rather than just language on its own;
(2) seeing all sorts of linguistic practices – including practices that were mixed, low-status or transgressive – as potentially relevant to social and economic well-being, accepting that it is very hard to predict any of this if you are just watching from the centre; and
(3) stressing the importance of grassroots activity on the ground, often on the margins of state control, outside formal institutions.

Going beyond the Linguistic Human Rights' arguments, Stroud's main contention is that an enhanced understanding of sociolinguistic processes should actually be central to emancipatory politics. LC 'aims to make visible the sociolinguistic complexity of language issues' (Stroud & Heugh, 2004: 192) and to promote 'the idea of language as a political and economic "site of struggle"', alongside 'respect for diversity and difference' and 'the deconstruction of essentialist understandings of language and identity' (Stroud, 2001: 353). This perspective, which should be 'inserted into political discourses and made into a legitimate form, target and instrument of political action' (2001: 343), has the potential to help marginalized people change their material and economic conditions for the better.

We will address several attempts to achieve this when we turn to language education in the UK. But before doing so, we should review the sociolinguistic and political ideas that LC draws on, try to clarify the combination of normative political position-taking and academic theory-and-description that LC entails, and point to some complications.

Sociolinguistic Underpinnings in Linguistic Citizenship

According to Dell Hymes, one of its founding figures, ethnographic sociolinguistics is a primarily analytical rather than a political or normative undertaking, focusing first on 'what is' rather than 'what should be'. But the careful comparative empirical study of communicative repertoires and practices ultimately serves the higher ethical aspiration of achieving *Liberté, Égalité, Fraternité* because it 'prepares [sociolinguists] to speak concretely to actual inequalities' (Hymes, 1977: 204–206, 1969; Santos, 2012: 46).

This interplay of the academic and the ethical/political can be seen in operation in Stroud's criticism of the way in which language and ethnicity are conceptualized in the Linguistic Human Rights' perspective (= [A], [B], (a) and (b) in the previous section). There is now substantial sociolinguistic research which challenges the idea that distinct languages exist as natural objects and that a proper language is bounded, pure and composed of structured sounds, grammar and vocabulary designed for referring to things (e.g. Heugh, 2004: 197; Joseph & Taylor, 1990; Makoni & Pennycook, 2007; Stroud, 1999; Stroud & Heugh, 2004: 197; Woolard *et al.*, 1998). The idea of named languages is obviously still very powerful in education, in immigration policy, in high and popular culture etc. and it is often also the object of passionate personal attachment. But contemporary sociolinguists argue that it is more productive *analytically* to focus on the very variable ways in which individual linguistic features with identifiable social and cultural associations get clustered together whenever people communicate (e.g. Blommaert, 2005; Hudson, 1980; Le Page, 1988). If we take any strip of communication and focus on the links and histories of each of the linguistic ingredients, we can soon see a host of forms and styles that are actually connected to social life in a plurality of groups – groups that vary from the very local to the transnational (Stroud, 2001: 350). From this, a differentiated account of the organization of communicative practice emerges, centring on identities, relationships, activities and genres that are enacted in a variety of ways. Both official and common-sense accounts often miss this, but it makes the ideological homogenization achieved in national language naming rather obvious.

This is one way in which developments in sociolinguistic theory 'prepare [sociolinguists] to speak concretely to actual inequalities' more effectively. Politically, both Linguistic Human Rights and LC oppose the exclusion of people who do not have officially approved linguistic resources in their repertoires. But while Linguistic Human Rights focuses on the recognition of named or nameable languages associated with specific groups judged to have been marginalized, LC works with developments in sociolinguistics that allow a more open and inclusive position, attending to the diversity of linguistic practices that people use/need to get themselves heard in arenas that affect their well-being.

But this 'actor-oriented' focus on 'practice' raises a question about the potential effectiveness of LC as a political idea. Are not the processes that it addresses rather small-scale (Petrovic & Kuntz, 2013: 142), relinquishing the wide-angle view and the potential to affect relatively large numbers of people identified in the debates about Linguistic Human Rights? Not necessarily. Both in sociolinguistic and social theory, practices are seen as basic building blocks in the production of society, and turning the argument around, it is now often said that studies of *state-level* policy run into problems if they neglect practice, because they miss all the unpredictable complexity that the formulation and implementation of policy actually entails (Ball *et al.*, 2012; Jessop, 2007): 'policy never just "is", but rather "does" … We do not restrict our analysis to … official policy declarations and texts... but place these in context as part of a larger sociocultural system... inferred from people's language practices, ideologies and beliefs' (McCarty, 2011: 2).

At the same time, however, if we are to understand how units 'both larger and smaller than the traditional nation-state' (Stroud, 2001: 350) enter the account, we need to move beyond practice to the networks in which it is embedded. In fact, this is implied in the notion of voice itself.

In the first instance, we might define 'voice' as an individual's communicative power and effectiveness within the here-and-now of specific events. But beyond this, there is the crucial issue of whether and how their contribution is remembered and/or recorded and subsequently reproduced in other arenas, travelling through networks and circuits that may vary in their scale – in their spatial scope, temporal durability and social reach (Blommaert, 2005, 2008; Kell, 2015; Maybin, 2017). This is studied in research on 'text trajectories' which focuses (a) on the here-and-now activity in which some (but not other) aspects of what is said get turned into textual 'projectiles' that can carry forward into other settings ('entextualization'); and then (b) the ways in which they are interpreted when they arrive there ('recontextualization'). This kind of account can cover both 'top-down' and 'bottom-up' trajectories, involving a variety of people, practices, media and types of text, working in cooperative and/or conflictual relationships within and across specific events, and it can of course be turned to political processes. So, for example, we could focus on directives formulated in government offices that are turned into curriculum documents, transmitted to schools, and then interpreted by teachers interacting with children in class, or alternatively, we could look at parents complaining at a school meeting, the local press reporting the matter, and local politicians then taking it up or dismissing it (see e.g. Kell, 2015; Mehan, 1996). These are obviously simplified sketches, but the essential point is that a 'trans-contextual and multi-scalar' framework of this kind allows us to investigate the resonance of particular communicative practices (or 'voices'). This then has two further implications.

First, this view of voice and text trajectories means that sociolinguists actually have to be flexible in their response to named languages and the essentialization that they involve, accepting that there may be occasions when the discourse of Linguistic Human Rights is strategically warranted. Certainly, when faced with data on linguistic practice situated in the here-and-now, sociolinguists first listen for the diversity of the communicative resources in play. But selection and reduction are unavoidable parts of the entextualization process, and if someone's viewpoint is to be heard elsewhere in unfamiliar situations, it needs to be represented in a repeatable form that, regardless of its eloquence, inevitably simplifies the first-hand experience that motivated it (see e.g. Haarstad & Fløysand, 2007). Named languages may form part of persuasive rhetorics that travel, and even though sociolinguists may worry about the negative (side-)effects and watch out for opportunities to reassert the ideological constructedness of named languages (Stroud & Heugh, 2004: 212), an analytic interest in the trajectory of voices has to accept the possibility that in certain circumstances, the invocation of named languages helps to advance political causes that sociolinguists deem progressive. So, although Stroud's account of LC includes mixed, low-status and transgressive language practices, we certainly should not assume that notionally purer, higher status and more standard ones are thereby necessarily excluded (Blommaert, 2004: 59–60; Stroud & Heugh, 2004: 191).

Second, it is necessary to move beyond the 'freedom to have one's voice heard' to what Hymes (1996 [1975]: 64) calls the 'freedom to develop a voice worth hearing'. People in the particular networks through which a voice seeks to resonate inevitably have their own ideas of what's important, and if its message is to be taken seriously, it needs to understand and connect with these concerns. As the word 'develop' implies, it usually takes time, effort, imagination and the support of others to learn how to say things that are relevant to people who you want to persuade but don't yet know, and this brings education – formal and/or informal – into the reckoning. Stroud's (2001) discussion of LC centres more on the taking of control over language education programmes than on what these programmes actually teach (though see e.g. Bock & Mheta, 2014; Kerfoot, 2018; Stroud & Heugh, 2004: 201). But if the practices that promote democratic participation and persuasive voices from the grassroots are to sustain themselves, it is vital to consider the organization of institutionalized arenas for learning and socialization that are at least partly sheltered from the front-line struggle.

So the central ideas that Stroud and colleagues' LC builds on – the deconstruction of named languages and the focus on linguistic repertoires and practice – find a great deal of support in ethnographic sociolinguistics, where Hymes also outlined broadly comparable objectives at the interface of research and politics. At the same time, these links qualify LC's radical force: if claims and voices want people elsewhere to listen to them, they have to make themselves relevant, and the entextualization required to do so often results in messages that simplify and partly compromise the original intention. It can also take time to develop a 'voice worth hearing', and this raises the question of institutional support. There are similar effects when ethnographic sociolinguistics is drawn into interaction with discussions of citizenship in political theory.

Sociolinguistics and Citizenship in Political Theory

Two political theorists feature especially prominently in the accounts of Stroud and colleagues. Right from the start, Stroud (2001, 2018), draws on Nancy Fraser's (1995) distinction between 'affirmative remedies for injustice [which are] aimed at correcting inequitable outcomes of social arrangements without disturbing the underlying framework that generates them', and 'transformative remedies [which are] aimed at correcting inequitable outcomes precisely by restructuring the underlying generative framework' (1995: 82).[2] While Linguistic Human Rights takes the affirmative path, LC makes the case for transformative politics, since as we have seen, it challenges traditional ideas about the distinctiveness and homogeneity of language groups and named languages, 'interrogat[ing] the historical, sociopolitical, and economic determinants of how languages are constructed' (Stroud, 2018: 20).

This commitment to transformation can also be seen in more recent references to Isin's work on citizenship (Isin, 2017; Isin & Nielsen, 2008; Stroud, 2018; Williams & Stroud, 2015). Like Fraser, Isin speaks of a politics that transgresses established frameworks (e.g. Isin, 2008: 18), but Isin also looks at how struggles over citizenship have been complicated and intensified by global mobility, arguing for an account of citizenship that reckons with the political agency of people like asylum-seekers and undocumented immigrants who occupy very precarious positions in the states where they reside (2008: 15–16; Isin, 2017: 504–505). To achieve this, Isin and Nielsen (2008: 2) speak of 'acts of citizenship', in which people actively constitute themselves as citizens by making claims to particular rights and duties, even though they are not formally seen as citizens by the law, and so they fall outside the realm of those eligible to claim such entitlements. The focus, therefore, is 'not only on the exercise of rights and duties as they exist [for ratified citizens] but also on claiming rights and duties yet to come as a result of social struggles' (Isin, 2017: 506). Claiming rights is a performative act and for analysis, this means 'asking questions not simply about what a right is but also about what it is we do when we make rights claims' (Isin, 2017: 506).

This concern with 'what we do when we make rights claims' means that philosophical, legal and system-focused accounts are insufficient – they need to be supplemented with empirical investigation of particular cases (e.g. Neveu, 2015; Oliveri, 2014). In fact, these investigations promise to qualify and complicate the idea of 'transformation' itself. In a distinction that resembles Fraser's 'affirmative' vs. 'transformative' politics, Isin starts out differentiating 'active' citizens who 'follow scripts' ($\approx$ affirmative) and 'activist' citizens who 'engage in writing' them ($\approx$ transformative) (Isin, 2008: 38). But later when he contemplates the key issues that empirical work on performative citizenship should tackle, he wonders whether acts of citizenship actually *break* conventions or just change them *incrementally*. The word 'rupture', Isin (2017) says, sometimes refers to 'revolution, regime change, or revolt' (2017: 519), but it can also refer to a 'quotidian and ordinary' act which simply 'draws people out of themselves to take notice of the taken for granted nature of a given state of affairs and turn critical attentiveness toward it' (2017: 519).

The analytic difficulties involved in determining whether change is major or minor, radical or merely adaptive, have in fact been widely noted (e.g. Williams, 1977: 123),[3] and linguistic ethnography also presents claims about rupture and transformation with a series of quite acute questions. As sociolinguists know well, every communicative act entails a huge range of partly autonomous and partly interwoven structures (themselves 'generative frameworks'), operating at the linguistic, interactional and institutional levels.[4] Saying for any given intervention which of these generative frameworks is and isn't being ruptured, for and by whom, and with what subsequent effects, is hard, and of course it is likely to become even harder with the introduction of analytic schemes from sociology, politics, economics and so forth. Analysis has an *invaluable* part to play *alerting* us to the intricacies of change, but in the end, the assessment of whether an action is transformative, affirmative, reproductive or indeed repressive is likely to involve a holistic, all-round judgement that is inevitably also informed by understandings and commitments that go well beyond the scientific expertise of the observer. This kind of shift from the technical to the ethical and subjective is wholly compatible with Hymes's view of an ethnographic sociolinguistics aligned with political values like *Liberté, Égalité, Fraternité* (e.g. Hymes, 1977: 194). At the same time, however, a strictly *analytic* lens from sociolinguistics puts the brake on romantic over-readings in which the observer attributes radical creativity to actions that participants see as rather mundane and inconsequential (Blommaert & Rampton, 2011: 9; Rampton, 2014). So it asks: exactly what aspects of the 'underlying generative framework' are challenged in an activity described as transformative, and what stays the same? The ideas expressed? The genre in which they are articulated? The interactional relationships etc? And how does it really ramify in subsequent events?

With this elaboration of Linguistic Citizenship's ties to ethnographic sociolinguistics in place, together with a clarification of the inescapable uncertainties that emerge in the encounter with politics and political theory, we can now move to the second part of the chapter. Stroud characterizes 'the concept of Linguistic Citizenship [as] a Southern and de-colonial concept', arising from the contradictions surrounding educational programmes in the geopolitical south (2018: 18). So how far and in what ways can it be transferred to a rich country like Britain in the North, where a relatively high degree of political continuity means that a notion like 'transformation' lacks the currency in public discourse that it has in a country like South Africa (see Burawoy & von Holdt, 2012)?

Projects Promoting Sociolinguistic Citizenship in England

In the UK in recent years, there have been two state-level discourses that have linked language to citizenship, but these are very hard to reconcile with LC in Stroud's sense (Rampton *et al.*, 2018a: Section 4). One refers to the learning of European standard languages (Moore, 2011), and the other emphasizes the need for immigrants to learn English for social cohesion and national security (Khan, 2017). On the ground, however, language repertoires and practices in England often involve the kinds of variety and mixing that Stroud and colleagues describe (e.g. Rampton, 2015a, 2016), and discussions of superdiversity in the UK also recognize that contemporary sociocultural heterogeneity challenges the demographic categories that public policy has traditionally relied on (Fanshawe & Sriskandarajah, 2010). This terrain has generated a range of relatively small-scale education and arts projects that can be aligned with Stroud's LC[5] (although to avoid confusion with the two official conceptions in the UK context, it is probably worth referring here to '*Socio*linguistic Citizenship'). In what follows, we sketch two projects in which we have been involved, but before doing so, it is first briefly worth considering the notion of transformation in education, referring to debates about 'translanguaging', an umbrella term for hybrid language mixing that has a good deal in common with LC (Pennycook, 2016).

'Translanguaging' has gained a lot of currency in recent years, and it is sometimes said that its recognition in education can be transformative. According to García and Li (2014: 66), translanguaging in education is associated with 'creativity, criticality and transformations': creativity is 'the ability to choose between following and flouting the rules and norms of behaviour' (2014: 66); criticality 'is the ability… appropriately, systematically and insightfully to inform considered views of cultural, social, political and linguistic phenomena [and] to question and problematize received wisdom' (2014: 67); and their combination in the kinds of practice that García and Li describe makes translanguaging 'transformative for the child, for the teacher and for education itself' (García & Li, 2014: 68). The question of whether practices targeting change are transformative or not is very important, but it is also very hard because of the unpredictability of outcomes generated by particular pedagogies. As Jaspers (2017) notes, 'all classrooms must be approached as complex interactive settings where, rather than simply accepting what is offered, pupils always negotiate what is put on the table (curricula, teaching styles, teachers) and develop different strategies depending on their short- and long-term ambitions, the classroom climate and local socio-economic conditions' (2017: 11; see also Charalambous *et al.*, 2016). Jaspers also draws attention to the wide range of sociologists who 'question the idea that interventions at school can transform society in any significant way' (2017: 7, 11). So we will take a relatively cautious line in the ensuing account, linking the projects we describe to LC through the political *intentions* driving them (democratic participation, voice, linguistic inclusivity, sociolinguistic understanding), focusing more on questions of scale and sustainability than transformative impact.

The first project was a course in ESOL (English for Speakers of Other Languages) entitled *Our Languages*. It took place within a small charitable organization called English for Action (EfA) that was set up in 2006, motivated by the vision of 'UK migrants hav[ing] the language, skills and networks they need to bring about an equal and fair society' (EfA, 2016: 7). According to its 2015–16 Annual Report (EfA, 2016), EfA is 'absolutely committed to community organising; that is listening to people's concerns in our classes and communities, connecting people, training people to listen and take action, taking action to effect change and building power-ful groups to be able to hold powerful people and organizations to account. Our approach is above all, to develop the capacity of our stu-dents to effect change. Campaigns, such as to secure better housing or living wages, emerge from classroom work and our community organis-ing' (EfA, 2016: 5). During 2015–16, 391 people accessed the 19 free of charge ESOL courses that EfA ran in seven London Boroughs, and 'over 100 students took action on a range of social justice issues' (EfA, 2016: 11). The courses were taught by a staff team of ten, with volunteers attending 85% of the classes, and this activity was supported with an income of £178,000, mostly raised from about a dozen charitable foundations.

Our Languages ran in 2017 as one strand in a three-year linguistic ethnography on 'Adult Language Socialization in the Sri Lankan Tamil diaspora in London' funded by the Leverhulme Trust (2015–2018) to the tune of £227,500. The course was designed to explore how far the linguis-tic experience of the Sri Lankan Tamils studied in the ethnography reso-nated with other migrant groups, and it involved participatory education (aligned with Freire [1970], critical pedagogy and democratic education). This takes an over-arching theme and then allows the exact shape of the course to emerge from session to session.[6] Working in two classes (36 students from 18 countries), the courses began by playing the recording of someone from Sri Lanka talking about how he'd practiced his English working in an off-license, and by the end of the eight weeks, the students had covered: non-standard language varieties; bi/multilingual language practices; language identities; intergenerational language transmission; multilingual communicative repertoires; language ideologies; language discrimination and the social processes of learning English in the UK. In this way, the course addressed what Stroud and Heugh (2004: 209–210) see as a substantial problem for Linguistic Citizenship: the 'problem ... is that much current theorisation of language and politics is often unavail-able to those communities who are theorised ... [L]inguistic knowledge needs to be built in dialogue with communities'.

At the end of course, there were gains in language learning, in prag-matic and 'multilingual narrative' competence and in vocabulary, and one of the students reported 'jokingly but proudly – that her family had com-mented that she was coming home from class "sounding like a dictionary", [using] research related terms such as "theme", "data" and "participant"' (Cooke *et al.*, 2018: 25). One of the groups also made representations to the All Party Parliamentary Group (APPG) on Social Integration, which was conducting an inquiry into the integration of immigrants. They invited its chair (who happened to be the local MP) to talk to them and told him that the APPG's interim report (2017a) overlooked the government's 60% cuts to ESOL funding since 2007 and also lent itself to negative stereotyping. He appeared to listen: when the final report came out, it was entitled *Integration not Demonisation*, discussed the cuts (All Party Parliamentary Group on Social Integration (2017b: 69–70; hereafter APPG), and acknowledged EfA and 'the testimony of... community group members' (2017b: 9, 83). Whether this political action was transformative, affirmative or trivial could produce a range of answers, depending on whether the focus was on state policy for ESOL, on the APPG's committee deliberations, or on the development of particular individuals making representations. On occasion, students themselves expressed racist ideas; the session on intergenerational language transmission generated quite a lot of frustration and guilt when students talked about their children's lack of heritage language competence; and there was also quite strong support for an 'English Only' policy in ESOL lessons, even though students had been encouraged to draw on their multilingual repertoires. Even so, the course's alignment with the ideas of LC outlined by Stroud etc. is clear.

English for Action aims to encourage the growth of participatory ESOL by sharing best practice (and has developed multilingual ESOL teaching materials [www.ourlanguages.co.uk]). The sharing of pedagogies committed to the fluidity of language and identity, sociolinguistic understanding, linguistic inclusivity and voice was also central to the second project, *Multilingual Creativity* (www.kcl.ac.uk/Cultural/-/ Projects/Multilingual-Creativity.aspx). This project ran from January 2015 to November 2016, and the question guiding it was: 'How can plurilingualism among young people be harnessed for creativity?' It recognized that there were a lot of unconnected projects in universities, schools and arts and cultural organizations which engaged with young people's hybrid multilingualism, and it set out to build links between them, seeking to develop something of a 'sector' for this kind of work.

There were three elements in the programme: research on current practice, the development of a website (www.multilingualcreativity.org. uk), and a series of events which focused on language communities, multilingual projects, performing and visual arts, print and multimedia texts, networking. These involved 52 cultural organizations (from education, museums, libraries, publishing and the arts sector), 17 artists, 12 academics and 32 members of the public. The research part surveyed existing projects and identified five pedagogic principles in something of a manifesto, illustrating them with examples of film making in Arabic supplementary schools, German teaching with hand-puppets for primary children, three-day workshops in creative translation, and a national language challenge (Holmes, 2015). The five principles were: plurilingualism over monolingual usage (the use of different 'languages' within the same utterance or activity); exuberant smatterings over fluency ('bits of language' as opposed to 'fluency' as a legitimate goal in language learning);

reflexive sociolinguistic exploration over linguistic 'common sense' (focusing on participants' own language practices); collaborative endeavour over individualization (drawing on the pooling of repertoires within a group); and investment over 'immersion' (fostering a genuine desire to participate, rather than insisting on exclusive use of the 'target' language). The politics was less explicit than in *Our Languages* (though see Holmes, 2015: 10). But even though the issue of actual *outcomes* is more complex, the involvement of arts organizations pointed to a contrast with schools that speaks back to questions about change, with pedagogy looking more transformative in the arts and more affirmative in education:

> A [school] teacher's approach can be very focused on building. It often starts with planning out the edifice of knowledge and skills that a child needs according to the prescriptions of the curriculum, then takes stock of what foundations they already have, before using all this to design the scaffolding required to support the next bricks.... The approach of arts practitioners... often starts with an element of destruction. Those foundations a child has can be a prison of limited and limiting conceptualisations which stymie creative potential. Once this is exposed children are empowered to become architects as well as brick-layers. (Holmes, 2015: 3)

Like *Our Languages* and most of the organizations it surveyed, *Multilingual Creativity* depended on relatively short-term, project-specific funding from charitable foundations and local communities and institutions (five or six grants, amounting to about £67,000). All these projects depend(ed) on the initiative of a few dedicated individuals and their perseverance and success in raising income from a plurality of funding sources, and this raises the crucial issue of sustainability, both for the projects and for the linguistic repertoires and capacities that the projects seek to develop. As noted by one of the organizations quoted by Holmes, 'creativity is not simply a matter of letting go. Serious creative achievement relies on knowledge, control of materials and command of ideas' (2015: 14). Is one intensive three-day workshop in the course of a 12-year school career, or a couple of hours a week for five weeks, really enough to develop sophisticated plurilingual writing and 'a voice worth hearing'? It would be optimistic to say 'yes', and this in turn raises the question: is civil society really the only place for educational programmes committed to the development of powerful but unorthodox voices and the sophisticated acceptance of mixed and non-standard language? Or could LC be incorporated within state provision? There are actually precedents, as we shall see in a historical glance back at language education in English schools in the 1960s–80s.

Sociolinguistic Citizenship in English State Education from the 1960s to the 1980s

Calls for language education to focus on standard English, grammar and correctness have a long pedigree in the UK (Rosen, 1981), but the period from the 1960s to the late 1980s was dominated by 'progressive' pedagogies. During this period, local authorities, teaching unions and subject associations had much more influence than central government, and they were supported major Committees of Inquiry (DES, 1967, 1975), which stated for example that the 'aim is not to alienate the child from a form of language with which he [*sic*] has grown up … It is to enlarge his repertoire so that he can use language effectively in other speech situations and use standard forms when they are needed' (DES, 1975: paras 10.6, 20.5).

Admittedly, there were different lines of thinking within broadly progressive language education during this period (Cox, 1990: 21; Rampton *et al.*, 1988: 10; Stubbs, 1986: 78), and not all would fit the model of LC outlined by Stroud. But there was an awareness of contemporaneous developments in ethnographic sociolinguistics (Burgess, 2002; Rosen & Burgess, 1980: 140), and a great deal of attention was given to voice and to pupils' own language use, which for many, brought the politics of gender, class and ethnicity into lessons (Gibbons, 2017: 30). In 1979, the ILEA English Centre published *Our Lives: Young People's Autobiographies* saying that 'community publishing groups have begun to show that local working-class autobiographies can contribute to the making of history every bit as forcefully as the autobiographies of the rich and powerful' (Ashton *et al.*, 1979: v). Rosen (1981: 17) noted this and spoke of 'sympathetic vibrations between ventures in popular theatre and drama in schools, between new black literature and the writing of dialect stories and poetry in schools, between a revitalized interest in the oral tradition and the classroom extension of this tradition'. Initiatives of this kind were supported by the National Writing Project (1985–89) and the National Oracy Project (1987–93), two very large-scale curriculum development initiatives 'that saw central funding being used to enable teachers, working with local authority advisers, their subject associations and higher education colleagues, to explore and investigate their own practice and develop new approaches rooted in the evaluation of their own experiences in collaboration with peers. Genuinely bottom up, these projects mirrored the ways in which associations like LATE and NATE had been working for 40 years' (Gibbons, 2017: 53).

A third curriculum development project of this kind, which focused on language itself, was called the Language in the National Curriculum project (LINC). This was supported with £21 million from central government (cf. £165 million at current values), and it ran from 1989 to 1992, involving 25 coordinators and more than 10,000 teachers in over 400 training courses (Carter, 1992: 16; Gibbons, 2017: 73). The project drew on applied linguistics as well as the experience of teachers, but 'recognise[d] that some aspects of language resist systematisation', and that 'language and its conventions of use are permanently and unavoidably unstable and in flux. Much of the richness, pleasure and creativity of language use inheres in such play with these conventions' (Carter, 1990: 17). LINC's six main principles included the idea that '[b]eing more explicitly informed about the sources of attitudes to language, about its uses and misuses, about how language is used to manipulate and incapacitate, can *empower* pupils to see through language to the ways in which messages are mediated and ideologies encoded' (Carter, 1990: 4, original emphasis), and it drew explicitly on Critical Discourse Analysis. It also recognized that 'many bilingual children operate naturally... switching between languages in speech or writing in response to context and audience' and encouraged teachers in multilingual classrooms to 'create the conditions which enable children to gain access to the whole curriculum by encouraging them to use, as appropriate, their strongest or preferring language' (Morrison & Sandhu, 1992; Savva, 1990: 260, 263). All these ideas were turned into professional development materials for teachers – 12 flexible units supported by BBC TV and radio, each designed to take up one to 1.5 days of course time, organized into sections on development in children's talk, reading and writing, together with a block devoted to language and society (Carter, 1990: 2).

These values did not go unopposed. During the 1980s, the cultural politics around English teaching had intensified, with critics advocating meritocratic individualism, the needs of industry and/or going 'back to basics' (spelling, grammar and punctuation) (Cameron & Bourne, 1988; Rampton *et al.*, 2007). This struggle came to a spectacular climax in 1991 when the government refused to allow proper publication of the LINC training materials, objecting, among other things, to a chapter on multilingualism (Abrams, 1991), and asking, in the words of the minister of state: 'Why ... so much prominence [is] given to exceptions rather than the norm – to dialects rather than standard English, for example ... Of course, language is a living force, but our central concern must be the business of teaching children how to use their language correctly' (Eggar, 1991). In fact, more generally over the 1990s, the Conservative government closed down on the idea of using school to develop creative critical voices. It introduced a centrally planned national curriculum and a system of national tests for 7, 11 and 14 year olds, and shifted power away from Local Education Authorities. These changes also saw the demise of large-scale, teacher-driven language curriculum development initiatives like LINC and the National Writing and Oracy Projects, and in a recent review of English teaching from the 1950s to the present, Gibbons (2017: 3) concludes that 'the legacy of nearly thirty years of top-down reform has been profound de-professionalization – leaving English teachers with the underlying sense that the critical decisions about what to teach and how to teach are no longer theirs to make. So hegemonic seems the discourse around standards, accountability, performance and attainment that it can appear that this is just the way things are'.

It is important, of course, not to romanticize language education in England from the 1960s to the 1980s. Jaspers' (2017) call for caution about transformation in education is needed here too, and after all, this historical sketch only describes the thinking of educationalists – it is far harder to know what young people themselves actually made of it all. Indeed, there were educationalists on the political left who argued that far from empowering students, pedagogies committed to voice masked the stratification and social filtering that schooling entailed, and that they failed to provide students with access to the genres that held greatest power in society (Kress, 1982; Reid, 1987; Rampton *et al.*, 1988). But we can still say: (a) that these ideas about developing creatively independent voices 'worth hearing' wouldn't have lasted as long as they did if they had not worked with at least some of the students; and (b) that the students who were affected positively in this way must have been far greater in number, over much longer in their educational careers, than anything that the non-profit, 'third sector' projects described in the previous section can hope to achieve.

Stroud (2008: 45) himself recognizes the 'shifting significance of language in citizenship across time and space, and across different political and economic structures', and the story of language education in England shows that political and economic structures can, at any given time, be either more or less conducive to realizing the ideals of LC. But Stroud's starting assumption is that traditional, state-based institutions are antipathetic to non-standard language mixing, and he focuses on grassroots activity at some distance from the centres of power. Perhaps because of this, in a recent paper looking at how the idea developed, he stresses LC's 'utopian' qualities: '[t]he contestations played out in "acts of citizenship" frequently *prefigure* a better world ... tantamount to anticipating or imagining a world in which harmful categories and systems of othering are deconstructed ... These foreshadowings may often be experienced as aesthetic or euphoric resonances of subjectively experienced events or states: Linguistic Citizenship carries a utopian surplus in this sense' (Stroud, 2018: 23; see also Hymes, 1972: 204–6; von Holdt, 2012: 172).

Compare this, however, with the view of Michael Stubbs (1986) in *Educational Linguistics* in England in 1986, who also envisaged '[a] reconstructionist [language] curriculum [which] sees education as a way of understanding and improving society', which would give students 'the ability to analyse, criticize, and possibly reconstruct social norms and practices', and which was 'essentially democratic in that all children have the right of access to such means of cultural analysis' (1986: 78). This vision fits with LC, but Stubbs insisted that '[n]o utopian assumptions are necessarily made: it need not be assumed that there is one ideal kind of society, or that perfection will be attained' (1986: 78). This pragmatism was well judged – just two years later, he was appointed to a government Working Group tasked with designing a national curriculum for English, and this committee soon produced a document that combined well with LINC and was well received by teachers (DFE, 1989; Cox, 1992: 264).

Admittedly, their text did not survive the transformations of the 1990s and it was soon overtaken by 'a series of events which should not have occurred in a democratic society. From 1991 to 1995, a small group of Conservatives interfered with the National Curriculum in order to impose an extreme right-wing version of the knowledge and skills necessary for the education of our children' (Cox, 1995: 185). Even so, in this context, it was tactics in the corridors of power that mattered, more than utopian aspiration at the margins. More than just working with utopian aspirations, Cox, Stubbs and their associates were fighting pragmatically for *specific proposals, building on existing* language education practices at least in part, targeting a clearly identified citizenry (5 to 16 year olds in England).

So the struggle for LC doesn't have to be confined to relatively short-term projects, and it is possible to work on a scale which reaches far beyond local initiatives involving critical pedagogy or creative production that symbolically challenges the linguistic status quo. But this is likely to require the penetration of (whatever is left of) the state, with all the practical compromises that this entails. The kinds of abstraction and strategic simplification described in the discussion of entextualization, hearability and the effective circulation of ideas in the second Section of this chapter inevitably form part of this, and the challenge is to ensure that the core commitments of LC remain intact – commitments to democratic participation, to voice, to the heterogeneity of the linguistic resources that these entail, and to the political value of sociolinguistic understanding.

Conclusion

According to Stroud (2018: 18), LC is a southern and de-colonial concept. But it chimes well with the programme for ethnographic sociolinguistics outlined by Hymes in the United States, which he himself hoped would be politically productive, overcoming 'scientific colonialism' (1969: 49, 55). It is also congruent with a line of thinking in language education that was very influential in English state schooling for more than two decades. Central government shut this down in the 1990s, but there are still small-scale projects promoting LC principles, even though they tend to rely on relatively short-term project-specific funding raised from non-state sources. In fact, with sustained pressure to increase the non-academic impact of research, collaborations like the ones described, involving university-based sociolinguists and teachers, arts organizers and community activists, are likely to continue (Rampton, 2015b).

Sociolinguists cannot predict or 'scientifically' assess the effects produced by practical initiatives promoting LC, and obviously, the more there are and the longer they last, the harder this gets (even though the expansion would itself be welcome). Nevertheless, over the last few years, a set of overarching terms seem to have crystallized in sociolinguistics that start to answer Fanshawe and Sriskandarajah's (2011: 5) call for 'a new way of talking about diversity in the UK'. *Superdiversity* characterizes the linguistic terrain, *translanguaging* points the kinds of communicative practice we find there, and *linguistic ethnography* identifies the stance and methods needed to understand them. To these, *Linguistic Citizenship* – or in the UK, 'Sociolinguistic Citizenship' – adds the need to strengthen democratic participation with political and educational efforts tuned to the significance of language. Of course, each of these concepts can and should be interrogated, unpacked, refined, applied and compared with different frameworks and situations (Burawoy & von Holdt, 2012). We have tried to do this in this chapter, and this interrogation is also grist to the academic/non-academic collaboration. But despite their flexible generality, these four broad concepts coalesce in a loosely coherent perspective on language and social change that denaturalizes the traditional equation of language, culture and nationality, and instead promotes a clearer understanding and a more constructive engagement with both the patterning and the unpredictability of contemporary sociolinguistic experience.

Notes

(1) The arguments and illustrations in this chapter are developed in much greater detail in Rampton *et al.* (2018a).

(2) Fraser and Stroud illustrate this in different political responses to discrimination against gay people. Affirmative action in the 1970s and 80s gave legitimacy to claims for equal treatment by giving positive recognition to gay identity, while transformative politics would follow queer theory and question 'the very basis of the distinction between heterosexual and homosexual, acknowledging instead the variable and amorphous sexuality of each individual ... destabilising sexual identities in the process' (Fraser, 1995: 85; Stroud, 2001: 344).

(3) '[N]ew meanings and values, new practices and relationships and kinds of relationship are continually being created... but it is exceptionally difficult to distinguish between those which are really elements of some new phase of the dominant culture ... and those which are substantially alternative or oppositional to it' (Williams, 1977: 123)

(4) Pronunciation, grammar, lexis, proposition, text organization etc ⇔ turn sequence and construction, participation and production format ⇔ media, genre, role, etc.

(5) In fact, educational projects that, like Linguistic Citizenship, promote the voice of relatively marginalized people through the recognition of mixed/non-standard language practices and sociolinguistic awareness have a substantial pedigree in critical pedagogy and beyond (e.g. Freire, 1970; Heath, 1983). There has been, for example, a good deal of work with pedagogies involving hip hop in the US (Alim, 2009), Hong Kong (Lin, 2009), Finland (Pietikäinen & Dufva, 2014) and Denmark (e.g. Madsen & Karreb, 2015; www.rapolitics.org), to name just a few of the locations.

(6) Sub-themes are drawn out and elaborated on through the use of a range of tools, activities and texts – see the accounts of two previous short courses in *Whose Integration?* (Bryers *et al.*, 2013) and *The Power of Discussion* (Bryers *et al.*, 2014; Cooke *et al.*, 2014).

References

Abrams, F. (1991) Accents and dialects still unmentionable subjects. *Times Educational Supplement*, 14 June.

Alim, S. (2009) Creating 'an empire within an empire': Critical hip hop language pedagogies and the role of sociolinguistics. In S. Alim, A. Ibrahim and A. Pennycook (eds) *Global Linguistic Flows: Hip Hop Cultures, Youth Identities and the Politics of Language* (pp. 213–230). London: Routledge.

APPG (All Party Parliamentary Group on Social Integration) (2017a) *Interim Report*. London.

APPG (All Party Parliamentary Group on Social Integration) (2017b) *Integration not Demonisation*. London.

Arnaut, K., Blommaert, J., Rampton, B. and Spotti, M. (eds) (2015) *Language and Superdiversity*. London: Routledge.

Ashton, P., Simons, M., Denaro, D. and Raleigh, M. (1979) *Our Lives: Young People's Autobiographies*. London: ILEA English Centre.

Ball, S.J., Maguire, M. and Braun, A. (2012) *How Schools Do Policy: Policy Enactments in Secondary Schools*. London: Routledge.

Blommaert, J. (2004) Rights in places: Comments on linguistic rights and wrongs. In D. Patrick and J. Freeland (eds) *Language Rights and Language Survival* (pp. 55–65). Manchester: St Jerome.

Blommaert, J. (2005) *Discourse: A Critical Introduction*. Cambridge: Cambridge University Press.

Blommaert, J. (2008) *Grassroots Literacy*. London: Routledge.

Blommaert, J. and Rampton, B. (2011) Language and superdiversity. Paper 70, *Working Papers in Urban Language and Literacies*. See www.academia.edu.

Bock, Z. and Mheta, G. (eds) (2014) *Language, Society and Communication*. Pretoria: Van Schaik.

Bryers, D., Winstanley, B. and Cooke, M. (2013) Whose Integration? Paper 106, *Working Papers in Urban Language and Literacies*. See www.academia.edu.

Bryers, D., Winstanley, B. and Cooke, M. (2014) The power of discussion. In D. Mallows (ed.) *Language Issues in Migration and Integration: Perspectives from Teachers and Learners* (pp. 35–54). London: British Council.

Burawoy, M. and von Holdt, K. (2012) *Conversations with Bourdieu: The Johannesburg Moment*. Johannesburg: Wits University Press.

Burgess, T. (2002) Writing, English Teachers and the new professionalism. In T. Burgess, C. Fox and J. Goody (eds) *When the Hurly-Burly's Done: What's Worth Fighting for in English Education?* Sheffield: NATE.

Cameron, D. and Bourne, J. (1988) No common ground Kingman, grammar and the nation. *Language and Education* 2/3, 81–160.

Carter, R. (1990) Introduction. In R. Carter (ed.) *Knowledge about Language* (pp 1–20). London: Hodder and Stoughton.

Carter, R. (1992) LINC The final chapter? *BAAL Newsletter* 42, 16–20.

Charalambous, P., Charalambous, C. and Zembylas, M. (2016) Troubling translanguaging: Language ideologies, superdiversity and interethnic conflict. In J. Jaspers and L. Madsen (eds) *Sociolinguistics in a Languagised World*. Special issue of *Applied Linguistic Review* 7 (3). DOI: https://doi.org/10.1515/applirev-2016-0014. (A version of this is also available as Paper 190, *Working Papers in Urban Language and Literacies*. See www.academia.edu.)

Cooke, M., Bryers, D. and Winstanley, B. (2018) 'Our Languages': Sociolinguistics in multilingual participatory ESOL. Paper 234, *Working Papers in Urban Language and Literacies*. See www.academia.edu.

Cox, B. (1990) *Cox on Cox: An English Curriculum for the 1990s*. London: Hodder and Stoughton.

Cox, B. (1992) *The Great Betrayal*. London: Chapmans.

Cox, B. (1995) *Cox on the Battle for the English Curriculum*. London: Hodder and Stoughton.

DES (Department of Education and Science) (1967) *Children and their Primary Schools*. (Plowden Report) London: HMSO.

DES (Department for Education and Science) (1975) *A Language for Life*. (Bullock Report) London: HMSO.

DES (Department of Education and Science) (1989) *English for Ages 5 to 16* (Cox Report) London HMSO.

Eggar, T. (1991) Correct use of English is essential. *Times Educational Supplement*, 28 June.

English for Action (EfA) (2016) *Annual Report 2015–16*. See http://apps.charitycommission.gov.uk/Accounts/Ends68/0001133268_ AC_20160731_E_C.pdf (accessed 7 December 2019).

Fanshawe, S. and Sriskandarajah, D. (2010) '*You Can't Put Me in a Box': Super-diversity and the End of Identity Politics in Britain*. London: IPPR.

Fraser, N. (1995) From redistribution to recognition? Dilemmas of justice in a 'post-socialist' age. *New Left Review* 212, 68–93.

Fraser, N. (2003) From discipline to flexibilisation? Rereading Foucault in the shadow of globalisation. *Constellations* 10 (2), 160–171.

Freire, P. (1970) *Pedagogy of the Oppressed*. Harmondsworth: Penguin.

García, O. and Li, W. (2014) *Translanguaging*. Basingstoke: Palgrave.

Gibbons, S. (2017) *English and its Teachers: A History of Policy, Pedagogy and Practice*. London: Routledge.

Haarstad, H. and Fløysand, A. (2007) Globalisation and the power of rescaled narratives: A case of opposition to mining in Tambogrande, Peru. *Political Geography* 26, 289–308.

Heath, S.B. (1983) *Ways with Words*. Cambridge: Cambridge University Press.

Holmes, S. (2015) Promoting multilingual creativity: Key principles from successful project. Paper 182, *Working Papers in Urban Language and Literacies*. See www.academia.edu.

Hudson, R. (1980) *Sociolinguistics*. Cambridge: Cambridge University Press.

Hymes, D. (1969) The use of anthropology: Critical, political, personal. In D. Hymes (ed.) *Reinventing Anthropology* (pp. 3–82). Ann Arbor, MI: University of Michigan Press.

Hymes, D. [1975] (1996) Report from an underdeveloped country: Toward linguistic competence in the United States. In D. Hymes *Ethnography; Linguistics, Narrative Inequality: Toward an Understanding of Voice* (pp. 63–106). London: Taylor and Francis.

Hymes, D. (1977) *Foundations in Sociolinguistics: An Ethnographic Approach*. London: Tavistock.

Isin, E. (2008) Theorising acts of citizenship. In E. Isin and G. Nielsen (ed.) *Acts of Citizenship* (pp. 15–43). London: Zed Books.

Isin, E. (2017) Performative citizenship. In A. Shadhar, R. Bauboeck, I. Bloemraad and M. Vink (eds) *The Oxford Handbook of Citizenship*. (pp. 500–523). Oxford: Oxford University Press.

Isin, E. and Nielsen, G. (ed.) (2008) *Acts of Citizenship*. London: Zed Books.

Jaspers, J. (2017). The transformative limits of translanguaging. Paper 226, *Working Papers in Urban Language and Literacies*. See www.academia.edu.

Jessop, B. (2007) From micro-powers to governmentality: Foucault's work on statehood, state formation, statecraft and state power. *Political Geography* 26 (1), 34–40.

Joseph, J. and Taylor, T. (eds) (1990) *Ideologies of Language*. London: Routledge.

Kell, C. (2015) Ariadne's thread: Literacy, scale and meaning making across space and time. In C. Stroud and M. Prinsloo (eds) *Language, Literacy and Diversity: Moving Words* (pp. 72–91). London: Routledge. (Also available as Paper 118, *Working Papers in Urban Language and Literacies* [2013]. See www.academia.edu.)

Kerfoot, C. (2018) Making and shaping participatory spaces: Resemiotisation and citizenship agency in South Africa. In L. Lim, C. Stroud and L. Wee (eds) *The Multilingual*

Citizen: Towards a Politics of Language for Agency and Change (pp. 263–288). Bristol: Multilingual Matters.

Khan, K. (2017) Citizenship, securitisation and suspicion in UK ESOL policy. In K. Arnaut, M.S. Karrebaek, M. Spotti and J. Blommaert (eds) *Engaging Superdiversity: Recombining Spaces, Times and Language Practices* (pp. 303–320). Bristol: Multilingual Matters.

Kress, G. (1982) *Learning to Write*. London: RKP.

Le Page, R. (1981) *Caribbean Connections in the Classroom*. London: Mary Glasgow Language Trust.

Le Page, R. (1988) Some premises concerning the standardisation of languages, with special reference to Caribbean Creole English. *International Journal of the Sociology of Language* 71, 25–36.

Lin, A. (2009) 'Respect for da chopstick hip hop': The politics, poetics and pedagogy of Cantonese verbal art in Hong Kong. In S. Alim, A. Ibrahim and A. Pennycook (eds) *Global Linguistic Flows: Hip Hop Cultures, Youth Identities and the Politics of Language* (pp. 159–178). London: Routledge.

Language in the National Curriculum Materials for Professional Development (LINC) (1992) Nottingham: Department of English Studies, University of Nottingham.

Madsen, L. and Karrebæk, S. (2015) Hip hop, education and polycentricity. In J. Snell, S. Shaw and F. Copland (eds) *Linguistic Ethnography: Interdisciplinary Explorations* Palgrave Advances Series (pp. 246–265). Basingstoke: Palgrave MacMillan.

Makoni, S. (2003) From misinvention to disinvention of language: Multilingualism and the South African constitution. In S. Makoni, G. Smitherman, A. Ball and A. Spears (eds) *Black Linguistics: Language, Society and Politics in Africa and the Americas* (pp. 132–152). London: Routledge.

Makoni, S. and Pennycook, A. (2007) (eds) *Disinventing and Reconstituting Languages*. Clevedon: Multilingual Matters.

Maybin, J. (2017) Textual trajectories: Theoretical roots and institutional consequences. *Text and Talk* 37 (4), 415–435.

McCarty, T. (2011) Introducing ethnography and language policy. In T. McCarty (ed.) *Ethnography and Language Policy* (pp. 1–28). London: Routledge.

Mehan, H. (1996) The construction of an LD student: A case study in the politics of representation. In M. Silverstein and G. Urban (eds) *Natural Histories of Discourse* (pp. 253–176). Chicago: University of Chicago Press.

Moore, R. (2011) Standardisation, diversity and enlightenment in the contemporary crisis of EU language policy. Paper 74. *Working Papers in Urban Language and Literacies*, 74. See www.academia.edu.

Morrison, M. and Sandhu, P. (1992) Towards a multilingual pedagogy. In K. Norman (ed.) *Thinking Voices: The Work of the National Oracy Project* (pp. 100–107). London: Hodder and Stoughton.

Neveu, C. (2015) Of ordinariness and citizenship processes. *Citizenship Studies* 19 (2), 141–154.

Oliveri, F. (2014) Acts of citizenship against neo-liberalism: The new cycle of migrant struggles in Italy. In N.K. Kim (ed.) *Multicultural Challenges and Sustainable Democracy in Europe and East Asia* (pp. 221–242). Basingstoke: Palgrave Macmillan.

Pennycook, A. (2016) Mobile times, mobile terms: The trans-super-poly-metro movement. In N. Coupland (ed.) *Sociolinguistics: Theoretical Debates* (pp. 201–216). Cambridge: Cambridge University Press.

Petrovic, J. and Kuntz, A. (2013) Strategies of reframing language policy in the liberal state: A recursive model. *Journal of Language and Politics* 12 (3), 126–146.

Pietikäinen, S. and Dufva, H. (2014) Heteroglossia in action: Sámi children, textbooks and rap. In A. Blackledge and A. Creese (eds) *Heteroglossia as Practice and Pedagogy* (pp. 59–74). Dordrecht: Springer.

Rampton, B. (2014) An everyday poetics of class and ethnicity in stylisation and cross-ing. In M. Fludernik and D. Jacob (eds) *Linguistics and Literary Studies: Interfaces, Encounters, Transfers* (pp. 261–268). Berlin: Mouton de Gruyter.

Rampton, B. (2015a) Superdiversity and social class: An interactional perspective. In C. Stroud and M. Prinsloo (eds) *Language, Literacy and Diversity: Moving Words* (pp. 149–165). London: Routledge.

Rampton, B. (2015b) The next ten years for applied linguistics? Paper 165, *Working Papers in Urban Language and Literacies*. See www.academia.edu.

Rampton, B. (2016) Drilling down to the grain in superdiversity. In K. Arnaut, J. Blommaert, B. Rampton and M. Spotti (eds) *Language and Superdiversity* (pp. 91–109). London: Routledge.

Rampton, B., Bourne, J. and Cameron, D. (1988) The Kingman Inquiry A briefing docu-ment. *Politics and Linguistics Newsletter* 5, 3–21.

Rampton, B., Cook, M. and Holmes, S. (2018a) Promoting Linguistic Citizenship: Issues, problems and possibilities. Paper 233, *Working Papers in Urban Language and Literacies*. See www.academia.edu.

Rampton, B., Harris, R. and Leung, C. (2007) Education and languages other than English in the British Isles. In D. Britain (ed.) *Language in the British Isles* (2nd revised edn) (pp. 417–35). Cambridge: Cambridge University Press.

Rampton, B., Leung, C. and Cooke, M. (2020) Education, England and users of languages other than English. Paper 275, *Working Papers in Urban Language and Literacies*. See www.academia.edu.

Reid, I. (ed.) (1987) *The place of genre in learning: Current debates*. Geelong: Centre for Studies in Literary Education, Deakin University

Rosen, H. (1981) *Neither Bleak House nor Liberty Hall: English in the Curriculum*. London: University of London Institute of Education.

Rosen, H. and Burgess, T. (1980) *The Languages and Dialects of London Schoolchildren*. London: Ward Lock.

Santos, B. de S. (2012) Public sphere and epistemologies of the South. *Africa Development* 37 (1), 43–67.

Savva, H. (1990) The rights of bilingual children. In R. Carter (ed.) *Knowledge about Language* (pp. 248–68). London: Hodder and Stoughton.

Stroud, C. (1999) Portuguese as ideology and politics in Mozambique: Semiotic (re)con-structions of a postcolony. In J. Blommaert (ed.) *Language Ideological Debates* (pp. 343–380). Berlin: Mouton de Gruyter.

Stroud, C. (2001) African mother-tongue programmes and the politics of language: Linguistic citizenship versus linguistic human rights. *Journal of Multilingual and Multicultural Development* 22 (4), 339–355.

Stroud, C. (2008) Bilingualism: Colonialism and post-colonialism. In M. Heller (ed.) *Bilingualism: A Social Approach* (pp. 25–49). Basingstoke: Palgrave.

Stroud, C. (2010) Towards a post-liberal theory of citizenship. In J. Petrovic (ed.) *International Perspectives on Bilingual Education: Policy, Practice and Controversy* (pp. 191–218). New York: Information Age Publishing.

Stroud, C. (2018) Linguistic Citizenship. In L. Lim, C. Stroud and L. Wee (eds) *The Multilingual Citizen: Towards a Politics of Language for Agency and Change* (pp. 17–39). Bristol: Multilingual Matters.

Stroud, C. and Heugh, K. (2004) Linguistic human rights and linguistic citizenship. In D. Patrick and J. Freeland (eds) *Language Rights and Language Survival* (pp. 191–218). Manchester: St Jerome.

Stubbs, M. (1986) *Educational Linguistics*. Oxford: Blackwell.

von Holdt, K. (2012) The symbolic world of politics. In M. Burawoy and K. von Holdt (eds) *Conversations with Bourdieu: The Johannesburg Moment* (pp. 169–174). Johannesburg: Wits University Press.

Williams, R. (1977) *Marxism and Literature*. Oxford: Clarendon Press.

Williams, Q. and Stroud, C. (2015) Linguistic citizenship: Language and politics in post-national modernities. *Journal of Language and Politics* 14 (3), 406–430.

Woolard, K., Schieffelin, B. and Kroskrity, P. (1998) *Language Ideologies*. Oxford: Oxford University Press.

Part 2

Multilingual Narratives and Linguistic Citizenship

5 'I Am My Own Coloured': Navigating Language and Race in Post-Apartheid South Africa

Lauren van Niekerk, Keshia R. Jansen and
Zannie Bock

Introduction

Language in South Africa has a long history of contestation, subjugation, oppression and resistance. Centuries of colonialism, followed by the more recent Apartheid era (1948–1994), have resulted in a diversity of linguistic forms and practices, a multiplicity of languages organized into a hierarchy from marginal to powerful, from invisible to dominant, all closely correlated with race, ethnicity, class, power and status. This chapter explores how this history plays out in one context – a focus group interview held at the University of the Western Cape (UWC). The topic is race, in particular, the racial positioning of people who self-identify as 'coloured', the label used by the Apartheid government to refer to people of complex heritage arising out of a history of colonialism and slavery, who were not easily classifiable as 'white' or 'black'. Throughout the Apartheid years, it was a fraught category, and remains so today (Adhikari, 2004; Erasmus, 2001; Erasmus & Pieterse, 1999; Rassool, 2019). The data are rich in stories about the students' experiences of being racially positioned, and they provide an insight into the complexities, ambiguities and layered nuances of being 'coloured' in the post-Apartheid era, or, in the words of one of the participants, of being 'in the middle' (that is, caught between black and white, the two 'dominant' racial groups).

In this chapter, we explore how these participants talk about 'colouredness' as a fluid, evolving identity, moulded by, yet pushing against, the historical and contemporary discourses which attempt to 'fix' and 'constrain' it in particular ways. We explore how, in these stories of everyday life, the old Apartheid boundaries of language and race are troubled and made visible as participants move in and through different geographical and social spaces. With the demise of Apartheid and its laws of spatial segregation and control, young South Africans of all races have enjoyed much greater social and physical mobility. Some (with financial means) have been able to attend better (formerly white) schools, live in more upmarket suburbs and make use of public amenities once reserved for 'whites only'. However, these spaces remain in many ways 'colour-coded' (Bock & Stroud, 2018). The stories in the data recount the participants' experiences of mobility; at the same time as they show how they are often positioned or 'put back' into historical categories which continue to act as powerful forces shaping the options available to them. These stories provide valuable counter narratives to the dominant ones that circulate in the public sphere and bring into focus the diversity and complexity of voice and racial positioning in post-Apartheid South Africa. The analysis uses Bakhtin's (1981) notion of the chronotope, and narrative theory, in particular, Georgakopoulou's (2007, 2015) 'small story' lens, to show how the stories are layered, with chronotopes from the past intruding onto the present, forcing participants into stereotypical positionings, causing them to feel uncomfortable, unsafe or vulnerable (Blommaert & De Fina, 2017). It traces the way in which reflection on these moments enables new 're-figurings' (or re-imaginings) of what it might mean to be 'coloured', or indeed, simply South African, to emerge.

A third theoretical angle that has proved useful in this analysis is Linguistic Citizenship. It has been described as 'an approach to a politics of language and multilingualism that departs from a notion of vulnerability, in the sense of the emergent and sensitive process of disinhabiting, stepping out of, imposed and linguistically mediated and entangled subjectivities' (Stroud, 2018a: 5). This chapter adds to this emerging body of work by exploring how a focus on small stories – as an analytical lens – can contribute to the 'disinhabiting' and 'stepping out of' inherited ethnolinguistic subjectivities. In particular, it focuses on how, in these stories, 'spaces of vulnerability' are central to the unsettling of historical and sedimented hierarchies of exclusion (Bock et al., 2019). According to Stroud (2018b: 18), these are spaces 'where speakers meet different others in disruptive and unsettling encounters that interrupt the status quo (Pinchevski, 2005), and where senses of self may be juxtaposed and refashioned as part of the deconstruction of dominant voices and more equitable linguistic engagement with others'. Reflecting on these spaces and moments, and the kinds of insights they engender, is part, we would argue, of de-constructing these historical 'boxes', and finding a way to re-imagine ourselves as fellow citizens in a non-racial future.

A brief history of language and race in South Africa

The story of South Africa is one of successive waves of Dutch and British colonialism, followed by white Afrikaner nationalism, which culminated, after 1948, in the system of legalized racism known as Apartheid. Language has been (and continues to be) central to all these struggles. During the colonial era, Dutch and English vied for supreme position, while Afrikaans emerged as a creole, a mix of European settler languages, the languages of local inhabitants (now dispossessed of their land) and the slaves brought from South East Asia and different parts of Africa to the Cape to work in the colony (Kriel, 2018). Later, Afrikaans – the version spoken by the white descendants of the Dutch farmers who moved away from the Cape Colony – was elaborated and elevated as 'the standard', and, together with English, served as one of the two official languages during the Apartheid years. Kaaps, the local variety of Afrikaans spoken predominantly by working-class coloured communities around Cape Town, was stigmatized and branded as inferior, in contrast to the 'pure' white Afrikaans variety (Hendricks, 2016). Similarly, the many languages of the African majority were relegated to lower levels in this language hierarchy and used as tools of governmentality to regiment and divide the population into distinct 'ethnic' groups. After 1994, in an attempt to build an inclusive national identity, nine of these African languages were recognized as 'official', alongside English and (standard) Afrikaans. However, since then, English has become the *de facto lingua franca*, and has gained considerable currency and prestige as the (perceived) gateway to social and global mobility, quality education and better jobs. A distinguishing feature of many newly middle-class homes has been the desire for English schooling for their children, and a shift from Afrikaans, Kaaps, or any number of African languages, to English as the dominant home language.

Just as centuries of colonialism and Apartheid have bequeathed South Africa a complex hierarchy of language varieties, so too has race been inscribed as a primary marker of identity. While racial segregation existed prior to 1948, racial categories were more variably and flexibly deployed. But with the advent of Apartheid and the enactment of the Population Registration Act of 1950, each individual was assigned a single racial label, e.g. 'black', 'white', 'coloured' or 'Indian'. The historian, Deborah Posel (2001a: 51) argues that these classifications were based on 'readings of bodily difference closely [aligned] with differences of class, lifestyle and general repute', often carried out by loyal party officials or small-town magistrates. Social criteria (e.g. occupation, education, religious affiliation) were somewhat arbitrarily defined and applied as they related to 'social standing', 'way of life' and 'acceptance' into a racially defined community. Physical criteria generally related to skin tone, but they included practices like the notorious 'pencil test' which was used to differentiate whites from coloureds: 'If a person's hair was sufficiently tightly curled to hold a pencil, then supposedly that person was not white' (Posel, 2001b: 105).

These classifications fixed a person's position within a racial hierarchy, firmly associating whiteness with power, privilege and opportunity, and blackness with poverty, dispossession and inferiority. Being coloured meant a rank somewhere 'in the middle'. Although coloureds shared a number of linguistic and cultural commonalities with whites (e.g. both spoke varieties of English and Afrikaans as their home languages), they were accorded 'second class' status under Apartheid. While they were granted some privileges (e.g. job preferences, limited voting rights) those classified 'black' (or 'native' or African) were not, they were discriminated against as people of colour, had no meaningful democratic rights and were excluded from the privileges and resources reserved exclusively for those classified white. In this way, the racial category of a person became a key determinant of all aspects of their public and private lives.

Posel (2001a, 2001b) documents how a number of individuals contested their classifications, and applied to be re-classified, usually, although not always, to 'improve' their ranking on the racial ladder. Thus, coloureds could become white, or blacks could become coloured, if they could convince the local magistrate of their 'racial purity'.[1] However, a change in classification meant you had to leave your home and cut off ties with your family and community, lest you lose your new racial status by association with the former. The rejection, loss, betrayal and shame that this traumatic practice inflicted on many families and individuals is beautifully and poignantly explored in Zoë Wicomb's novel about a young coloured couple who successfully 'tried for white' in 1960s Cape Town (Wicomb, 2006). Erasmus (2001) also explores the contested, ambiguous, at times compromised, but also agentive and constantly renewing conception of colouredness in her seminal book on coloured identity.

Despite the legal dismantling of Apartheid in 1994, race has continued to have a profound effect on people's lives and is still very much a 'lived experience' (Adhikari, 2004; Erasmus & Pieterse, 1999; Lefko-Everett, 2012; Soudien, 2013). As many scholars have argued, institutionalized racism entrenches structures of privilege and disadvantage which shape families for decades even after the legal system has been abolished (Bundy, 2014). One of the ways in which the post-Apartheid government has sought to transform this legacy is through a policy of affirmative action that gives preferential employment to people from previously disenfranchised groups. To this end, many institutions use racial quotas to regulate admissions or employment. A consequence of this is that all South Africans are required to identify themselves in terms of the old Apartheid categories on all official application forms. Thus, another reason why race is still so pervasive in contemporary South Africa is that it has been reinvigorated in the name of redress and used to favour applicants who were disadvantaged by Apartheid. In particular, black applicants, by nature of belonging to a group deemed 'more disadvantaged' than coloureds, have preferential status. Hence, this is a further reason for the young coloured participants in this study to complain that they are 'still in the middle': under Apartheid, they were not white enough, now they are not black enough

(Adhikari, 2004). As a result of this ambiguity and 'in-between-ness', argue Petrus and Isaacs-Martin (2012), many coloured people feel caught between belonging and not belonging. The resultant sensitivity about race, suggests Adhikari (2004) and Erasmus (2001), stems from the vulnerability that many coloured people experience from feeling marginalized and 'intermediate'.

This chapter uses these racial labels conscious of their history and contested meanings. Erwin (2012) cautions that their use inevitably runs the risk of further entrenching these same categories, and researchers should work to critique and destabilize these naturalized classifications. This chapter thus aims to draw attention to the ways in which language and race still feature in the stories of young South Africans, as part of a broader project which seeks to explore those moments or spaces where some kind of shift or re-imagining becomes visible, or begins to seem possible (Bock, 2017, 2018; Bock & Hunt, 2015).

Narrative and Chronotopic Identities

Given the complexities and sensitivities inherent in racial positioning, we chose a narrative approach with a 'small stories' analytical lens. Small stories may refer to events in the distant or recent past, or to incidents that are imagined or hypothetical. They may serve as 'reworked slices of life' arising as participants recount experiences (Georgakopoulou, 2007: 150), or as a way of elaborating or backing up an argument in conversation. They provide a sense of how people interact with the social discourses in their everyday contexts and provide counter positions and ambivalences often lost in the homogenizing master narratives. In this way, argues Georgakopoulou (2015), they are an important epistemology for capturing the silenced, under-represented voices and subjectivities which are not yet fully articulated.

Blommaert and De Fina (2017) use Bakhtin's notion of the 'chronotope' – or the 'intrinsic connectedness of temporal and spatial relationships that are artistically expressed in literature' (Bakhtin, 1981: 84) – as a way of thinking about narrative and identity in everyday interaction. They show how it can bring into analytical focus 'the ways in which specific forms of identity enactment are conditioned by the timespace configurations in which they occur' (Blommaert & De Fina, 2017: 4). Chronotopes, they argue, are characterized by different norms, roles, identities, discourses and behaviours, and may operate at any given level or scale – from the momentary, interactional context, to the broader historical *long durée*. Thus each chronotope refers to 'socially shared, and differential complexes of value attributed to specific forms of identity' which can be activated by the 'looks, behaviours, actions, and speech of certain characters', thus serving to 'invoke orders of indexicality valid in a specific timespace frame' and mark particular modes of behaviour as desirable, compulsory or deviant (Blommaert & De Fina, 2017: 3). These changes in timespace arrangements may 'trigger complex and sometime massive shifts in roles, discourses, modes of interaction, dress, codes of conduct and criteria for judgement of appropriate versus inappropriate behaviour, and so forth' and redefine 'what is possible and allowable' in identity work in that context (Blommaert & De Fina, 2017: 4, 5).

Williams and Stroud (2015) also use the chronotope to explore how language can be used in a staged performance (comedy) to make visible marginal voices – in other words, to enact Linguistic Citizenship. Their analysis shows how the performer uses small indexical linguistic features to 'reference higher order contextualizations', or chronotopes and 'provide the spatial and temporal parameters for the successful realisation' of particular subjectivities and voices (Williams & Stroud, 2015: 425). They argue that it is in the local, often transgressive and counter-discursive encounters of the everyday that ordinary people construct and deconstruct, negotiate and challenge the ways in which they are positioned and contained by more powerful, hegemonic and institutional social discourses (Williams & Stroud, 2015: 407).

From these perspectives, then, people can be seen as inhabiting a world of layered chronotopes, some reaching into the past, some new and emergent. Particular words, actions or behaviours can trigger or 'make visible' one or other of these layerings, bringing them into dialogue with other configurations currently in operation. In the analysis which follows, we see how the storyteller's social and geographical mobility in the post-Apartheid triggers different timespace frames, bringing these and their related discourses into conflict, causing him much discomfort, but also insight and awareness into his own (emerging) racial identity. These moments become visible in the small stories that he tells. Because small stories 'hold' the complexity of the experience without the teller having to distil one unitary interpretation or meaning, we suggest that this lens is a productive means to explore the complex and subtle ways in which the teller 'feels raced' and discursively positioned, and seeks to negotiate a different, emerging identity for himself.

Interactional context and data

The two stories for analysis are drawn from a focus group interview (73 minutes) held in 2018 at UWC.[2] The group consists of four participants – two males, two females and the interviewer (also first author of this chapter). They were selected by the latter (who is herself a student). They all self-identify as coloured. The data was elicited using open-ended questions which asked participants for their views on 'being coloured': what it means to them, how they feel about it, have they ever felt discriminated against because of their race, etc. Despite the fact that this is a focus group interview, their interaction is more akin to casual conversation, with highly interactive turn taking and co-constructed evaluations. As Lambrou (2003: 171) has argued, when the participants in a focus interview are friends, conversational story telling becomes 'an inevitable feature' as well-established patterns of convivial interaction 'take over'.

The data are rich in stories which explore the students' experiences of being 'raced' and policed in different spaces. This chapter focusses on two stories which bring into focus the nexus of racialized bodies, language and place. Both are told by one participant (pseudonym, Lee), who is a 23-year-old final-year Law student. While he speaks some Afrikaans, his dominant language is English. He grew up in a poor, working-class, coloured area of Cape Town, and while, for the first few years, he went to a local school, his mother later managed to send him to a better, English medium one in a neighbouring area, which, he says, opened his eyes to the opportunities that a good education can offer. He is well informed about the history of the country, and politically conscious, indicating that he thinks 'coloured' is a derogatory term and would prefer to describe himself as 'black' as it is a politically 'generic term [which] we coloureds are supposed to form part of'.[3] However, in the stories he tells, he clearly identifies as coloured as evidenced by his frequent use of the inclusive pronoun 'we' to refer to himself and the other participants in the focus group. At the same time, he claims that he is his 'own coloured' as he does not fit the stereotypical norms of colouredness.

Story 1: The Niemandsville Bar

This story was told about 13 minutes into the interview in response to the interviewer's question: 'Was there ever a time when being perceived as coloured has held you back, or worked to your advantage?' Niemandsville (also a pseudonym) is a small farming community near Cape Town – and the location is a key influence in the story. It is the arrival of Lee and his friend, young coloured men, in a local, predominantly white bar in this small rural town, which brings into conflict two chronotopes with clashing notions of race, language and class, and makes visible the ways in which language is used to impose, challenge and resist racial positioning in South Africa.

At the beginning of his story, Lee makes a bid for the floor by stating: 'I have a story like just maybe it just – it made me shook', where his use of 'shook', a colloquial version of 'shake' or more specifically 'stunned', creates some mirth among the audience, and foreshadows the threat that is to come. He then proceeds to narrate the encounter below.[4]

Extract 1: The Niemandsville bar

a.	Lee:	Uhm I was – I was in Niemandsville in Worcester
b.		so I was at this bar (1.0) right
c.		so I just decided

d.		I'm gonna have a drink there at this bar
e.		and I went in
f.		and I walked in
g.		I was just like – lots and lots of white men
h.		like I was like 'okay'
i.		and like three Indians sitting there [some laugh]
j.		and I proceed to drink
k.		and this white guy comes over to me right
l.		and he's like uhm 'hi'
m.		like almost like 'wat doen julle hier' [*what are you (plural) doing here?*]
n.		so I'm like 'uh ek drink net uhm ja' [*uh I'm just drinking uhm yes*]
o.		and then my Afrikaans game isn't too strong really
p.		it isn't like I can't say I'm coloured
q.		I have to speak Afrikaans
r.		I am my own coloured uhm
s.		and I drink
t.		and then he comes over to me
u.		and he says uhm 'kom ons speel a game' – it's darts – [*Come let's play a game*]
v.		'Kom ons speel a game coloureds teen blanke' (1.0) [*Come let's play a game coloureds against whites*]
w.	Ellen:	Wow
x.	Lee:	and himself
y.		so I'm like 'okay let's play'
z.		so we winning my friend and I
aa.		we winning
bb.		and then he basically – I'm starting to speak English now
cc.		cause my Afrikaans airtime is running up [Everyone laughs]
dd.		and then he basically tells me
ee.		'Nee wat doen jy [*No what are you doing*]
ff.		praat Afrikaans saam met my' [*speak Afrikaans with me*]
gg.		so I was like 'why must I speak …'
hh.		just because you see…
ii.		'Nee djy's van die Kaap [*No you're from the Cape*]
jj.		djy praat Afrikaans [*you talk Afrikaans*]
kk.		and djy's coloured [*and you're coloured*]
ll.		djy praat Afri….' [*you talk Afri …*]
mm.		I'm like 'ha ah ek praat Engels' [Everyone laughs] [*no I talk English*]
nn.		at that time – at that time I knew I had to leave because –
oo.		and before that he like I saw like his T-shirt
pp.		so I said 'Oh you work there blah blah'
qq.		I won't mention the company
rr.		he's like 'oh djy weet' [*oh you know*]
ss.		so I'm like almost like I'm not suppose to know
tt.		but the reason why his perception of coloured people are like that is because in Niemandsville there's a lot of farm workers that work there

uu.	Lauren:	and they all coloured
vv.	Lee:	and they all coloured
ww.		now I'm not saying this
xx.		I might be wrong but assumptions
yy.		but the farm workers they aren't given maybe as many opportunities in terms of education as us coloureds in the urban setting
zz.		so his setting or his mindset mentality of coloureds is 'okay farm workers
aaa.		this is how we going deal with you'
bbb.		and now someone from the urban city comes in
ccc.		and then now he's like huh? taken aback
ddd.		so at time I knew I had to leave
eee.		because if I had to open my mouth again
fff.		and defend my (2.0) [gestures to himself]
ggg.		it would have been a major problem
hhh.		so it was just the thing
iii.		of how people <u>see</u> coloured people
jjj.		I mean it just like if you there in their place per se

The first ten lines (a–j) serve, in classic Labovian (1972) terms, as the orientation by setting the scene and describing how Lee enters a bar for a drink – an event which would normally suggest relaxation and leisure. He signals, however, that he immediately feels like an outsider, by mentioning that there were 'lots and lots of white men' present, and only 'three Indians sitting there'. This racial labelling implies that he and his companion were the only coloureds and felt outnumbered and uncomfortable in this predominantly white space. The insertion of his somewhat cautionary 'okay' (in line h) signals to his audience his awareness that they are probably not welcome in the bar. In line k, he recounts how 'this white guy comes over' and says 'hi', a greeting which he interprets as a hostile interrogation of his right to be in that space (almost like 'wat doen julle hier' – line m). His code-switch to Afrikaans for the man's imagined speech would, for his audience, clearly invoke the Apartheid chronotope in which Afrikaans was strongly associated with white masculinity and power, and further identify the bar as a 'whites only' space, hostile to people of colour. Note, however, that it is *imagined* speech (signalled by 'almost like') – but its inclusion here in this story speaks to Lee's sense of being unwelcome.

Lee's response (line n) is full of hesitations and dysfluencies ('uh ek drink net uhm ja') indicating not only that he perceives the man's stance as threatening, but also that he is struggling to switch into Afrikaans. In the following four lines (o–r), Lee steps out of the narrative to reflect on his lack of proficiency which he frames as a question mark on his authenticity as a coloured: 'and then my Afrikaans game isn't too strong really / it isn't like I can't say I'm coloured / I have to speak Afrikaans /

I am my own coloured'. Here Lee's racial anxiety becomes visible as he shifts between self-identifying as coloured (the double negative of 'it isn't like I can't say I'm coloured' signalling his anxiety), and acknowledging the broader social norm – shared by many coloured people – that the ability to speak Afrikaans is part of this identity ('I have to speak Afrikaans') and, by inference, that not being fully proficient in the language somehow disqualifies him from identifying as coloured. But then he rejects this stereotype with the bold assertion: 'I am my own coloured' (line r).

In the next 22 lines (s–nn), Lee picks up his narrative again and recounts how he is just settling down with his drink when the same man again approaches him, this time to challenge him – in Afrikaans – to a game of darts: 'Kom ons speel a game coloureds teen blanke' (line v). Tellingly, his interlocutor's use of the term, 'blanke' is an Apartheid term used to refer to 'whites', and his suggestion of a game between racially based teams ('coloureds against whites') echoes centuries of racial animosity. It, therefore, serves to activate, once again, the Apartheid chronotope in which Lee, as a coloured person, is positioned as the racial antagonist to the more powerful white man. The significance of this threat is not lost on Lee's audience as there is a moment of silence (end of line v) before Ellen exclaims 'wow' (turn w) in shock and disbelief at the blatant racial positioning underway.

Lee, however, is not cowered, and in the following line, we hear how he and his friend take up the challenge: 'okay let's play'. What's more, they begin to win, the significance of which is brought home by the repetition in lines z–aa: 'so we winning my friend and I / we winning'. They are *also* beginning to speak English, as Lee notes: 'cause my Afrikaans airtime is running up' (line cc). Here he uses humour to lighten the tension, both as a narrative device, but also, one can surmise, as a way to lessen the anxiety he feels about his own lack of proficiency in this language which he and others perceive as indexing colouredness. He then recounts how the man proceeds to question his choice to speak English over Afrikaans, insisting that as a coloured ('djy's coloured') from the Cape ('van die Kaap'), he (Lee) should be proficient in Afrikaans ('djy praat Afrikaans'):

dd.   and then he basically tells me
ee.   'Nee wat doen jy [No *what you are doing*]
ff.   praat Afrikaans saam met my' [*speak Afrikaans with me*]
gg.   so I was like 'why must I speak …'
hh.   just because you see…
ii.   'Nee djy's van die Kaap [*No you're from the Cape*]
jj.   djy praat Afrikaans [*you talk Afrikaans*]
kk.   and djy's coloured [*and you're coloured*]
ll.   djy praat Afri….' [*you talk Afri …*]
mm.   I'm like 'ha ah ek praat Engels' [Everyone laughs] [*no, I talk English*]

The man in the bar's insistence on the 'naturalness' of this ethnolinguistic identity inserts – into the interactional frame – a historical stereotype for colouredness, one which is increasingly irrelevant post-Apartheid as the next generation move out of their historical geographic and socioeconomic spaces and associated ethnolinguistic identities, and adopt English as a language of upward mobility (Anthonissen, 2013). But this man is doing more than questioning Lee's authenticity as a coloured. By rejecting Lee's choice of English and insisting on a particular language of communication and a particular racial identity, he, Lee's opponent, is invoking, once again, the Apartheid racial hierarchy in which he, the white man, gets to define the terms of the interaction.

What is interesting in this narrative is the place of Afrikaans, and the multiple positions that it indexes. While Lee is apologetic about his lack of proficiency in the language, which he feels somehow disqualifies him from 'authentic colouredness', the man in the bar uses Afrikaans as a means to invoke the old Apartheid hierarchy, put Lee 'in his place' and assert his right to police the bar as a space of whiteness. Because the different varieties of coloured and white Afrikaans are mutually intelligible, and Lee would have been familiar with both, Afrikaans has always played a complex role in the relationships between people historically classified as white and coloured. While, for many people, Afrikaans became, under Apartheid, 'the language of the oppressor', various varieties of Afrikaans remained a first language for many black and coloured people, or at least a highly significant language in their repertoires. English, as the language of the former colonizer, has played an equally complex role, both in terms of its hegemonic power to marginalize local languages, as well as to facilitate access to 'better' education, job opportunities, and social and global mobility. Here, by insisting on his choice of English ('ha ah ek praat Engels' – line mm), Lee is able to sidestep – and challenge – the white man's racial profiling of him, even as his lack of Afrikaans proficiency is a matter of some anxiety, as it disqualifies him from what he perceives as authentic colouredness.

This ambiguity is nowhere more evident than in Lee's pronunciation of the word, 'jy', meaning 'you'. In his first revoicing of the white man's words (turn ee), he uses the standard pronunciation, typical of white Afrikaans, namely, the palatal approximant, /j/ for 'jy', pronounced /jɛɪ/. However, in the subsequent revoicings (lines ii–ll, rr), he shifts to using the palate-alveolar affricate, /dʒ/, which is indexical for Kaaps. Perhaps he is using this small linguistic marker as a way to signal his resistance to being positioned, and to align himself with his audience, who would immediately recognize this pronunciation as indexing coloured belonging.

It is at this point that the concept of Linguistic Citizenship becomes a useful lens in the analysis. As Williams and Stroud (2015) have argued, it is the micro discourses and small linguistic markers that index particular chronotopes as challenges to the macro hegemonic discourses. In addition, the bar constitutes a 'space of vulnerability' for both Lee and the white man. In this space, the linguistic choices they make bring into the frame clashing chronotopes, some rooted in Apartheid ethnolinguistic identities, others carried by past and contemporary discourses of coloured-ness. Thus Lee's story reflects the complexities of the post-Apartheid iden-tity options for the current generation who are less bound by the old stereotypes and positions. Perhaps, we could argue, the sharing of this story and the insights it gives into the complexities of contemporary racial positionings, provide a means to acknowledge and deconstruct some of these powerful shaping discourses (such as: 'you must speak Afrikaans to be coloured') and unsettle some of the sedimented racial and social cate-gories, at the same time that it enables Lee to begin to assert a new, more fluid identity – in his words, to be his 'own coloured'.

Before Lee ends his story, however, he inserts a further anecdote, namely that he had noticed that his interlocutor was wearing a T-shirt which identified him as working for one of the companies in the area (lines oo–qq). He recalls that the man seems surprised that he should know of the company ('oh djy weet' – line rr). He then reflects that the reason for this surprise was probably because the only coloured people in Niemandsville are farm workers, while Lee, as a coloured person from an 'urban setting' with education, breaks this mould. Lee then completes his story with his evaluation of the white man as having a 'mindset mentality' that all coloureds are farm workers and 'this is how we gonna deal with you' (lines zz–aaa). The underlying threat in this imagined speech of his interlocutor is once again a reminder of the power that white people exer-cised over people deemed 'non-white' and, therefore, inferior during the Apartheid years. Thus, in addition to feeling interpellated as coloured and Afrikaans speaking, Lee feels further positioned as less powerful, unedu-cated and from the labouring class. As much contemporary research argues, social identities are multifaceted and race interacts with other social variables such as class in complex ways (Cho *et al.*, 2013). Similarly in this story, race, class and language intersect and reflect how the neat correlations that were promoted and imposed as part of the Apartheid ideology of racial segregation are being reconfigured.

At this point, however, Lee resolves the story by deciding to leave the bar before the confrontation becomes physical (line fff). He has clearly under-stood that his interlocutor has not taken kindly to being challenged in his 'own' bar and perceives him (Lee) as a threat. It is noteworthy that Lee does not 'name' his own body – merely gestures towards it in line fff – as though acknowledging not only the vulnerability of his physical self, but also the heightened significance that his racialized body has had in this story:

ddd. so at time I knew I had to leave
eee. because if I had to open my mouth again
fff. and defend my (2.0) [gestures to himself]
ggg. it would have been a major problem

The final clauses of the narrative act as a coda in which Lee sums up the significance of his story and highlights his awareness of how traces of the Apartheid landscape still shape and define how people can move through or inhabit different colour-coded spaces (Bock & Stroud, 2018). Once again, we see the friction caused when historical and contemporary chronotopes intersect, and people of colour, who are educated city dwellers, come into a conservative 'white space', choose not to speak Afrikaans, beat a white man at darts and challenge him and his sense of racial dominance in his own comfort zone:

hhh.　so it was just the thing
iii.　of how people see coloured people
jjj.　I mean it just like if you there in their place *per se*

This story, then, gives insight into how Lee navigates what it means to be coloured in a post-Apartheid South Africa in which he has to contend with the old-style racism of Apartheid whiteness. In the next story, Lee adds a further layer to this complexity when he recounts how he, as a child, was taunted by his coloured peers – this time, for being 'too white'. This story taps into another historical chronotope built on the narratives and practices of 'trying for white' under Apartheid (in order to be reclassified 'up' the racial hierarchy) and the resultant feelings of rejection, shame, loss and betrayal. Lee offers this anecdote as a follow up to a story told by Ellen about how her coloured neighbours look strangely at her when she brings white friends to her home. He uses this story to sketch the Apartheid context and the state classification machinery which organized people into racial categories and hierarchies which, he suggests, is still affecting the way people relate to each other and racially different bodies in 'their' spaces. Unlike Story 1, however, this time it is 'white in appearance' bodies in coloured spaces that are under scrutiny.

Story 2: 'Ou Boertjie'

a.　I just wanna say something just extra
b.　why – why maybe coloured people see white people in a certain light …
c.　it's because in Apartheid they had this whole thing
d.　where they – they would class you man
e.　if you either white or – or – or coloured
f.　so for example if you were like light of complexion like coloured
g.　and you had straight hair
h.　you had green eyes everything the works
i.　and they took a pencil hmm
j.　and the pencil fell out
k.　okay fine you can go on
l.　so certain coloureds became whites
m.　and because of that 'djy hou vir jou wit' [*you keeping yourself white*]

n.   that's where the whole stigma came out
o.   even as a light of complexion coloured it's – it's tough for me where I
      grew up
p.   'hou djy vir jou wit ou boertjie' all of these things [*are you keeping
      yourself white, little white/Afrikaans boy*]
q.   and I'm just like – I'm just like you guys
r.   I'm- I'm like you
s.   I - I we breathe the same
t.   we do the same
u.   but it's just that mindset
v.   that's passed on passed on
w.   and it just – it won't – it - it just feels like it won't stop

In Lee's description of how racial categorization was imposed, it is note-worthy that he uses the word 'they' four times to refer to the Apartheid regime. This strong signal of distancing indicates that he does not con-sider himself or anyone else in the room a member of this 'they'; he thus positions himself and the rest of the group as 'the in-group'. This is sig-nificant as his narrative deals with being cast out of the racial group to which he feels he belongs. Lee explains in lines c–e that 'they' would divide people in order to place them into a racial category according to certain physical criteria. He then illustrates this statement with an exam-ple which is directly related to the narrative he later tells. In lines f–k Lee explains how light-skinned coloureds who had all the features of 'white-ness' (light complexion, straight hair, green eyes, etc.) and who passed the infamous 'pencil test', could be reclassified as white, where 'okay fine you can go on' (line k) could be the imagined words of the Apartheid official, and where 'so certain coloureds became whites' (line l) was the outcome.

The next two lines get to the crux of his anecdote when he reports how the coloured community typically responded to these reclassifica-tions, with the widely known saying, 'djy hou vir jou wit' (line m), which can be translated as '*you keeping yourself white*', meaning: 'you think you are better or of higher standard [than us]'. The quotation is marked with the Kaaps affricate, /dʒ/, in 'djy' ('you') clearly marking this taunt as 'coloured speech'. It is noteworthy that he refers to this 'passing for white' as a 'stigma', as something shameful, a mark of disgrace that a person could not shake off. It is clear that the process of being racially reclassified was disapproved of by the rest of the coloured community who did not qualify for reclassification. Perhaps this stems from the envy they may have felt towards the 'white' coloureds who, after reclassification, had certain privileges which they did not have. Additionally, after reclassifica-tion they became members of the group who oppressed them. In this way, being reclassified was seen as a denial of the coloured community and identity.

In the next line, however, we hear that Lee is using this historical anecdote to speak about his own difficulties of being accepted as coloured:

he too has certain 'white' characteristics that caused the coloured community he grew up in to reject him.

o. even as a light of complexion coloured it's – it's tough for me where I grew up
p. 'hou djy vir jou wit ou boertjie' all of these things [*are you keeping yourself white, little white/Afrikaans boy*]

This switch to speaking about himself is signalled by the shift into the present tense (in line o) when he evaluates his experience of growing up with this 'stigma' as something he struggled to endure: 'it's tough for me where I grew up'. Here we see different chronotopes intersect as Lee shifts from the past to the present in the same statement, by referring to how his struggle is *still* tough even though he is now an adult. He then repeats the offensive taunt, this time framed as a question, and reveals that he was given the hurtful nickname, 'ou boertjie', which can be translated here as '*little white boy*', in particular '*little white Afrikaans boy*'. *Boer* is the Afrikaans word for 'farmer' which has historically been used to refer to white people in South Africa, typically but not exclusively Afrikaans speaking. It was also used by black and coloured communities to refer to the police during the struggle against Apartheid. Today, the use of this word may be derogatory, depending on the context. Perhaps this stems from the fact that it associates the named person with 'the oppressor'. Essentially, a person cannot be a *boer* and a coloured at the same time. It is therefore clear that Lee's peers used this taunt to position him as a member of the out-group, the white community.

In lines q–v, we notice a shift in Lee's story as the past and the present chronotopes intersect when he insists: 'I'm just like – I'm just like you guys' (line q). He could be recalling how he spoke to his coloured peers all those years ago, or he could be appealing to the focus group participants. It is significant that he addresses the audience as 'you' because they are coloured too. The false starts in lines q, r and s betray his anxiety. Perhaps this is an issue that he has never divulged to others. It is, therefore, possible that he is still figuring out how he feels about the situation while he is speaking. He might also be unsure of how what he is saying will be interpreted by the audience. Even though the events to which Lee referred in his story happened a long time ago, they obviously still cause him distress and he still experiences anxiety about his acceptance as 'coloured'. Therefore, he uses this story to assert his desire to belong:

q. and I'm just like – I'm just like you guys
r. I'm- I'm like you
s. I - I we breathe the same
t. we do the same
u. but it's just that mindset

v.   that's passed on passed on
w.   and it just – it won't – it – it just feels like it won't stop

In lines u–w, he returns to the present and sums up the coda-like significance of his story. He attributes his wrongful classification as an outsider to a 'mindset' (line u) that was, and still is 'passed on passed on' and which 'feels like it won't stop', an acknowledgement that he still experiences it as very real.

Both these stories were told 24 years after the dawn of democracy; yet in both, Apartheid's racial narratives and painful histories continue to intrude on the present. In both, Lee, as a young socially mobile South African on the path to achieving a middle-class professional lifestyle, recounts how he is 'read' and positioned by both white and coloured people who persist in placing him in historically defined 'racial boxes'. In both stories, he attributes this to a mindset or mentality forged under Apartheid which continues to shape the way people perceive and relate to each other. While in Story 1 Lee is confident about challenging the white man's racism, both stories reveal the anxiety he experiences about his own racial belonging. His anxiety stems from his lack of fluency in Afrikaans, his light skin and, perhaps, his good education and social mobility which have enabled him to 'move beyond' the socioeconomic conditions of his hometown's working-class community.

Conclusion

As Adhikari (2004), Erasmus (2001), Rassool (2019) and other scholars have argued, the meanings and identities associated with 'coloured' in South Africa are multiple, complex and contested. While many people choose to identify as 'coloured', the ongoing use of these racial labels as categories for identification continues to be rejected by others who argue that 'coloured' is an Apartheid label designed to 'divide and rule'. In Lee's stories, we see how he navigates these complexities in relation to his own lived experience of being racially positioned and his desire for a more flexible racial identity. These workings are made visible in the small stories he tells. In both stories, it is the reported speech (De Fina & Georgakopoulou, 2012) and translanguaging which play a critical role in bringing the multiplicity of voices into the narrative. These voices, and particular wordings (e.g. 'coloureds teen blanke', 'djy hou vir jou wit, ou boertjie') activate the different historical chronotopes which trigger certain identities and roles for Lee and mark his behaviour as desirable or deviant. The clashing of these timespaces creates considerable discomfort for Lee, and it is these feelings of vulnerability that become the focus of his stories. As Bock *et al.* (2019) argue, vulnerability comprises a condition of openness to others that offers the potential for alternative engagement with Selves.

When we look at these stories through the lens of Linguistic Citizenship, we see how linguistic varieties carry histories and values which are used to racially position and police Others in ongoing cycles of exclusion, rejection and shame. However, we also see how, in the post-Apartheid, language can be a 'transformative dynamic' (Stroud, 2018b: 35) serving to unsettle these boundaries and trigger disruptive moments which destabilize the dominant historical discourses. We see how these spaces of vulnerability bring about moments of reflection, which, we would argue, are a precursor to the stepping out of these historical positions and their racial designations. Furthermore, in this chapter, we have argued that small stories are a useful analytical lens in that they not only encapsulate the layered and nuanced complexity of the lived experience, but they also bring into focus the different historical and contemporary chronotopes shaping the story. Lastly, and perhaps most significantly, we suggest that it is through the sharing of these stories in contexts such as this focus group, in conversation with empathetic others, that racial identities can be refashioned and reconstituted in more inclusive ways, as part of the building of new political subjectivities and a more humane and inclusive society (Stroud, 2018b).

Acknowledgements

Our sincere thanks to the participants of this focus group, and especially to 'Lee', for their rich contributions to this project. We would also like to thank the University of the Western Cape and the National Research Foundation for funding which supported this project. Any opinions, findings, conclusions or recommendations expressed in this material are those of the authors and the NRF does not accept any liability in regard thereto.

Notes

(1) By 31 March, 1964, 3940 appeals had been lodged, of which approximately one-third were by persons wanting reclassification from 'coloured' to 'white', and the remainder from 'bantu' (or black/African) to 'coloured'. By June of that year, 2823 of these applications had succeeded, and 17 appeals against the Race Classification Appeal Board were due to be heard in the Supreme Court (SAIRR, 1964:137-38, cited in Posel, 2001b: 107).

(2) UWC was established in 1960 for coloured students, but the current student population is predominantly a mix of black and coloured students, with a handful of white students and a growing number of students from elsewhere in Africa.

(3) During the struggle against Apartheid, many coloured and Indian people/activists rejected the term 'coloured' as an Apartheid label and chose to refer to themselves as 'black', as an expression of solidarity with the oppressed majority. Others have argued for the need, post-Apartheid, to move beyond these racial categories in the interests of the building of a non-racial society (Alexander, 2006).

(4)   Longer pauses are indicated in round brackets in seconds, reported speech is indicated with quotation marks, laughter and other non-verbal gestures are indicated in square brackets, underlining is used to indicate emphasis, and translations are given in italics in square brackets next to each line.

References

Adhikari, M. (2004) 'Not black enough': Changing expressions of coloured identity in post-apartheid South Africa. *South African Historical Journal* 51, 167–178.

Alexander, N. (2006) Racial Identity, Citizenship and Nation-Building in Post-Apartheid South Africa. https://www.marxists.org/archive/alexander/2006-racial-identity-citizenship-and-nation-building.pdf (accessed 27 June 2012).

Anthonissen, C. (2013) 'With English the world is more open to you': Language shift as marker of social transformation. *English Today* 29 (1), 28–35.

Bakhtin, M. (1981) *The Dialogic Imagination* (M. Holquist, ed.). Austin: University of Texas Press.

Blommaert, J. and De Fina, A. (2017) Chronotopic identities: On the spacetime organization of who we are. In A. De Fina, I. Didem and J. Wegner (eds) *Diversity and Superdiversity: Sociocultural Linguistic Perspectives* (pp. 1–15). Washington, DC: Georgetown University Press.

Bock, Z. (2017) 'Why can't race just be a normal thing?' Entangled discourses in the narratives of young South Africans. In C. Kerfoot and K. Hyltenstam (eds) *Entangled Discourses: South-North Orders of Visibility* (pp. 59–76). New York: Routledge.

Bock, Z. (2018) Negotiating race in post-Apartheid South Africa: Bernadette's stories. *Text & Talk* 38 (2), 115–136.

Bock, Z., Abrahams, L. and Jansen, K. (2019) Learning through Linguistic Citizenship: Finding the 'I' of the essay. *Multilingual Margins* 6 (1), 72–85.

Bock, Z. and Hunt, S. (2015) It's just taking our souls back: Apartheid and race in the discourses of young South Africans. *Southern African Linguistics and Applied Language Studies* 33 (2), 141–158.

Bock, Z. and Stroud, C. (2018) Zombie landscapes: Apartheid traces in the discourses of young South Africans. In A. Peck, Q. Williams and C. Stroud (eds) *Making Sense of People, Place and Linguistic Landscapes* (pp. 11–28). London: Bloomsbury Press.

Bundy, C. (2014) *Short-Changed? South Africa since Apartheid*. Auckland Park: Jacana Media.

Cho, S., Crenshaw, K.W. and McCall, L. (2013) Toward a field of intersectionality studies: Theory, applications, and praxis. *Signs* 38 (4), 785–810.

De Fina, A. and Georgakopoulou, A. (2012) *Analyzing Narrative: Discourse and Sociolinguistic Perspectives*. Cambridge: Cambridge University Press.

Erasmus, Z. (2001) Introduction: Re-imagining coloured identities in post-Apartheid South Africa. In Z. Erasmus (ed.) *Coloured by History, Shaped by Place: New Perspectives on Coloured Identities in Cape Town* (pp. 13–28). Cape Town: Kwela Books.

Erasmus, Z. and Pieterse, E. (1999) Conceptualising coloured identities in the Western Cape Province of South Africa. In M. Palmberg (ed.) *National Identity and Democracy in Africa* (pp. 167–187). South Africa: Capture Press.

Erwin, K. (2012) Race and race thinking: Reflections in theory and practice for researchers in South Africa and beyond. *Transformation* 79, 93–113.

Georgakopoulou, A. (2007) Thinking big with small stories in narrative and identity analysis. In M. Bamberg (ed.) *Narrative – State of the Art* (pp. 145–154). Amsterdam: John Benjamins.

Georgakopoulou, A. (2015) Small stories research: Methods – analysis – outreach. In A. De Fina and A. Georgakopoulou (eds) *The Handbook of Narrative Analysis* (pp. 255–271). Oxford: Wiley-Blackwell.

Hendricks, F. (2016) The nature and context of Kaaps: A contemporary, past and future perspective. *Multilingual Margins* 3 (2), 6–39.

Kriel, M. (2018) Chronicle of a creole: The ironic history of Afrikaans. In J. Knörr and T.F. Wilson (eds) *Creolization and Pidginization in Contexts of Postcolonial Diversity: Language, Culture, Identity* (pp. 132–157). Leiden: Koninklijke Brill NV.

Labov, W. (1972) *Language in the Inner City*. Philadelphia: University of Pennsylvania Press.

Lambrou, M. (2003) Collaborative oral narratives of general experience: When an interview becomes a conversation. *Language and Literature* 12 (2), 153–174.

Lefko-Everett, K. (2012) Leaving it to the children: Non-racialism, identity, socialisation and generational change in South Africa. *Politikon* 39 (1), 127–147.

Petrus, T. and Isaacs-Martin, W. (2012) The multiple meanings of coloured identity in South Africa. *Africa Insight* 42 (1), 87–102.

Pinchevski, A. (2005) The ethics of interruption: Towards a Levinasian philosophy of communication. *Social Semiotics* 15 (2), 211–234.

Posel, D. (2001a) What's in a name? Racial categorisations under Apartheid and their afterlife. *Transformation* 47, 50–74.

Posel, D. (2001b) Race as common sense: Racial classification in twentieth-century South Africa. *African Studies Review* 44 (2), 87–113.

Rassool, C. (2019) The politics of non-racialism in South Africa. *Public Culture* 31 (2), 343–371.

South African Institute of Race Relations (SAIRR) (1964) A Survey of Race Relations. Johannesburg: SAIRR.

Soudien, C. (2013) 'Race' and its contemporary confusions: Towards a restatement. *Theoria* 60 (136), 15–37.

Stroud, C. (2018a) Introduction. In L. Lim, C. Stroud and L. Wee (eds) *The Multilingual Citizen: Towards a Politics of Language for Agency and Change* (pp. 1–14). Bristol: Multilingual Matters.

Stroud, C. (2018b) Linguistic Citizenship. In L. Lim, C. Stroud and L. Wee (eds) *The Multilingual Citizen: Towards a Politics of Language for Agency and Change* (pp. 17–39). Bristol: Multilingual Matters.

Wicomb, Z. (2006) *Playing in the Light*. Johannesburg: Umuzi/Random House.

Williams, Q.E. and Stroud, C. (2015) Linguistic citizenship: language and politics in postnational modernities. *Journal of Language and Politics* 14 (3), 406–430.

6 Linguistic Citizenship and Non-Citizens: Of Utopias and Dystopias

Marcelyn Oostendorp

> The future is already here. It's just unevenly distributed.
> (*Neuromancer*, William Gibson)

> We were the people who were not in the papers. We lived in the blank white spaces at the edges of print. It gave us more freedom. We lived in the gaps between the stories.
> (*The Handmaid's Tale*, Margaret Atwood)

> You have a house here. The house has two windows and a door. The door represent people can go in and people can go out. The window can be open for these people to have an air freshener. And outside out top there, we have a sun. When we have a sun, we have light for everyone. We having a tree outside. The road took me to South Africa and there's a road coming down here. I'm having another house here, it's very hectic. The house don't have a window and there is no door. Which means I am stuck somewhere. In this second house, I am very blocked according to my skills, according to what I studied and even here, I study. But still I am not fitting into the society, and I am struggling to get somewhere. And I cannot say that life is rosy. Because somewhere I am trying my best. We trying to fit into society, but is not easy. Here is a half moon, is like my half-life. You have to keep on moving and try again and again.
> (Interview 2 with 'Hydran', 2013)

The first two epigraphs in this chapter are from famous dystopian novels, and the last extract is from an interview in 2013 with Hydran (not his real name; pseudonyms are used for all of the participants in this chapter). Hydran is originally from the Republic of the Congo (note not from the Democratic Republic of Congo, previously known as Zaire), and his extract forms part of a larger multimodal narrative about his life in South Africa. Those of us who have read dystopian novels or watched dystopian movies will recognize the similarities between these film and novel genres, and Hydran's story. Lewis (2014: 19), drawing on the work of Moylan (2000), suggests that a dystopian society can be recognized by 'the totality of one relentless and overpowering experience'. This can be in the form of 'social oppression, governmental oppression and natural/scenic oppression'. This oppression is usually made visible through a focus on the tedious repetition of actions by the characters and the general bleakness of the landscape (Lewis, 2014: 14). Hydran is stuck in his South African house with no windows to give some much-needed air and light. He uses the metaphor of scenic oppression to talk about his social oppression. Like so many other non-citizens in South Africa, Hydran is trapped in a dystopia. He does not have a green South African identification book. He was the only one of his family to come to South Africa, so his friends, who are also mostly migrants, are his only support structure. His qualifications do not count, he has no job and the languages he speaks are not valued, admired or understood by most of the people in this country. He cannot go back home as he fled violent conflict so, as he states in his narrative, '[he is] stuck'.

According to Vieira (2010: 17), the primary aim of a dystopian novel is 'didactic and moralistic'. In this genre, a vision of the future is presented to scare the reader, and to make them aware that the future will not be bright if they do not take action to prevent the dystopian situation or event. Like a dystopian novel, this chapter will provide a frightening vision of how the lack of voice and agency and the wrong kind of multilingualism on the wrong kind of body lead to a nightmarish existence for migrants in South Africa. I am not the first to offer this kind of reading of migrant life. Jan Blommaert (2009) explores the ways in which language can trap asylum seekers in the in-between spaces. Particularly poignant is Blommaert's (2009) reading of Joseph's story, whose unusual polyglot repertoire was judged by authorities as not matching his country of origin. This led to his request for asylum being denied. Where my reading differs, however, is that I want to introduce explicitly the idea of 'dystopia'. This is done with the purpose of entering into a dialogue with Stroud's (2001) Linguistic Citizenship, and to move towards a theoretical understanding of what linguistic resources can and cannot do. Additionally, the chapter serves as a cautionary tale to sociolinguists that language activism alone cannot solve all of the world's problems. Instead, a broader engagement in social activism is needed.

I hope that this chapter will contribute to the notion of Linguistic Citizenship and to the recent introduction of 'utopia' into this framework. My central argument is that utopias should be part of a utopia/dystopia dialectic. This is implied in Stroud and Williams (2017) but not explicitly theorized. To do this conceptual work, I draw on literary theory, where the idea of dystopia has been extensively explored as a fictional genre. I also draw on decolonial theorists (Freire, 1998; Mbembe, 2001; Spivak, 1988)[1] to expand the possibilities of a dystopian reading of Linguistic Citizenship. In the next section, I provide some context on migrant life in South Africa. I introduce the central concepts of 'linguistic repertoire' and

'Linguistic Citizenship' before I briefly refer to the methods used to gather the data for the project which this chapter explores. Finally, I argue that utopia/dystopia should be an entangled dialectic in a theory of Linguistic Citizenship by presenting extracts from the migrant narratives of Ash, Dunbar, Hydran, Novel, Tshepo and Ulrich.

Being a Migrant in South Africa

'Migrants and refugees make a significant contribution'
(*Mail and Guardian*, 14 February 2019)

'ANC takes a hard line on migrants'
(*News24.com*, 20 January 2019)

'Thousands of "undocumented" children being deprived of basic right to education'
(*News24.com*, 19 February 2019)

'A life of anonymity – Migrants die, unnamed and unclaimed, in South Africa'
(*News24.com*, 1 November 2018)

'SA's contradictory laws discriminate against children of migrants'
(*Mail and Guardian*, 20 November 2018)

'Foreign migrant influx straining Gauteng's resources – govt report'
(*Citizen*, 25 September 2018)

These six headlines appeared in the South African media between September 2018 and February 2019. Of the six, only one can be described as positive. Quite a substantial body of research confirms that these headlines paint an accurate picture of the experience of African migrants (Crush & Tawodzera, 2011; McDonald, 1998) in South Africa. Migrants are regularly discriminated against, deprived of basic human rights, and subjected to violence. Before the onset of the democratic dispensation in South Africa, migration policies were highly selective and racist. Since 1994, migrants from other African countries have been able to enter South Africa more freely, although there has not all that much high-level support for 'legal immigration', and it is becoming increasingly difficult to obtain residency permits (see the body of work done by the Southern African Migration Programme). Nevertheless, the number of African migrants entering South Africa has increased significantly. Since 2008, there have been sporadic waves of intense xenophobic violence. Dodson (2010) reports that these outbreaks are not isolated or sudden, but that xenophobic attitudes towards migrants of African descent are obdurate. Therefore, xenophobia will have to be dealt with systematically to change such widely-held and longstanding attitudes.

In addition to the physical forms of violence that African migrants in South Africa experience, they are subjected to discrimination and human rights abuses in the legal, medical and educational sectors (Crush & Tawodzera, 2011; Lefko-Everett, 2007). Some of these abuses can be attributed to general structural failures (such as state medical facilities that are overstretched to begin with) and/or language differences and mis-communication. However, many of these human rights abuses occur because of the deeply held beliefs about and attitudes to migrants (Crush & Tawodzera, 2011). As recently as 2013, Crush *et al.* (2013: 34) reported that nearly 80% of surveyed citizens either support prohibition of the entry of migrants or would like to place severe restrictions on it.

Despite the substantial body of work on African migrants in South Africa, the role of language in establishing identity, in social inclusion and exclusion, and in accessing goods and services has not been sufficiently explored (Siziba & Hill, 2018). This is surprising considering that lan-guage has been used as a marker of 'foreignness' by both officials and general members of the public. As Siziba and Hill (2018: 118) recount, during the May 2008 xenophobic attacks, 'shibboleths were used to iden-tify' foreigners. The research that does investigate language in migrant contexts tends to provide essentialist readings of language and culture (Siziba & Hill, 2018: 118) without engaging with recent retheorization(s) of language. The project that this chapter is based on uses current recon-ceptualizations of language to understand how African migrants use their linguistic repertoires to navigate social spaces where their linguistic resources did not necessarily match the preferred ones.

Linguistic Repertoires

In this chapter, I draw on the notion of 'repertoire' (Blommaert, 2009; Busch, 2012), which has been favoured as a way of working outside 'named languages' to embrace the diversity of varieties, styles and regis-ters to which individuals and communities have access (see also similar arguments around translanguaging, e.g. Otheguy *et al.*, 2015). Clearly, within mainstream sociolinguistics, a 'sociolinguistics of repertoires' is steadily gaining ground on 'a sociolinguistics of languages' (Blommaert, 2009: 425). This shifts to a focus on 'the real bits and chunks of language' (Blommaert, 2009: 425).

With the resurrection of this concept, which has been around since the 1960s, additional foci have been added to turn linguistic repertoire into 'an empirically more useful and theoretically more precise notion, helpful for our understanding of contemporary processes of language in society' (Blommaert & Backus, 2013: 12). This has led to an increased focus on mobility (Blommaert & Backus, 2013), biographical dimensions, lived experience (Busch, 2012, 2017) and space (Pennycook & Otsiju, 2014). Central to this reconceptualization is the view that repertoires do not only include linguistic dimensions but also include all meaning-making resources that individuals can use to make themselves understood (Rymes, 2014). One context in which repertoires have been extensively investigated is in educational spaces. In this educational research, the fact that linguistic repertoires are not used to their full potential is bemoaned, and recommendations are often made that closer attention to the linguistic repertoire, and better use of it, will make for a more socially-just educational experience (Bristowe *et al.*, 2014; Rymes, 2014). Otheguy *et al.* (2015: 305) suggest, for example, that translanguaging increases equality by providing bilingual students with the opportunity to learn while having the benefit of all their linguistic resources. There seems to be an underlying premise that a more inclusive use of linguistic varieties can go a long way in addressing issues of discrimination, social injustice and the breach of linguistic human rights.

Other research points out how individuals deploy their linguistic repertoires to resist institutional structures and practices (Banda & Bellononjengele, 2010; Busch, 2016). This is exactly where Linguistic Citizenship resonates with linguistic repertoire – focusing on how the semiotic resources people have available to them can deploy voice and agency in everyday life and within a broader political process.

Linguistic Citizenship: On Utopias

Stroud first introduced Linguistic Citizenship in 2001. His central concern in that seminal text was finding alternative explanations as to why African mother-tongue educational programmes often fail. These programmes usually do not deliver on issues such as cognitive enhancement and language maintenance. At that time of writing, the failure of mother-tongue programmes was often blamed on the lack of material resources or on bad programme management. Stroud (2001: 340) proposed that what was needed was a theoretical rethink which located the problems of mother-tongue programmes within the 'social fabric of the postcolonial community itself'. The dominant model for language policy and planning at the time, namely linguistic human rights, was described by Stroud (2001: 344) as an 'affirmative model'. Affirmative models tend to add rights for marginalized groups in pre-determined categories, thus leaving these categories intact rather than breaking them down. Instead, Stroud suggested that what was needed was a 'transformative' model located within a broader politics of citizenship. Transformative models deconstruct the categories on which rights are based. Stroud's proposal for a transformative model is Linguistic Citizenship. Drawing on Weeks (1997: 4), Stroud (2001: 345) refers to Linguistic Citizenship as an attempt to include language issues in a way in which citizenship is discussed in the 'sense of broadening the definition of belonging, equal protection of the law, equal rights in employment, parenting, [and] access to social welfare provision and education'. Since this introduction, the uptake of Linguistic Citizenship has been much more wide-ranging than in educational contexts, and it is now considered a broader sociolinguistic theory of how inequality can be opposed both in local interactions and on a bigger scale in wider sociopolitical encounters. Subsequently, Linguistic Citizenship has been used as a central concept in such diverse terrains as ethnographic studies of Hip Hop (Williams & Stroud, 2010) and the study of language ideologies (Shaikjee & Milani, 2013).

More recently, Stroud (2015) has emphasized the utopian qualities of Linguistic Citizenship. Drawing on Bloch's (1968) notion of 'utopia', Stroud (2015: 25) argues that 'a productive sense of utopia is not the conventional non-place in a non-time usually associated with the concept, but the condition ... that references a better way of living that is foreshadowed in the present (and past) but [is] as yet unrealized'. Claeys (2010) states that, although myriad conceptualizations of utopia exist, a common thread is a commitment to conviviality which is sometimes connected to principals of friendship. It is this common thread within utopian understanding that Stroud uses to conceptualize his current iteration of Linguistic Citizenship. Stroud and Williams (2017: 184) argue that a Linguistic Citizenship approach to language allows for the focus on possibilities to re-figure language and to challenge power relations by reinserting voice. Glimpses of these utopian visions of language can be seen when participants engage in language practices that use multi-semiotic resources which challenge and disrupt common and dominant ideologies of language (Stroud & Williams, 2017: 184). The importance of the linguistic repertoire within a conceptualization of Linguistic Citizenship is thus apparent. Stroud and Williams (2017: 184) further argue that Linguistic Citizenship is 'a way of thinking through the potential of language, thinking about a space where language could be used "otherwise"'. It is this recent emphasis on the utopian qualities of Linguistic Citizenship that this chapter will draw on, specifically by focusing on African migrants in South Africa, and their linguistic repertoires.

Linguistic Repertoires and Arts-Based Methodology

The empirical examples used in this chapter come from a project that used arts-based methods to collect multimodal narratives on the experiences of African migrants. Arts-based research methods seek to make active connections between theories, emotions, thoughts and ideas. Leavy (2015: 14) states that arts-based practices have the goal of evoking meanings, rather than denoting them. Bochner and Ellis (2003: 509) argue that arts-based research produces narratives that show characters going about the complexities of their daily lives which include 'moments of struggle, resisting the intrusions of chaos, disconnection, fragmentation, marginalization and incoherence, trying to preserve or restore the continuity, and coherence' of their lives. The research team found that this description poignantly resonated with the complex and precarious lives of the African migrants they were exploring.

Two groups of migrants participated in the project. The intention was not to focus on national groups, but when initially establishing networks, our contacts were asked to bring friends along who are also migrants. We ended up with two homogenous groups in terms of country of origin: seven participants who were originally from the Republic of Congo (all men) and eight participants originally from Zimbabwe (six men and two women). An interdisciplinary team consisting of sociolinguists and visual artists developed the arts-based research methods. We completed two art-based tasks together with the participants, which included filling in a language portrait (Busch, 2012) and producing a drawing on a scraperboard – a piece of black cardboard which, when scratched with a sharp object, reveals its white underlayer. In the language-portrait task, participants were invited to display their linguistic repertoires on a blank body silhouette, which they filled in with different colours on different parts of this body silhouette. We asked the migrants to depict their journeys on the scraperboard, using any metaphor, picture or other representation. They were free to take the scraperboard home to work on their depictions. In the next class, the migrants discussed their creations in English, which was not the first language of any of the migrant participants or the researchers (see Anthonissen *et al.*, forthcoming), for more information on the methodological processes and pitfalls). The migrants constructed several narratives featuring linguistic repertoires, both from the task that specifically focused on linguistic repertoires and the task which did not.

Dystopian Linguistic Repertoires

In this section, I illustrate how linguistic repertoires, even when exemplified by multiplicity and diversity, are often still not enough to resist inequalities. I will evoke the idea of a 'dystopia' to make sense of this. First, I will very briefly refer to the linguistic repertoires of the participants in general before concentrating on the position of English within these repertoires. All the participants in our study had linguistic repertoires consisting of multiple registers and varieties. These repertoires consist of bits and pieces of language (Blommaert, 2009). Participants readily admitted not knowing the languages in their repertoires perfectly (see e.g. the extract from Tshepo's narrative). The repertoires also consisted of language ideologies (Busch, 2012), with participants using descriptions such as 'national language', 'vernacular', 'metropole languages', or 'community languages' in their narratives of their language portraits (see e.g. Figure 6.1).

Tshepo

By the time I was in Botswana, I started to stay in Botswana from 2005 up to November, I speak maybe Tswana maybe 50%. Then I was in Joburg, I speak Sotho. Then I move to Kwazulu-Natal, I speak Tswana and in Cape Town I speak Xhosa. I speak 70%, maybe I speak Tswana 80% now.

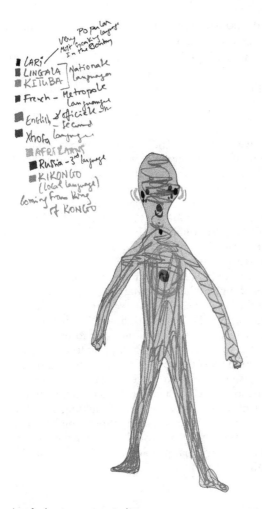

Figure 6.1 Example of a language portrait

In the narratives told by the participants, there was scant recounting of how their repertoires might have ruptured the *status quo* or allowed them to navigate a new sense of self. Instead, as Stroud and Williams (2017: 168) argue, multilingualism in their retellings is viewed as a '[tool] of colonial governmentality' used to order languages and people hierarchically, with languages such as Lari identified as community languages and French as a school language. English emerged even more strongly from the narratives, as did silence, which occupied important places in the participants' linguistic repertoires while in South Africa. Interestingly, English played a very different role for the two groups.

For the participants from the Republic of Congo, English represented a utopia, not in the Blochian sense in which Stroud uses it, but as a non-place in a non-time. Scott and Bell (2016: 11) state that, when used in a negative sense, utopia is regarded as 'an impossible dream'. English is seen as the magical quality or characteristic which will unlock possibilities in South Africa. Ash's small story and the extract from Ulrich's narrative is illustrative of this group's general sentiments about English.

Ash

When I arrived in South Africa, things was very difficult for me, because I was coming from the French country to the new society. Things were very tough to be connected to the society and especially the language; language was a big issue for me. English was a big problem. I went to library. My friend used to push me, he used to say 'Ash, without English you won't get any job, you won't get any money, you won't survive in this country'. Otherwise you will be back to where we coming from. And I try my best. He gave me some books, some dictionaries. I try to read, to study, to learn about English. From 2007, I came down to Cape Town, to the Western Cape; I was in Gauteng and then I come to Western Cape. Things were tough at the beginning, but afterwards things got more open because of the language. I started to communicate to people. I got opportunity, I got a job. That was my first job – it was a little bit difficult. Sometimes when they say get some stuff to put there, I did not understand. I had to turn to people from my country, who got more experience and was talking nicer than me. It was difficult; I didn't understand. Now I am getting somewhere. Now we are getting somewhere can communicate with people. There is a people who is happy. Not totally, but a little bit happy. Unfortunately, we are still struggling. As a foreigner in a country, there is many things man, many things you have to been on line, you have to be on time. You have to follow the law of the country to join the society. We still have that problem. We do our best. Things are going a little bit OK.

Ulrich

We have to be focused on the books to learn more. When we come from our place to South Africa, most of us were busy learning. When we come to South Africa, our diploma was not valid. What we supposed to do to get a normal life? We have to go back to school to get some knowledge and skills. Because when you learn more, you also get more skills and knowledge and you have the ability to struggle or defend your live anywhere. Because you are unable to speak English. You have a border inside yourself. There is no way you can get there – only in books.

However, despite great effort, taking classes, and eventually acquiring English, things are only 'a little bit OK' (Ash) for the Congolese migrants. For the Zimbabwean migrants, English does not have this kind of utopian potential, since the schooling system in Zimbabwe requires proficiency in English. Instead, it marks them as 'other' in the spaces in which they move. Scott and Bell (2016: 14) state that 'the term dystopia', meaning 'bad place', is often regarded as the direct opposite of 'utopia'. Instead, they argue that there is no clear separation between the two. Gordin *et al.* (2010: 1) state that, whereas a true opposite of a utopia would be 'a society that is either completely unplanned or is planned to be deliberately terrifying and awful', a dystopia is not either of these. Rather, 'it is a utopia that has gone wrong or a utopia that functions only for a particular segment of society' or, perhaps, a particular part of one's life. English might provide the Zimbabwean participants with work (all of the Zimbabwean participants were employed, while only one of the Congolese participants had permanent employment), but it is also the language that marks them as outsiders and thus subjects them to violence. Generally, for life in a Western Cape township – where all of our Zimbabwean participants reside – isiXhosa becomes the ideal language and, retrospectively, many of them regretted not learning isiNdebele, a minority language in Zimbabwe related to isiXhosa. The Zimbabwean participants believe that proficiency in isiNdebele would have made it easier to learn isiXhosa. Siziba (2015) similarly reports on the 'usefulness' of isiNdebele. He found that isiNdebele-speaking Zimbabwean migrants often try to pass for Zulu with interlocutors who do not have the necessary skills to recognize the fact that these migrants are not Zulu, but they remain silent with those who can call their bluff. For Nolan and Dunbar, as is evident in their respective anecdotes below, the migrants' proficiency in English combined with their lack of proficiency in isiXhosa is what marked them as foreigners, and thus they chose to remain silent.

Nolan

> To me, it was difficult. Just because I come from Masholand-West. I don't know Ndebele. I know only Shona. It was a very big problem to me to understand each other. When I talk to somebody, they don't like to speak in English. They shout me. But I want to learn. I take it easy. I am scared of people. I am a foreigner. I have to take it easy here. If somebody shout me or beat me, I take it easy.

Dunbar

> At first it was very difficult for me to speak Xhosa. I was forced to learn that language. So Xhosa and Ndebele, they are very close together. If you speak English, they become rude to you. They say: 'You guys, we are going to chase you back. You don't want to speak our language'.

According to Lewis (2014: 19), a dystopia is 'usually conceived of as a "social elsewhere", either implicitly or explicitly framed as a future into which the reader's current society has devolved'. Here, similarities with Stroud and Williams' (2017) 'utopia' are drawn upon, where Lewis emphasizes the 'not yet' quality of utopias. Dystopias have similar qualities as a 'social elsewhere', with the current situation having the potential of turning into this dystopia. According to Gordin *et al.* (2010: 2), whereas a utopia takes us into the future, dystopia places us in a depressingly dark reality, evoking a terrible future if we do not address the current dystopia. In this case, the reality is that English is seen as the magic language by some migrants. Yet using English in spaces and/or ways in which it should not be used can mark them as 'the other'. Stroud and Williams (2017: 173) powerfully illustrate the dystopian possibilities of Afrikaans in their analysis of *Luister*, a recent documentary which maps the experiences of black students at Stellenbosch University. The authors argue that their analysis illustrates the 'power of language to determine the parameters along which the body appears visible and is experienced subjectively' (Stroud & Williams, 2017: 173). A similar function is performed by English emplaced on the migrant body, with specific bodies evoking different types of social exclusion. As Busch (2017: 356) argues, the linguistic repertoire is chronotopic with the 'co-presence of different spaces and times in speech' that are transferred to the linguistic repertoire. English evokes an imperial or colonial chronotope. According to Tlostanova (2007: 407), this is part of a 'particular condition of transcultural subjectivity – that of restless non-belonging and a specific double consciousness'. This is the case for both migrant groups in the study: for the group from the Republic of Congo, this is a more traditionally colonial chronotope – the imposition of a colonial language as the most important language to find employment. For the group from Zimbabwe, this chronotope plays out differently. Here we find the colonial chronotope which divided black people and positioned them against each other. Similarly, Stroud and Williams (2017: 169) talk about how Afrikaans can 'reproduce Apartheid frameworks', with the use of languages other than Afrikaans requiring validation at Stellenbosch University and constraining the mobility of people. It is thus clear that the idea of dystopia is present in Stroud and Williams' (2017) work, but the possibilities of what a dystopian understanding of language offers are not laid out to the same extent as those of a utopian understanding.

Dystopia/Utopia

In the preceding section, I have argued that, instead of the migrants tapping into the utopian dimensions of Linguistic Citizenship, they are trapped in a dystopian society regarding their linguistic repertoires/abilities. This dystopia is created through their 'non-citizenness', in the traditional sense, and their lack of appropriate voice. Theoretically, what does this exposition add to the development of Linguistic Citizenship and, specifically, the utopian qualities thereof? According to Scott and Bell (2016: 14):

> In pointing us towards the worst possible scenario, dystopias provide a warning of what will happen if we continue to follow current trends and practices. In pointing us towards the worst possible scenario, dystopias provide a warning from the future in our present. They give us new eyes to look at how current developments may evolve.

From the snippets of data that are provided, the following questions come to mind: which trends can be identified, and which should we pay attention to in sociolinguistics in order to avoid a full-on dystopia? Firstly, language is still seen in a hierarchical sense, with English being the language that gives one access to employment while a local indigenous language helps one to fit in. Secondly, it is not only *what* one speaks but *who* speaks it. English means different things to the two groups and evokes different reactions. Thirdly, for these migrants, it is a linguistic 'lose-lose' situation: it does not matter how well one speaks English, the odds of being accepted into the community are still against them because they are perceived as 'outsiders' or 'foreigners' by the indigenous community members. These are, of course, not new sociolinguistic insights, and are not restricted to migrant contexts. However, the current reconceptualizations of linguistic repertoire, agency and voice (with some exceptions), spotlight the individual possibilities for mobilization. The emphasis seems to be on showcasing how, despite overwhelming social forces, people can carve out resistance and a new way of being through language. This seems to be a characteristic not only of sociolinguistic research but also of other research within the broader humanities. For example, Mbembe (2001: 5) states that with the rediscovery of 'the subaltern subject', there has been great emphasis on this subject's 'inventiveness'. As such, scholars have invoked notions such as 'hegemony, moral economy, agency and resistance' to describe subaltern subject positions. Thus, he says, the subaltern subject is seen as 'capable of challenging [their] oppression; and that power, far from being total, is endlessly contested, deflated, and re-appropriated by its targets' (Mbembe, 2001: 6). Less attention has consequently been paid to social formations of power and more to individual efforts to subvert power. Snell (2013: 123) remarks that we have to 'take account of voice' and also pay attention to 'how and why some speakers make themselves heard in educational settings while others fail to do so'. It is in the latter part of Snell's assertion that an engagement with dystopia can play a role. Glimpses of utopias are essential as they show us the positive possibilities. However, we also get glimpses of dystopias in the present, with both being equally possible as a future status quo. According to Gordin *et al.* (2010: 2), the dialectic between utopia and dystopia, 'the dream and the nightmare[,] begs for inclusion together'. The authors claim that 'by considering utopia and dystopia together, we are able to consider just how ideas, desires, constraints and effects interact simultaneously' (Gordin *et al.*, 2010: 2).

By introducing dystopia explicitly into the toolkit of Linguistic Citizenship, we learn which conditions and which bodies (do not) make it possible for people to express their voice and agency. The migrants, as shown in the data generated during this study, wish to conform, either by learning English or by hiding their English language proficiency because the imminent threat of harassment, violence and deportation. We can, therefore, ask what conditions would allow for those extreme

circumstances to be subverted, even in conditions of fear. A focus on dystopias allows us to look at old questions in a different way, and to foreground themes which might have been prominent before in sociolinguistics
but have now drifted into the background. Three specific themes that I see
emerging from the narratives of this chapter, which I interpreted through
a dystopian lens, include a focus on *silence, hope* and *vigilance*.

Two kinds of silence can be found in the migrants' narratives: silence as
a result of not being able to speak because they do not have the specific linguistic resources necessary to do so, and silence as a form of survival, where
the migrants refuse to speak to avoid being revealed as a foreigner. Both
examples can be described as being silenced rather than being silent, where
Fivush (2010: 88–89) describes the difference between the two as follows:

> [W]hen being silenced is contrasted with voice, it is conceptualised as
> imposed and it signifies a loss of power and self. But silence can also be
> conceptualised as being silent, a shared understanding that need not be
> voiced, and in this sense, silence can be a form of power, and the need to
> speak, to voice, represents a loss of power.

In an interview with Steve Paulson (2016) for the *Los Angeles Review
of Books*, Spivak expands on the meaning of 'subaltern', from her famous
essay *Can the Subaltern Speak?* (in Nelson & Grossberg, 1988). She states
that the 'subaltern' refers to 'those who don't give orders; they only receive
orders', but this term can also denote 'those who do not have access to the
structures of citizenship'. In her case, she refers to people who might have
voting rights but no 'access to the structures of citizenship'. The migrants
referred to in the data for this chapter are subaltern in that they have neither voting rights nor access to structures of citizenship. To paraphrase
Spivak (1988), being black, migrants and poor, they get it three ways. By
focusing more on silences, we can stress the importance of what cannot
be said (Spivak, 1988: 82).

According to Gordin *et al.* (2010: 12), dystopias are just as vulnerable
as utopias. Just as utopias can disintegrate, so too can dystopias. This
reminds us that there is *hope*. Van Heertum (2006: 46) draws attention to
Freire's (1998) ideas on hope which, he suggests, point to the need to 'help
people recognize not only their oppressed situation, but their position as
subjects in history with the power to change it'. Hope is what makes
utopia possible, and dystopias are what call for hope. One can argue that
utopias cannot exist without dystopias and are both visions that we need.

In the data that I have presented, there are some glimpses of hope.
Hydran uses the metaphor of a half-moon when he says:

> There is also a positive side. The positive thing I am speaking a language
> today. Yesterday I did not speak the language. But I am proud today.
> When was at home I was to be lawyer, but now I am in the hospitality
> industry. I got that knowledge here and I have skills. Tomorrow when I

go home, I can take this skills with me. That's why you see the little moon here, a half moon. I have a little light that is coming.

Similarly positive, Nolan says:

Now, for now, I am trying. I am trying. When I am trying to talk to each other, they know what I'm trying to say. At least now it's better, it's better.

Hydran's half-moon metaphor show us that it is possible for communality to be achieved. Hope allows us to think through the possibilities of Nolan and Hydran's positions if their efforts to make themselves understood were reciprocated by a society who wanted to understand them.

The last important focus that dystopia adds is vigilance. According to Vieira (2010: 17), 'dystopia rejects the idea that man can reach perfection'. This vision of the future is expected to evoke a positive reaction from readers, namely that human beings will always have flaws and that the way of building a better world is through social improvement rather than individual improvement. In addition, readers should react by understanding that a dystopia is a possibility that we can still learn to avoid (Vieira, 2010: 17). Acknowledging the fact that we will always have flaws will ensure that we never become complacent in our activism. This vigilance will allow us to scrutinize our practices of placing language at the centre of social problems (despite theoretical arguments to the contrary) and will remind us that we will never have an ideal society – just a better one, provided that we work to make it so and maintain our progress. And here perhaps lies the greatest use of dystopia within Linguistic Citizenship: the fact that it puts the emphasis on social improvements – not individuals – thus returning our attention to Stroud's (2001: 353) original idea that '[mother tongue] education needs to be part of a general emancipatory social context, where affirmations of diversity in the form of local knowledge structures and systems of language might find their appropriate sociopolitical place in a regional and national context'. I am not calling for an abandonment of utopia because, as Stroud himself shows, utopia and dystopia are always simultaneously present. Rather, I am calling for a better understanding of the utopia/dystopia dialectic, and an explicit theorization of it, in order to unpack the possibilities of dystopia and thus the possibilities of utopia and Linguistic Citizenship.

Note

(1) I have lumped together Mbembe, Spivak and Freire as decolonial theorists, knowing that this oversimplifies things. Mbembe's work would perhaps be positioned as postcolonial, while Spivak is associated with subaltern studies. Freire, although used in some decolonial theorizing, did not identify himself as a decolonial scholar. I follow Bhambra (2014) here in seeing the similarities in these related movements in the 'intellectual resistance' they offer to 'epistemological dominance' and the possibilities of a 'new geopolitics of knowledge'.

References

Anthonissen, C., Costandius, E., Oostendorp, M. and Perold, K. (forthcoming) *Exploring Methodology An Arts-Based Approach to Multilingualism Research in South Africa*.

Banda, F. and Bellononjengele, B.O. (2010) Style, repertoire, and identities in Zambian multilingual discourses. *Journal of Multicultural Discourses* 5 (2), 107–119.

Bhambra, G.K. (2014) Postcolonial and decolonial dialogues. *Postcolonial Studies* 17 (2), 115–121.

Blommaert, J. (2009) Language, asylum, and the national order. *Current Anthropology* 50 (4), 415–441.

Blommaert, J. and Backus, A. (2013) Superdiverse repertoires and the individual. In I. Saint-Georges and J.J. Weber (eds) *Multilingualism and Multimodality: The Future of Education Research* (pp. 11–32). Rotterdam: Sense Publishers.

Bochner, A.P. and Ellis, C. (2003) An introduction to the arts and narrative research: Art as inquiry. *Qualitative Inquiry* 9 (4), 506–514.

Bristowe, A., Oostendorp, M. and Anthonissen, C. (2014) Language and youth identity in a multilingual setting: A multimodal repertoire approach. *Southern African Linguistics and Applied Language Studies* 32 (2), 229–245.

Busch, B. (2012) The linguistic repertoire revisited. *Applied Linguistics* 33 (5), 503–523.

Busch, B. (2016) Regaining a place from which to speak and be heard: In search of a response to the 'violence of voicelessness'. *Stellenbosch Papers in Linguistics Plus* 49 (1), 317–330.

Busch, B. (2017) Expanding the notion of the linguistic repertoire: On the concept of 'Spracherleben' – The lived experience of language. *Applied Linguistics* 38 (3), 340–358.

Claeys, G. (2010) The origins of dystopia: Wells, Huxley and Orwell. In G. Claeys (ed.) *The Cambridge Companion to Utopian Literature* (pp. 107–134). Cambridge: Cambridge University Press.

Crush, J. and Tawodzera, G. (2011) Medical xenophobia: Zimbabwean access to health services in South Africa. In J. Crush (ed.) *Migration Policy Series (Vol. 54)*. Cape Town: South African Migration Programme.

Crush, J., Ramachandran, S. and Pendleton, W. (2013) Soft targets: Xenophobia, public violence and changing attitudes to migrants in South Africa after May 2008. In J. Crush (ed.) *Migration Policy Series (Vol. 64)*. Cape Town: South African Migration Programme.

Dodson, B. (2010) Locating xenophobia: Debate, discourse, and everyday experience in Cape Town, South Africa. *Africa Today* 56 (3), 2–22.

Fivush, R. (2010) Speaking silence: The social construction of silence in autobiographical and cultural narratives. *Memory* 18 (2), 88–98.

Freire, P. (1998) *Pedagogy of Freedom*. Lanham: Rowman & Littlefield.

Gordin, M.D., Tilley, H. and Prakash, G. (eds) (2010) *Utopia/Dystopia: Conditions of Historical Possibility*. Princeton, NJ: Princeton University Press.

Leavy, P. (2015) *Method Meets Art: Arts-Based Research Practice*. New York: Guilford Publications.

Lefko-Everett, K. (2007) Voices from the margins: Migrant women's experiences in Southern Africa. In J. Crush (ed.) *Migration Policy Series (Vol. 46)*. Cape Town: South African Migration Programme.

Lewis, D. (2014) Melancholia and machinery: The dystopian landscape and mindscape in Hard Times. *Dickens Quarterly* 31 (1), 17–32.

Mbembe, A. (2001) *On the Postcolony*. Berkley, CA: University of California Press.

McDonald, D. (1998) Left out in the cold? Housing and immigration in the new South Africa. In J. Crush and D. McDonald (eds) *Migration Policy Series* (Vol. 5). Cape Town: South African Migration Programme.

Moylan, T. (2000) Look into the dark: On Dystopia and the Novum. In P. Parrinder (ed.) *Learning from other Worlds: Estrangement, Cognition and the Politics of Science Fiction and Utopia* (pp. 51–71). Liverpool: Liverpool University Press

Otheguy, R., García, O. and Reid, W. (2015) Clarifying translanguaging and deconstructing named languages: A perspective from linguistics. *Applied Linguistics Review* 6 (3), 281–307.

Paulson, S. (2016) Critical intimacy: An interview with Gayatri Chakravorty Spivak. Los Angeles Review of Books website. See https://lareviewofbooks.org/article/critical-intimacy-interview-gayatri-chakravorty-spivak/ (accessed 16 August 2020).

Pennycook, A. and Otsuji, E. (2014) Metrolingual multitasking and spatial repertoires: 'Pizza mo two minutes coming'. *Journal of Sociolinguistics* 18 (2), 161–184.

Rymes, B. (2014) Communicative repertoire. In C. Leung and B.V. Street (eds) *The Routledge Companion to English Language Studies* (pp. 287–301). Abingdon: Routledge.

Scott, D. and Bell, E. (2016) Reawakening our radical imaginations: Thinking realistically about utopias, dystopias and the non-penal. *Justice, Power and Resistance*. Capel Dewi: EG Press.

Shaikjee, M. and Milani, T. (2013) 'It's time for Afrikaans to go' ... or not? Language ideologies and (ir)rationality in the blogosphere. *Language Matters* 44 (2), 92–116.

Siziba, G. (2015) 'Cross-identification': Identity games and the performance of South Africanness by Ndebele-speaking migrants in Johannesburg. *African Identities* 13 (4), 262–278.

Siziba, G. and Hill, L. (2018) Language and the geopolitics of (dis)location: A study of Zimbabwean Shona and Ndebele speakers in Johannesburg. *Language in Society* 47 (1), 115–139.

Snell, J. (2013) Dialect, interaction and class positioning at school: From deficit to difference to repertoire. *Language and Education* 27 (2), 110–128.

Spivak, G.C. (1988) Can the subaltern speak? In C. Nelson and L. Grossberg (eds) *Marxism and the Interpretation of Culture* (pp. 271–313). Basingstoke: Macmillan.

Stroud, C. (2001) African mother-tongue programmes and the politics of language: Linguistic citizenship versus linguistic human rights. *Journal of Multilingual and Multicultural Development* 22 (4), 339–355.

Stroud, C. (2015) Linguistic citizenship as utopia. *Multilingual Margins* 2 (2), 20–37.

Stroud, C. and Williams, Q.E. (2017) Multilingualism as utopia: Fashioning non-racial selves. *AILA Review* 30 (1), 167–188.

Tlostanova, M. (2007) The imperial-colonial chronotope. *Cultural Studies* 21 (2–3), 406–427.

Van Heertum, R. (2006) Marcuse, Bloch and Freire: Reinvigorating a pedagogy of hope. *Policy Futures in Education* 4 (1), 45–51.

Vieira, F. (2010) The concept of utopia. In G. Claeys (ed.) *The Cambridge Companion to Utopian Literature* (pp. 3–27). Cambridge: Cambridge University Press.

Weeks, J. (1997) The sexual citizen. Paper presented at the Norwegian Research Council's Gender in Transition Conference: Sexing the Self: Sexuality, Gender, Ambiguity (Oslo, 13–14 October).

Williams, Q.E. and Stroud, C. (2010) Performing rap ciphas in late-modern Cape Town: Extreme locality and multilingual citizenship. *Afrika Focus* 23 (2), 39–59.

Part 3

Linguistic Citizenship for Linguistic Knowledge, Digital Activism and Popular Culture

7 The Travels of Semilingualism: Itineraries of Ire, Impact and Infamy

Linus Salö and David Karlander

Introduction

Some ideas travel well. Ideas are more or less stable objects of knowledge and are, as such, capable of moving through networks of actors to eventually end up somewhere new (Howlett & Morgan, 2010; Latour, 1986, 2004). Indeed, they may even morph into policy innovations. This chapter focuses on the travels of the idea of 'semilingualism' in its original Swedish context. It is thus concerned with how the movements of an academic idea unfold in science–society interaction, focusing on the way the idea of semilingualism informed educational policies governing minority languages in the Swedish curriculum.

A reasonably old idea, semilingualism (Swedish, *halvspråkighet*; Hansegård, 1962, 1968) refers to a form of imperfect language-knowledge; more specifically, a purported 'half-competence' among bilingual individuals whose acquisition and mastery of any of their languages is seen as 'incomplete'. While it was already being contested in the 1970s, semilingualism is still what Latour (2004) refers to as a recurrent 'matter of concern'. In 2017, for example, it surfaced in a media debate waged over Sweden's educational provisions for immigrants and autochthonous linguistic minorities, most saliently over *Mother-tongue instruction*. The debate was initiated in an op-ed by local centre-right *Moderate Party* politicians, who argued in the tabloid *Aftonbladet* (AB) that mother-tongue instruction should be abolished since it deprives minority children of 'sufficient knowledge of the Swedish language' and puts them 'at risk of becoming semilingual' (AB, 17 October 2017).[1] Their proposal spawned critical reaction in defence of the educational policies at issue. In one reply, some 250 teachers, educationalists and academics denounced the politicians' use of arguments unsupported by 'science and established practice' (AB, 19 October 2017). Other critics targeted the term 'semilingual'. In academic contexts, semilingualism is widely considered to be an obsolete, theoretically dubious, and potentially harmful idea (e.g. Martin-Jones & Romaine, 1986; Stroud, 1978, 2004). Already by the 1980s, semi-lingualism was being decried as 'a dirty word in the Scandinavian debate', capable of inciting 'an almost moral indignation in other researchers' (Skutnabb-Kangas, 1984 [1981]: 248). Tellingly, in the 2017 media debate, another academic, a researcher at the Swedish Language Council, stated that 'the term [semilingualism] has long been passé in research; people do not have half languages but linguistic competence in areas where they have been given the opportunity to develop' (AB, 18 October 2017). Although some commentators at the debate suggested that mother-tongue instruction could 'cure' semilingualism (ETC, 20 October 2017), most agreed that semilingualism was a flawed idea, 'unheard of since the turn of the millennium' (*Dagens Nyheter* [DN], 18 October 2017). The critique eventually prompted the Moderate Party to denounce the proposal (Skolvärlden, 18 October 2017).

Much can be said about these exchanges. In late-modern Sweden, the governing of what Stroud (2010: 195) labels 'non-mainstream speakers' – precarious migrants, indigenous minorities and socioeconomically mar-ginalized groups – remains a central public and political concern, and mother-tongue instruction is deeply implicated in such forms of concern. For some 40 years, mother-tongue instruction has been a tenet in Sweden's institutional setup for minority education, i.e. instruction in and about languages other than Swedish.[2] Moreover, while the idea of semilingual-ism appears to matter to some politicians, teachers and linguists, it none-theless seems beset with varying understandings of its relationship to mother-tongue instruction. For some, it seems, semilingualism may arise if mother-tongue instruction *is* provided, but for others, it may arise if mother-tongue instruction *is not* provided. To some actors, mentions of semilingualism by others acts as a shibboleth of detachedness from up-to-date research and general incompetence in minority education. In rela-tion to mother-tongue instruction, semilingualism thus matters.

In exploring this terrain, this chapter argues that the idea of semilin-gualism has not only had an impact on present-day debates but also at a much earlier stage. We maintain that the notion played an integral part in shoehorning bilingual education into Sweden's national curriculum in 1977. Without doubt, as a policy innovation, mother-tongue instruction in Sweden owes much of its existence to the impactful idea of semilingualism. We do not argue that the first debates on semilingualism single-handedly resulted in the introduction of mother-tongue instruction. As historical accounts of Sweden's mother-tongue instruction make clear, other condi-tions – notably, a general turn towards pluralism in immigration policy – clearly contributed to this reform (e.g. Hyltenstam & Milani, 2012). Nonetheless, while some authors have pointed to the linkage between semi-lingualism and mother-tongue instruction (e.g. Borevi, 2012; Hyltenstam & Arnberg, 1998; Wickström, 2015), the impact of semilingualism as a policy-driver has not been subjected to a thorough analytical treatment. Such a historical account has three motivations, all pertaining to strengthening the epistemological aspirations of linguistics, especially with regard to the need to add meta-knowledge to this undertaking. Firstly, in the spirit of philosopher of science Gaston Bachelard (2002 [1938]), the language sciences should aim to grasp the knowledge that they produce, including the effects that this production engenders. Centring particularly on these effects, secondly, a historical approach to semilingualism adds nuanced knowledge to the ways in which ideas become entrenched in policy, notably in mother-tongue programmes (Stroud, 2001). Thirdly, the same case points to a rarely recognized mode of the societal impact of research, in which a fairly subtle interaction between science and politics is at play. Irrespective of later re-evaluations, the case of semilingualism elucidates the ways in which the impact of the human sciences buttress institutional action (e.g. Benneworth, 2015; Meagher et al., 2008).

Accordingly, this chapter traces the pathways of semilingualism and their links to mother-tongue instruction. Adding a historical epistemological lens to these issues, we seek to better understand the relationship between mobile ideas and policy innovations. The timespan extends from the late 1950s to the early 1980s and so encompasses the formation and early circulation of the idea of semilingualism in Sweden, rather than the global travels of the idea that ensued in the 1980s (but see e.g. Martin-Jones & Romaine, 1986). To this end, we analyse a set of texts through which the idea was prefatorily forged, subsequently mobilized, acted upon and finally contested. We draw on journalistic and non-journalistic material from regional and national print media: news items, opinion pieces and letters to the editor. We also draw on motions and minutes from the Swedish parliament, as well as on a range of academic texts.[3] In analysing this material, we use the notion of 'traveling ideas' (Howlett & Morgan, 2010) as a conceptual lens. Through this lens, the idea of semilingualism is envisioned as moving through networks of actors comprising academics, the general public, press actors, politicians and policymakers. In line with this vision, the analysis pins down the crucial transition points where the idea found new uses and new users, and where it, accordingly, was authoritatively acted upon.

Ideas In and Out of Science

It is widely acknowledged that language is intimately linked to processes of granting or denying group membership, and thereby to the reproduction of social order. The notion of *Linguistic Citizenship* sets out to grasp some of these processes critically (e.g. Stroud, 2007, 2010). It develops a critique of predefined conceptions of language, and of the rigid categories of belonging that such conceptions postulate or naturalize. As critically noted in Linguistic Citizenship, the idea of mother tongue is a paradigm case of this mode of thinking. Unsurprisingly, the Linguistic Citizenship framework remains sceptical of mother-tongue programmes, insofar as they supposedly reify this gaze, downplay ontological multiplicity and obstruct the voiced participation of marginalized actors (Stroud, 2001). While Linguistic Citizenship typically engages with postcolonial settings, kindred processes are at work in the geographical north. By exploring mother-tongue instruction in Sweden, insights may be gained about the ways in which policy innovation for mother-tongue programmes is contingent upon 'entextualized' ideas that have found their way into certain institutional settings. However, we are not merely interested in the production and lexical labelling of *semilingualism,* but also in its circulation, uptake and effects, as well as in its demise. To accomplish this, we utilize perspectives from science studies, particularly those concerned with the production and the communicative flow of scientific knowledge (Bucchi, 1998; Howlett & Morgan, 2010; Meagher *et al.,* 2008), and with science brokering in political decision-making (Pielke, 2007). Science studies have long been interested in the emergence of scientific *facts.* While this agenda resembles ours, we treat facts as being heralded by and contingent upon *ideas.* Following Bachelard (2002 [1938]: 27), we 'take facts as ideas and place them within a system of thought'. More specifically, we take 'ideas' to denote more or less stable objects of knowledge, which often comprise claims about how things work, about causal conditions, and the like. Under certain conditions, ideas may acquire the quality of being fact-like and, by this merit, attach a high degree of certainty to a given truth claim (Latour, 2004; Morgan, 2010). Fact-like ideas, then, may become significantly mobile and travel in manifold ways (Howlett & Morgan, 2010). They may travel because people travel, or, because they are exchanged through interpersonal communication or disseminated as artefacts. Their pathways are often transmodal, forming a cyclic movement from interaction to text to interaction. Texts may be products of talk (e.g. minutes, transcribed interviews), and talk often draws on texts. In either case, text is central to the travel of ideas, allowing ideas to precipitate in various outlets and be physically distributed to various actors. In these processes, ideas not only become mobilized but substantially fixed (Latour, 1986) and 'sufficiently fact-like to enable people to act upon them' (Morgan, 2010: 24).

To speak of travelling ideas entails a focus not only on the ways in which ideas transmit from one place to another, but also on how the transmission of ideas through time and space may create *transformation.* As Morgan (2010) stresses, successful travelling is attested by a circulation 'far and wide', with *new users* and *new uses* being key parameters for gauging the efficacy of that travel. While 'new users' refers to an expansion of the social network where the idea is used, 'new uses' refers to a multiplication of the idea's applications, often beyond the original intent. Through such processes, academic ideas may blend with political language, and eventually seep into policy innovations. Such transformative moments presuppose that the idea has informed the beliefs and practices of politicians and policymakers. Moreover, as Pielke (2007: 151) states, '[p]olitical advocates will always seek selectively to use science in support of their agendas.' Conversely, science often reaches politicians through byroads such as the media. There is more to this movement than suggested by traditional linear models, according to which knowledge is produced in science and straightforwardly disseminated through press channels. Although academics regularly use mass media for reaching out to various publics, media does not simply *mediate* scientific knowledge, but determines the content and scope of the mediation (Bucchi, 1998). In sum, the view opted for here downplays rigid boundaries between science and other knowledge-yielding practices, foregrounding instead the networks of actors that link science to media to politics.

The Roots and Routes of Semilingualism

Prefatory debate

Semilingualism embarked on its travels in the margins of the far north – in Tornedalen,[4] a region that extends across the borderland of Sweden and Finland. Tornedalen is a historically multilingual area where Finnish and Swedish varieties, as well as Sámi languages, have long remained in varying degrees of contact.[5] The area has experienced various state-backed regimes of language. Following the creation of the Swedish–Finnish border in 1809, Finnish speakers dwelling in Sweden were increasingly subjected to a newfound nation-state agenda. As is often the case, state-funded education was one of several crucial instruments for enforcing linguistic cohesion. By the late 19th century, most far north school districts had introduced Swedish-only policies, sometimes sustaining them by physically violent means. While the strictest assimilatory policies were gradually diluted from the mid-1930s, Finnish was barred from being used in most institutional contexts until the mid-1950s (Elenius, 2001; Slunga, 1965).

It was in immediate relation to these conditions that the Swedish Finno-Ugrist Nils Erik Hansegård (1918–2002) began to formulate his idea of semilingualism. Born in Stockholm, he lived in the far north town of Kiruna from 1953 to 1966, working as an upper secondary teacher. Beginning in the late 1950s, Hansegård began to campaign in public lectures for an increased use of Finnish in local schools. As noted in a late retrospective, Hansegård (1990: 19) regarded Sweden's policies as 'ethnocentric, nationalist and racist'. Throughout his career, he maintained that this minority politics had ravished the linguistic competence of the non-Swedish population of Tornedalen, as well as their general intelligence and emotional life. Semilingualism, or, more accurately 'double semilingualism', Hansegård came to argue, was an effect of this historical order.

Hansegård (1990) advocated the introduction of minority mother tongues in education. The public impact of Hansegård's agenda was significantly augmented by reports of his lectures in print media. However, serving initially as an arena for disseminating his ideas, the press gradually developed into an area for critical debate and contention. The first surge of such exchanges materialized in a number of northern Swedish dailies, such as *Norrländska Socialdemokraten* (NSD), *Norrbottenskuriren* (NK), *Norrlandsfolket* (NF) and *Haparandablade*t (HB). In February 1957, Hansegård addressed 'the linguistic oppression in the north' in a radio talk, which was advertised, reported on, and, subsequently, critically debated on in local (and occasionally national) print media (NSD, 22 February 1957; NSD, 23 February 1957; NSD, 6 March 1957; NSD, 10 April 1957; SvD, 15 February 1957). As one of his adversaries, a district physician, exclaimed: 'it is better to know one language well than two incompletely' (NF, 14 March 1957). While agreeing, Hansegård responded that a minimal share of formal instruction in Finnish was unlikely to hamper children's acquisition of Swedish (NF, 20 March 1957).

Over the coming years, the press continually gave voice to Hansegård's explanations of the relation between pupils' language difficulties and their 'spiritual development' (NK, 8 January 1962). Yet, it also published letters that were critical of Hansegård's position (NK, 15 February 1962). Hansegård (1990: 111 ff) recalls first using the term 'semilingualism' in a radio appearance in the late 1950s, but not seeing it in print before 1962 (*Röster i radio*). When his 25 April radio appearance 'Tvåspråkig eller halvspråkig?' [Bilingual or semilingual?] was announced and briefly discussed in the press, the idea of semilingualism was recapped, albeit disparagingly: some of Hansegård's comparisons with the Swiss sociolinguistic situation were dismissed as being farfetched, and his critique of Sweden's policies as being overtly polemic (NSD, 27 April 1962). Although the idea of semilingualism was incidentally reused by some academics (Ringbom, 1962), it was yet not 'packed' to travel far and wide. By publishing in a periodical with a non-academic readership, Hansegård (1962) subsequently attempted to anchor semilingualism more thoroughly in scholarly discourse, with frequent references to German linguist Georg Schmidt-Rohr, and Austrian psycholinguist Friedrich Kainz, who Hansegård had visited in Vienna in 1961 (see Hansegård, 1961). While Hansegård's own position in the scientific field was still marginal – he received his doctorate in 1967 – his argument was quite convincingly dressed in scientific language. At the time, research on bilingualism was a new subfield of the language sciences and engaged only a few Swedish linguists (e.g. Els Oksaar, Bertil Malmberg, Björn Collinder). As the field was still in the making, academic authority was, thus, up for grabs.

Beginning in 1963, the ever more recurring northern media reports on 'the problem of bilingualism' depicted Hansegård as an *urstockholmare* ('inborn' or 'proto-' Stockholmer) with ample academic knowledge of linguistics, who had started attacking the Swedish-only education policies in bilingual Tornedalen (NK, 12 August 1963). Indeed, Hansegård was criticizing the shaky research grounding of bilingual education. In succeeding accounts, he gathered support for his views from 'American expertise', in the guise of pioneering bilingualism scholar Einar Haugen, to argue that the northern region was in dire need of expertise on bilingualism (NSD, 10 March 1964). While the term 'semilingualism' was mostly absent in media reports on Hansegård's lectures (but see NSD, 27 April 1962), these articles nonetheless reiterated Hansegård's pedagogical, sociological and psychological arguments in relatively technical terms (HB, 16 April 1964; HB, 25 April 1964). However, although the media positioned Hansegård as an expert on the issues at hand, it is possible that Hansegård himself underestimated their vexed nature, as well as the political force of his viewpoints, inserted as they were into a conflict-ridden space where language was a vector of struggle, oppression, and abuse. Accordingly, his media accounts were soon met with intensifying scepticism from readers responding with letters to the editor signed with pseudonyms as well as real names. Some writers heckled Hansegård's efforts (HB, 17 September 1964a), whereas others adopted an academic or matter-of-fact style (HB, 5 September 1964). Hansegård attempted to respond to the criticism, referring to the 'extensive experiments' that spoke in favour of mother-tongue programmes (HB, 17 September 1964b) and downplaying occasional parental resistance to the use of Finnish in education. Presenting himself as an issue advocate for mother-tongue programmes, he used 'scientific authority as tool of advocacy' (Pielke, 2007: 135). For instance, he equated the abandonment of a mother tongue to volitional self-harm:

> Just as one has the right to smoke oneself to death, one should have the right to linguistic suicide. [...] Responsible persons consider themselves obliged to inform smokers about produced research findings [on the matter]. Similarly, there exists extensive bilingualism research abroad (and an incipient Swedish one) and the same obligation should apply in providing citizens with other mother tongues than Swedish information about that [research]. (HB, 17 September 1964a).

Hansegård appears to have made it his duty to enlighten the people of Tornedalen of their own subordination. Speaking to and imposing his academic knowledge onto the group, he cared little about its own voice. That said, the group's voice was far from unison. As seen in the press debate, the initiatives had been limited thus far to introducing Finnish in the educational system were applauded by some speakers and berated by others. Hansegård's standpoints were celebrated in contributions that defended the right to mother-tongue programmes (NSD, 24 August 1965; NSD, 28 August 1965; NSD, 29 September 1965). Hansegård was attentive to positive appraisals of his opinion and used these to clarify his stance (NSD, 11

September 1965). His own discourse was rhetorically rich, and he did not hesitate to engage fiercely with his antagonists. His responses to bantering commentators were occasionally affective, lashing out, for instance, at their 'infantile' critique or at 'the backward school system' (HB, 28 September 1965). Unsurprisingly, such arguments did not silence Hansegård's opponents, many of whom were Finnish speakers, who denounced him as a 'learned fanatic' for his 'offensive scribblings' (HB, 22 January 1966) or for his 'propaganda for a greater-Finland' (HB, 24 March 1966), or simply exhorted him to 'travel back home' (NSD 30 September 1965). A few letter titles are illustrative of these sentiments: 'No Finnish for our children' (NSD, 30 September 1965), 'What does Mr Hansegård mean by his spying activities?' (HB, 22 January 1966), and 'Disaster for Tornedalen if Hansegård is believed' (NSD, 21 October 1965). By stressing that 'we want to feel like Swedes and be left alone' (HB, 24 March 1966), another group of detractors asserted that they belonged in the Swedish nation-state or even defended assimilatory policies. Furthermore, Hansegård's views were critiqued on more intellectual grounds: for being overly localist and presentist (HB, 13 January 1966), or for downplaying the complexity of the sociolinguistic issues in question (NSD, 1 October 1965). Attempting to silence his critics, Hansegård replied with a rhetorical question, asking whether the Tornedalians had the guts and strength to become their own 'linguistic masters' (HB, 29 August 1967). The prefatory debate in Tornedalen closed on a hostile note.

The national press debate

Throughout the exchange in the northern Swedish context, Hansegård had only partially succeeded in gaining acceptance for his views on mother-tongue programmes. While the exchanges of the early 1960s laid the foundations for Hansegård's endeavour, the term 'semilingualism' seldom occurred. There and then, few *new users* of the term were thus to be found. Yet, as we shall see, Hansegård's advocacy was more successfully received on a national plane, where it eventually fed into an incipient debate on immigration.

Towards the end of the 1960s, there was significant momentum for replacing Sweden's assimilatory policies with pluralistic frameworks. Debates on this matter germinated as a series of opinion pieces in the leading daily *Dagens Nyheter* (DN, 21 October 1964; DN, 24 October 1964; DN, 28 October 1964) that questioned the hitherto dominant ideology of cultural, religious, and linguistic assimilation. This view eventually gained a foothold on DN's editorial page (DN, 24 December 1964) and was subsequently debated in various forums. One of these was the influential volume *Swedish Minorities* (Schwartz, 1966), to which Hansegård (1966) contributed a chapter on the 'forgotten Finnish minority' of Tornedalen, or, as he also put it, the 'linguistic cripples' (*språkliga krymplingar*) (Hansegård, 1966: 180) of the far north. This contribution effectively invigorated the question of mother-tongue programmes in Tornedalen. Hansegård's efforts to influence educational policy were reported in DN (11 January 1966), where Hansegård was given an opportunity to voice his agenda. Additionally, Bertil Malmberg, a leading Swedish linguist, wrote an extensive piece on language politics in *Svenska Dagbladet* (SvD), which criticized Sweden's far north policies for violating UNESCO's recommendations on mother-tongue programmes. He noted that '[t]he youth up here are not bilingual, they are 'semilingual' – this is more or less how a teacher in a Norrbotten school put it in a conversation when I visited the school a few years ago' (SvD, 11 October 1966).

Malmberg's intervention added considerable weight to these concerns. Although a new user of the idea, he commanded authority in the language sciences. His mentioning of 'semilingual' speakers was among the first ones to appear in the national press, thus marking a crucial transition point in the route of semilingualism. However, the idea would see its major breakthrough later on, when Hansegård's book *Tvåspråkighet eller halvspråkighet?* [Bilingualism or Semilingualism?] was published (Hansegård, 1968). Here, Hansegård discussed his ideas in relation to the work of Schmidt-Rohr and, particularly Kainz, who he cited alongside the work of scholars like Uriel Weinreich, Heinz Kloss, Einar Haugen, Robert Lado, Ferdinand de Saussure and Joshua Fishman. Hansegård (1968: 111) depicted the prevailing Swedish language politics as a 'cultural genocide', interpreting its historical patterns of domination in psycholinguistic terms, impinging upon the minds of the region's Finnish-speaking inhabitants. Maintenance of the mother tongue was seen as a determinant of minorities' cultural, cognitive and spiritual development, and consequently their educational success more generally (Hansegård, 1968: 97–133). In this vein, Hansegård (1968: 110) regarded monolingual education as imposing mental constraints on the social advancement of minority children, leaving them with a 'deficient command' of both their languages, that is, 'semilingual'.

It is apparent that Hansegård's idea of semilingualism resonate with the notion of *halvbildning* ('semi-learning') (*Halbbildung*; see Adorno, 1972 [1959]). In fact, Malmberg (1964: 156) had argued that a failure to provide mother-tongue instruction for minorities nourished 'the worst enemy of all learning – semi-learning'. Be that as it may, Hansegård's work was seen as solid due in significant part to its anchorage in the burgeoning area of bilingualism research (Wande, 1996: 226). Indicatively, the book received markedly positive reviews from Swedish linguists. Per Linell (SvD, 18 January 1969) referred to the work as 'matter-of-fact and exhaustive, yet accessible' and commended its 'well-developed theoretical foundation.' Alvar Ellegård spoke of 'our [Swedish] language imperialism' and praised Hansegård's discussion for being 'thoughtful and balanced' (DN, 3 June 1969). Around this time, Hansegård's efforts yielded results, as mother-tongue programmes were expanded in Tornedalen. As DN reported on this event, Hansegård was called upon as an expert and an honest broker of policy alternatives (Pielke, 2007). He asserted that a 'deep-reaching educational overhaul' was needed to avoid the risk of creating 'tens of thousands "linguistic cripples", victims of double semilingualism' (DN, 23 June 1968).

It was soon clear that Hansegård's argument had broader implications, which extended beyond his original intent. In the national arena, the idea of semilingualism found new users, attracting attention from a range of political actors. Here, and importantly so, semilingualism also found *new uses* as it interlaced with issues pertaining to new patterns of immigration, and with a general shift towards a pluralistic stance in immigrant and minority politics. Among actors in the media, as well as in politics and in policymaking, an acceptance of pluralism was gaining ground, paving the way for semilingualism to travel. In 1970, an article in SvD (4 January 1970) reported on immigrants' sociolinguistic predicaments, highlighting problems purportedly linked to the absence of mother-tongue programmes. Here also, Hansegård figured as an expert, warning against the lurking perils of semilingualism and assuring the validity of his theories for linguistic issues of immigrants, too. He thereby extended the itinerary of semilingualism, propelling it further into the educational debate. Revealingly, DN (8 April 1970) published a full-page piece on the 'language barrier' among immigrant children soon afterwards, explaining the importance of mother-tongue programmes for alleviating the latent risk of semilingualism. *Lärartidningen/Svensk skoltidning*, the journal of Sweden's largest teachers' union, also published an article on immigrant primary education, titled 'Can auxiliary teachers save immigrant children from semilingualism and isolation?' (LT, 1970[43]). The concern was circulating widely. For example, DN published a piece titled '[It is] dangerous to become semilingual' (24 April 1972), and SvD one called 'They learn "half" languages' (26 March 1974).

Entering politics

Clearly, the idea of semilingualism worked in favour of pro-mother-tongue programme agendas, as well as pluralistic policies more generally. Since 1968, the government commission *Invandrarutredningen* (the Immigrant Commission, henceforth IC) had been outlining Sweden's new immigration policy. In parliamentary politics, this area was characterized by a notable absence of opposing views: all political parties welcomed a pluralistic shift in minority politics (Borevi, 2012). Consensus and certainty are features that Pielke (2007) regards as being profitable for the trustworthiness of science in decision-making. Absence of political conflict facilitates the use of scientific knowledge in arguments for a particular course of action. Indicatively, in the run-up to the 1973 elections, all party leaders generally agreed on the importance of allowing immigrants to maintain their culture and language when exhaustively questioned on the matter in *Vårt Nya Land* (VNL). Social democratic Prime Minister Olof Palme reiterated the preceding academic exchange, noting that '[s]everal researchers have also demonstrated the importance of possessing skills in the mother tongue before[immigrant] school children move on to studies about Swedish and in Swedish' (VNL, 1972[6]: 7). In this climate, preventing semilingualism was a real and urgent concern. In a parliamentary motion on increased funding to immigrant education, opposition leader Torbjörn Fälldin and his Center Party colleagues stressed the need for mother-tongue programmes for immigrant children, arguing that:

> Without proper skills in [their mother tongue], immigrant children are less well-placed to learn Swedish satisfactorily. They may be at risk of becoming so-called semilinguals, i.e. not learning any language satisfactorily. (Motion, 1973:702: 18)

This motion shows that semilingualism had travelled into politics, reaching a group of new and powerful users. For many political actors, tacking onto the idea served to vest their ethos and agenda with scientific authority. Left Party MP Karin Nordlander noted that 'semilingual pupils' had become a major educational concern, since it was doubtful 'that even if pupils were able to read Swedish and the mother-tongue, they might not understand what they read' (Minutes, Riksdag, 1973:79: 147). The same stance was, importantly, expressed in numerous similar motions, produced by all political camps and in cross-party collaborations. For instance, a motion on Sámi education, jointly filed by right, center-right and social democratic MPs, maintained that adult Sámi often were 'what one calls semilingual' (Motion, 1974:1381: 4).

In 1974, the final report of the IC was presented (SOU 1974:69). It stated that limited mother-tongue use in primary education could cause 'intellectual and emotional distress,' and lead to serious 'linguistic and intellectual and impairments'. The IC report stated additionally that a '[d]efficient mastery of the mother tongue leads to deficient skills also in the other language, so-called *semilingualism*' (SOU, 1974:69: 241) As a countermeasure, the IC strongly favoured introducing *Home Language Instruction* (effectively mother-tongue instruction; see Note 2) as an additional subject in the national curriculum. This position gained acceptance among the parliamentary committee members only six weeks before the launch of the IC's final report (Jacobsson, 1984: 78). Thus, since at least 1973, the political uptake of semilingualism was truly influential in the development of pluralistic language policies. Under such conditions, public and political pressure to realize the intentions of IC was strong. Mother-tongue instruction was vocally promoted by parties on both the left and the right (Minutes, Riksdag, 1975/76:141, 1975/76:87; Motion,

1975/76:1394, 1975/76:1501). Print media continuously featured articles about the perils of semilingualism (SvD, 19 September 1974; DN, 4 September 1975; DN, 17 October 1976), and research continuously affirmed the reality of the phenomenon (e.g. Jaakkola, 1973).

The 1977 *Home Language Reform* (Prop. 1975/76:118) principally followed the IC directives, making mother-tongue instruction a general provision for all minority children. At this point, the idea of semilingualism had travelled into, or had enacted a major impact on, Swedish legislation. A claim made by IC chair Jonas Widgren, who was effectively one of the main architects of Sweden's new immigration policy, attests to this suggestion. Reflecting on the policy developments of the 1970s, Widgren (1982: 60) identified Hansegård's 1968 book, and the discussion on bilingual education it heralded, as a de facto contribution to the far-reaching changes in Swedish immigration policy.

The infamy of semilingualism

The political debate on semilingualism was paralleled by a domestic academic discussion, which pushed the idea into 'epistemic uncertainty' (Pielke, 2007). In this trajectory, semilingualism gradually changed into a profitable object to attack and a worthy object to defend. Reservations against it were first expressed by Loman (1974), who, drawing on his own research in Tornedalen, suggested that semilingualism in the region might well be a 'fiction'. Stolt (1975b) declared her support for mother-tongue instruction, but encouraged scrapping the *term* semilingualism, as it idealized the connection between mother tongue and emotional life. Conversely, Skutnabb-Kangas (1975) agreed that the term was difficult to define and apply, but nevertheless insisted on the importance of more research on semilingualism. Toukomaa (1975: 30), for his part, not only argued that 'semilingualism was an actual phenomenon' but that '[t]he risk of semilingualism [could] be avoided by providing immigrant children [...] with improved teaching in their mother tongue' (1975: 6). Notably, from the mid-1970s and on, these authors contributed to elevating the semilingualism debate to the international scale (e.g. Skutnabb-Kangas & Toukomaa, 1976). In the Swedish context, Hansegård (1975) responded to criticism from Loman (1974) and Stolt (1975b) by insisting that semilingualism was a reality in Tornedalen. Resorting to his habitual cutting rhetoric, Hansegård (1975) labelled the Swedish spoken there 'parrot Swedish' (*papegojsvenska*). In this wording, it is obvious that the idea of semilingualism served to pathologize certain minority speakers. The derogatory connotations were indeed criticized (Loman, 1975; Stolt, 1975a). Hansegård (1975) was rebuffed for being prejudiced (Wande, 1977), which spurred further debate (Hansegård, 1977; Loman, 1978).

While Loman's (1974) initial critique was empirically based, the objections delivered by subsequent critics of semilingualism were informed by other considerations. Stroud (1978) dissected semilingualism using a conceptual analysis paired with a review of literature that addressed relevant themes such as bilingualism and cognition, language learning and language testing. His critical examination of the alleged theoretical assumptions underpinning semilingualism sought to cast doubts on the internationally budding scholarly camp, represented by Jim Cummins and others, that asserted the reality of kindred ideas. In the Swedish academic discussion, a new type of criticism against semilingualism was raised by Öhman (1981). In contrast to the empiricist reservations of Loman and the theoretical deliberations of Stroud, Öhman (1981) drew attention to a set of ethical problems linked to the circulation of the idea in and beyond science. In framing his argument, he recounted a recent TV show in which a group of reportedly semilingual Turkish immigrant youth were put on show to the Swedish public. Öhman (1981) reacted against such denigrating applications of a linguistic idea, arguing that semilingualism had come to serve as a 'caste mark', that is, as a symbol of irrevocable linguistic, cognitive, and social marginalization. Taking issue with this ideological use, he admonished the language sciences for their failure to take responsibility for the ways in which the idea was being perceived and applied beyond the confines of academia. Addressing new, partially non-academic, networks of users, Hyltenstam and Stroud (1982) attempted to synthesize the previous thrusts of critique. Seconding Stroud's (1978) theoretical reservations and Öhman's (1981) ethical objections, Hyltenstam and Stroud (1982: 13) scorned the idea of semilingualism because of its capacity to stigmatize, and even fuel patronizing and xenophobic narratives about 'semilingual immigrants', arguing 'it is time we abandon the concept of semilingualism'. Through these exchanges, semilingualism had become an obsolete and even infamous idea in scholarly networks. Tellingly, Christina Bratt Paulston (1983: 56) concluded that '[s] emilingualism does not exist, or, to phrase it in a way that cannot be contested, semilingualism has never been proved empirically.' Yet, its effects in educational policy existed, and still exist.

Conclusion

Some ideas certainly travel well. This is true of the idea of semilingualism, which recurrently surfaces in societal and political debate. Whenever it does, it appears as a polysemic object of knowledge, affording different interpretations and gelling with different agendas (see Lainio, 2008; Stroud, 2004). As the present chapter has shown, semilingualism seems to have commanded this capacity ever since it began to travel. Several important insights can, accordingly, be drawn from the example it presents. The travels of semilingualism illustrate how a practically used idea may help to establish an understanding of deprivation and redress, and how the same idea may feed into policy innovation. Sweden's MT programme is a case in point. As shown empirically, the provision of mother-tongue instruction in Sweden's educational system is evidence of the impactful travels of semilingualism.

While the case at hand obviously speaks to the spatial politics of linguistic research, it also illuminates a somewhat unexpected unfolding of an idea's trajectory: it is striking that semilingualism emerged from a marginal position, but nevertheless travelled into the limelight of national policymaking. For this reason, it is appropriate to address the following questions: What conditions could help explain why the idea of semilingualism gained this kind of traction? What factors made it impactful in Swedish policymaking? The present study points to a number of interdependent causes. Notably, in the late 1960s, the idea of semilingualism appeared scientifically innovative and convincing, resonating with a growing mass of users – academics, journalists and policymaking. Moreover, its travels unfolded in a period of policy revision, rife with trust in scholarly expertise. Through this itinerary, it enjoyed certain scientific credibility but also support from a near-consensual call for more egalitarian minority politics. Expressed in more general terms, the effects of its travels depended on a wider social set of networked actors who were willing to use it (Benneworth, 2015: 56). Upon entering politics, the idea proved sufficiently sturdy for political actors who appropriated it and harnessed their agendas to it. Semilingualism, in short, received both *new users* and *new uses* when it was inserted into a new 'politics of difference' (Stroud, 2007: 27). Given the layeredness of this politics, it would be overly simplistic to argue that the wide acceptance of the idea of semilingualism singlehandedly *caused* mother-tongue instruction to be introduced. More accurately, the introduction of mother-tongue instruction was intricately bound up with the scrapping of Sweden's previous immigration and minority politics, and with the search for alternative models. As the assimilatory regime was abandoned, mother-tongue instruction surged as an emblem of minority inclusion, which simultaneously reasserted Sweden's self-image as a modern and progressive country (Borevi, 2012; Hyltenstam & Milani, 2012). At the same time, it is indisputable that the circulation and uptake of the idea of semilingualism accelerated this shift, and that the idea thus functioned as a policy-driver *in its own right*. In other words, this political shift was significantly aided by the idea of semilingualism, by the routes on which it had travelled and by the actors who had used it.

Given these circumstances, it should be noted that a 'flow of knowledge' (Meagher et al., 2008) runs unevenly: at some transition points, an idea may be acted upon in ways that may yield social or institutional change. It follows that the travel of semilingualism shows the importance of the societal impact of academic ideas. The 'birth, slow construction, fascinating emergence' (Latour, 2004: 242) of semilingualism stresses that the tangled interaction between the human sciences, the media and political actors may precipitate in durable institutional regimes. Exploring this condition, our analysis underscores that the *marks of science* (Latour, 1986) are not merely inscribed in technical innovations or economic growth, but also in policy innovations in the public sector. Here, the impact of the human sciences must not be underestimated. Yet, not only does the case of semilingualism beckon us to contrive research impact in terms of knowledge flows, but it also demonstrates the value of historical inquiry as a powerful lens for making policy impact visible.

It seems as if a strong indicator of successful travelling is attested in the leap of an idea into policy. Nonetheless, the impact of semilingualism notwithstanding, this leap was followed by a devaluing of the idea as its travels clearly lost momentum after mother-tongue instruction had been implemented. In this regard, the idea's consecutive itineraries of impact and infamy suggest that once a scholarly idea has travelled well, it can be terminated by actors of the kind – scholars – who first allowed it to travel. Yet, once the idea has been made obsolete, the effects of its travels may still prevail. On this note, the relationship between the field of sociolinguistics and semilingualism should be given attention. As far as mother-tongue instruction is concerned, the effects of the travels of the idea of semilingualism are tangible, and certainly held to be desirable, in the view of most sociolinguists familiar with the Swedish educational framework. In other words, while the scientific reality or validity of the idea is still perceived to be nil, the effects of its past circulation are widely appreciated. When seen from a historical point of view, the sympathies nourished among contemporary Swedish scholars for mother-tongue instruction appear increasingly as a distant effect of the travels of semilingualism – in fact, the dissociation of the historical connection between the idea, its trajectory and its institutional context is, it seems, a prerequisite for maintaining this mode of support. Put as starkly as possible, the scholarly support for the 'appealing' policy of mother-tongue instruction is concomitant with a scholarly dismissal of the 'appalling' idea of semilingualism.

This relationship has several implications. It is important to acknowledge, first, that Hansegård was guided by a narrow conception of linguistic normality, paired with a pathologization of perceived linguistic deviances in minoritized speech and writing. As his ideas of normality and pathology were largely modelled on a received view of an idealized native mother-tongue speaker, his work represents precisely the sort of scholarly and political legacy that the notion of Linguistic Citizenship seeks to combat and transform. At the same time, however, it is also important to recognize that Hansegård, much like later researchers of multilingualism, was driven by a sincere desire to elucidate, analyse, and redress deep-seated sociolinguistic inequalities in a marginalized population. Despite the apparent differences between Hansegård's engagement and more recent developments in the field, this ethos stands strong among most scholars who conduct research on or with minoritized speakers, in Sweden and elsewhere. In this respect, the case at hand speaks to the merit of meta-knowledge in the human sciences, and to the importance of taking responsibility for the knowledge that they handle. Unless we take into account the historical circulation, uptake, and use of an idea, we are at risk of overlooking the often-intricate relationships between linguistic ideas and policy innovations. An ahistorical understanding of the idea of semilingualism, congruently, leaves us with little possibility of grasping all political dimensions of the idea, of its travels, and its most salient effects. Not least for this reason, it is imperative to scrutinize the ways in which scholarly ideas of today are made to travel. In the spirit of the present volume, it is thus worth asking whether the appealing idea of Linguistic Citizenship is packaged to travel into policy. To what extent has this possible transposition been facilitated or obstructed? What are the social prerequisites of its mobilization? What effects could its movements potentially have on policy and institutional practice across different national contexts? To what extent would such effects rework or modify the actual idea? These questions are by no means simple but do nonetheless merit serious consideration. As the case of Hansegård shows, it is difficult to predict the impact of a mobile idea by attending exclusively to its intellectual or ideological content. Monitoring the movements of any policy-attuned linguistic idea should, for this reason, be a central priority for anyone invested in the production of such ideas. As Morgan (2010: 6) reminds us, scholars 'should be careful of the ways that they package their facts for successful travel and, as much as possible, take care about the company they keep while these facts are in their charge'. Knowledge about these processes *per se* is certainly important, not just in relation to old linguistic ideas, but also in relation to those currently in production.

Acknowledgements

We are grateful to Jürgen Jaspers, Lian Madsen, Stef Slembrouck, Piet Van Avermaet, Kirsten Rosiers, Christopher Hutton, Alexandra Jaffe, Kathleen Heugh, Kenneth Hyltenstam, Linnea Hanell, Monica Heller, Gunnar Norrman, Sverker Sörlin, Dag Avango, Adam Jaworski, David Nilsson, Nina Wormbs, Mats Benner, Pauline Mattsson and Ulrika Bjare, all of whom provided valuable comments on the manuscript. This work was partially funded by Sweden's Innovation Agency Vinnova (2015-04473; 2019-03679).

Notes

(1) All translations are our own.
(2) Here, *MT programs* (e.g. Stroud, 2001) denote educational models that use instruction in and about the mother tongues of minorities. Since 1977, *MTI* has been the standard MT programme in the Swedish national curriculum. MTI was termed *Home Language Instruction* until 1997, but the programme has remained largely unchanged.

(3) Press material was manually located and excerpted from the microfilm Newspaper Collection at The National Library of Sweden. Motions and minutes were retrieved from the digital collection of the Riksdag. In addition, unpublished academic text material was obtained from the N.E. Hansegård Archive at Carolina Rediviva Library in Uppsala.

(4) We use *Tornedalen (Torne Valley)* to denote the valley of the Torne river and its hinterlands in Norrbotten County in the Swedish part of Sápmi.

(5) Our use of glottonyms largely mirrors those of the periods and authors we discuss. Notably, the Finno-Ugric variety of Tornedalen, referred to as Finnish throughout this chapter, is today called Meänkieli. Since 2000, it has been recognized as a national minority language under this name.

Sources

AB 17.10.2017, *Avskaffa hemspråk – lär barnen svenska*, online; 18.10.2017, *Ni går emot forskning om språkinlärning*, online; 19.10.2017, *Utan hemspråk klarar sig inte våra elever*, online

DN 21.10.1964, *Utlänningsproblemet i Sverige*, 4; 24.10.1964, *Utlänningarnas traditioner*, 4; 28.10.1964, *Utlänningarnas anpassningsproblem*, 4; 24.12.1964, *Att vara utlänning*, 2; 11.1.1966, *Kirunalärare larmar om språkligt förtryck*, 19; 23.6.1968, *Ny språkpolitik i Tornedalen undervisning på finska*, 7; 3.6.1969, *Vår språkimperialism*, 4; 8.4.1970, *Språkbarriär skapar blyghet*, 50; 24.4.1972, *Farligt bli halvspråkig*, 13; 4.9.1975, *"Ett sätt att råda bot på halvspråkigheten"*, 58; 17.10.1976, *Invandrarbarnen och svenskan: en misshandlad generation*. 4; 18.10.2017, *Bygg en ramp bredvid skoltrappan för invandrarbarnen*, 5

ETC 20.10.2017, *Samer rasar mot Wengholm (M): "Kulturellt folkmord"*, 6–7.

HB 16.4.1964, *Tvåspråkigheten vetenskapligt belyst i Haparanda-föreläsning*, 1, 4; 25.4.1964, *Tvåspråkighetens positiva sidor i vetenskapligt ljus*, 4; 5.9.1964, *Språkfrågan i Tornedalen*, 3; 17.9.1964a, *Hr Lassinantti driver med tornedalingarna*, 3; 17.9.1964b, *Undervisningen i Tornedalen*, 3; 28.9.1965, *"Tornedalings" kritik infantil*, 6; 13.1.1966, *Svenskt eller finskt en föråldrad debatt*, 6; 22.1.1966, *Vad menar hr Hansegård med sin spionverksamhet?*, 2; 24.3.1966, *"Vi vill känna oss som svenskar och vara ifred"*, 2; 29.8.1967, *Vågar och orkar tornedalingarna bli sina egna språkliga herrar?*, 3

LT 43/1970, *Kan anpassningslärare rädda invandrarbarn från halvspråkighet och isolering?*, 24–27.

Minutes, Riksdag 1973:79, *Anslag till undervisning för invandrare i svenska språket m.m.*; 1975/76:87, *Studiesociala åtgärder*; 1975/76:141, *Hemspråksundervisning för invandrarbarn*

Motion 1973:702, *Om ökade anslag till invandrarundervisning*; 1974:1381, *Angående samernas folkhögskola*; 1975/76:1394, *Om hemspråksundervisning för invandrarbarn*; 1975/76:1501, *Om undervisning i samiska, m.m.*

NF 14.3.1957, *Kan Tornedalsbefolkningen bli tvåspråkig?*, 6; 20.3.1957, *Språklig medvetenhet i finskan behövs*, 6

NK 8.1.1962, *Kiruna-adjunkt först på "vitt" forskarfält*, 54; 15.2.1962, *Apropå adjunkt Hansegårds yttrande om undervisning på finska i Tornedalen*, 8; 12.8.1963, *Tvåspråkiga på undantag anser språkman i Kiruna*, 3;

NSD 22.2.1957, *Språkförtryck i norr*, 15; 23.2.1957, *Aktuellt porträtt*, 4; 6.3 1957, *Tornedalsfinskan än en gång*, 4; 10.4.1957, *Hansegård får en slutreplik*, 4; 27.4.1962, *Hansegård om språken*, 4; 10.3.1964, *Tvåspråkighetsexperten behövs i Norrbotten*, 15; 24.8.1965, *Nu är Hansegård i Kiruna ilsken igen: vi har fått skador för livet därför att vi fötts i Tornedalen*, 14; 11.9.1965, *Tack för inlägget om finskundervisning!*, 13; 1.10.1965, *Inte bara språket*, 6; 21.10.1965, *"Katastrof för Tornedalen om*

Hansegård blir trodd", 6; 28.8.1965, *Finsk undervisning i skolorna*, 13; 29.9.1965, *Språket i Tornedalen*, 7; 30.9.1965, *Ingen finska för våra barn*, 11
Skolvärlden 18.10.2017, *Förslaget att avskaffa modersmål sågas av egna partiet*, online
SvD 15.2.1957, *Uteätande, crazy och idrott i nästa veckas radioprogram*, 9; 11.10.1966, *Språkpolitik borta och hemma*, 4; 18.1.1969, *Tvåspråkighet*, 5; 4.1.1970, *Ung invandrare: Varför leva på annat sätt än det svenska när vi är bosatta i Sverige?*, 24; 26.3.1974, *De lär halva språk*, 1, *"Finländska barnen behärskar varken svenska eller finska"*, 9; 19.9.1974, *Halvspråkighet*, 14
VNL 1972[6], VNL:s *partiledarintervjuer: Gösta Bohman (m) Olof Palme (s)*

References

Adorno, T. (1972) [1959]) Theorie der Halbbildung. *Gesammelte Schriften* 8, 93–121. Frankfurt: Suhrkamp.

Bachelard, G. (2002 [1938]) *The Formation of the Scientific Mind. A Contribution to a Psychoanalysis of Objective Knowledge*. Manchester: Clinamen.

Benneworth, P. (2015) Tracing how arts and humanities research translates, circulates and consolidates in society. *Arts & Humanities in Higher Education* 14 (1), 45–60.

Borevi, K. (2012) Sweden: The flagship of multiculturalism. In G. Brochmann and A. Hagelund (eds) *Immigration Policy and the Scandinavian Welfare State 1945–2010* (pp. 25–96). New York: Palgrave.

Bratt Paulston, C. (1983) *Forskning och debatt om tvåspråkighet*. Stockholm: Skolöverstyrelsen.

Bucchi, M. (1998) *Science and the Media*. New York: Routledge.

Elenius, L. (2001) *Både finsk och svensk. Modernisering, nationalism och språkförändring i Tornedalen 1850–1939*. Umeå: Umeå University.

Hansegård, N.E. (1961) Reseberättelse. Studieresa till Österrike och Schweiz hösten 1961. Unpublished report.

Hansegård, N.E. (1962) Tornedalen – en svensk bygd utan språk. *Samtid och Framtid* 4, 215–219.

Hansegård, N.E. (1966) Finskt i Tornedalen, en glömd minoritet. In D. Schwartz (ed.) *Svenska minoriteter* (pp. 162–182). Stockholm: Aldus.

Hansegård, N.E. (1968) *Tvåspråkighet eller halvspråkighet?* Stockholm: Aldus.

Hansegård, N.E. (1975) Tvåspråkighet eller halvspråkighet? *Nordisk minoritetsforskning* 3, 7–13.

Hansegård, N.E. (1977) Loman och halvspråkigheten. *Invandrare och minoriteter* 3, 36–51.

Hansegård, N.E. (1990) *Den norrbottenfinska språkfrågan. En återblick på halvspråkighetsdebatten*. Uppsala: Uppsala University.

Howlett, P. and Morgan, M.S. (eds) (2010) *How Well Do Facts Travel?* Cambridge: Cambridge University Press.

Hyltenstam, K. and Arnberg, L. (1998) Bilingualism and education of immigrant children and adults in Sweden. In C. Bratt Paulston (ed.) *International Handbook of Bilingualism and Bilingual Education* (pp. 476–513). New York: Greenwood.

Hyltenstam, K. and Stroud, C. (1982) Halvspråkighet – ett förbrukat slagord. *Invandrare och minoriteter* 3, 10–13.

Hyltenstam, K. and Milani, T.M. (2012) Flerspråkighetens sociopolitiska och sociokulturella ramar. In K. Hyltenstam, M. Axelsson and I. Lindberg (eds) *Flerspråkighet – en forskningsöversikt* (pp. 17–152). Stockholm: Vetenskapsrådet.

Jacobsson, B. (1984) *Hur styrs förvaltningen?* Lund: Studentlitteratur.

Lainio, J. (2008) Ett segt begrepp i svensk tvåspråkighetsdebatt. In U. Börestam, S. Gröndahl and B. Straszer (eds) *Revitalisera mera!* Uppsala: Uppsala University.

Latour, B. (1986) Visualization and cognition. In H. Kuklick (ed.) *Knowledge and Society* (pp. 1–40). Greenwich: Jai.

Latour, B. (2004) Why has critique run out of steam? From matters of fact to matters of concern. *Critical Inquiry* 30 (2), 225–248.

Loman, B. (1974) *Språk och samhälle 2.* Lund: Gleerup.

Loman, B. (1975) Halvspråkighet eller papegojsvenska? *Nordisk minoritetsforskning* 4, 27–28.

Loman, B. (1978) Man kan inte skrämma folk till tvåspråkighet. *Invandrare och minoriteter* 3/4, 35–43.

Malmberg, B. (1964) *Språket och människan.* Stockholm: Aldus.

Martin-Jones, M. and Romaine, S. (1986) Semilingualism: A half-baked theory of communicative competence. *Applied Linguistics* 7 (1), 26–38.

Meagher, L., Lyall, C. and Nutley, S. (2008) Flows of knowledge, expertise and influence: A method for assessing policy and practice impacts from social science research. *Research Evaluation* 17 (3), 163–173.

Morgan, M.S. (2010) Travelling facts. In P. Howlett and M.S. Morgan (eds) *How Well Do Facts Travel?* (pp. 3–39). Cambridge: Cambridge University Press.

Öhman, S. (1981) Halvspråkighet som kastmärke. In K. Öberg (ed.) *Att leva med mångfalden* (pp. 216–227). Stockholm: Liber.

Pielke, R.A. (2007) *The Honest Broker.* Cambridge: Cambridge University Press.

Prop. 1975/67:118. *Om hemspråk för invandrarbarn.* Stockholm: Utbildningsdepartementet.

Ringbom, H. (1962) Tvåspråkigheten som forskningsobjekt. *Finsk Tidskrift* 6, 263–269.

Schwartz, D. (ed.) (1966) *Svenska minoriteter.* Stockholm: Aldus.

Skutnabb-Kangas, T. (1975) Vad är halvspråkighet? *Nordisk minoritetsforskning* 2, 12–14.

Skutnabb-Kangas, T. (1984 [1981]) *Bilingualism or Not: The Education of Minorities.* Clevedon: Multilingual Matters.

Skutnabb-Kangas, T. and Toukomaa, P. (1976) *Teaching Migrant Children's Mother-Tongue and Learning the Language of the Host Country in the Context of the Socio-Cultural Situation of the Migrant Family.* Geneva: UNESCO.

Slunga, N. (1965) *Staten och den finskspråkiga befolkningen i Norrbotten.* Luleå: Tornedalica.

SOU 1974:69. *Invandrarutredningen 3.* Stockholm: Arbetsmarknadsdepartementet.

Stolt, B. (1975a) Halvspråkighet och känslor. *Nordisk minoritetsforskning* 4, 24–26.

Stolt, B. (1975b) Om 'halvspråkighet' och 'språkens känslofunktion'. *Nordisk minoritetsforskning* 2 (1), 5–12.

Stroud, C. (1978) The concept of semilingualism. *Lund Working Papers in Linguistics* 16, 154–172.

Stroud, C. (2001) African mother-tongue programmes and the politics of language. *Journal of Multilingual and Multicultural Development* 22 (4), 339–355.

Stroud, C. (2004) Rinkeby Swedish and semilingualism in language ideological debates: A Bourdieuean perspective. *Journal of Sociolinguistics* 8 (2), 196–214.

Stroud, C. (2007) Bilingualism: Colonialism and postcolonialism. In M. Heller (ed.) *Bilingualism: A Social Approach* (pp. 25–49). London: Palgrave.

Stroud, C. (2010) A postliberal critique of language rights: Toward a politics of language for a linguistics of contact. In J. Petrovic (ed.) *International Perspectives on Bilingual Education* (pp. 195–221). Charlotte, NC: IAP.

Toukomaa, P. (1975) Om finska invandrarelevers språkutveckling och skolframgång i den svenska grundskolan. *Nordisk minoritetsforskning* 2 (2), 4–6.

Wande, E. (1977) Hansegård är ensidig. *Invandrare och minoriteter* 3/4, 44–51.

Wande, E. (1996) Tvåspråkighet eller halvspråkighet – det var frågan. In R. Raag and L.G. Larsson (eds) *Finsk-ugriska institutionen i Uppsala 1894–1994* (pp. 209–238). Uppsala: Uppsala University.

Wickström, M. (2015) Making the case for the mother-tongue: Ethnic activism and the emergences of a new policy discourse on the teaching of non-Swedish mother tongues in Sweden in the 1960s and 1970s. In M. Halonen, P. Ihalainen and T. Saarinen (eds) *Language Policies in Finland and Sweden: Interdisciplinary and Multi-sited Comparisons* (pp. 171–195). Bristol: Multilingual Matters.

Widgren, J. (1982) *Svensk invandrarpolitik.* Stockholm: Liber.

8 Turbulent Twitter and the Semiotics of Protest at an Ex-Model C School

Amy Hiss and Amiena Peck

Introduction

This chapter draws on linguistic citizenship as a theoretical framework when investigating a racially driven protest at Winterberry Girls' High School[1] (henceforth WBGHS), an all-girls school catering for the daughters of middle-class parents in Cape Town. In 2016 the learners' protest against alleged institutionalized racism at the school made its online debut on Twitter and swiftly led to rapid transformation in the language policy and processes of the school.

In this chapter, we demonstrate how semiotics of protest at the school (pictures, placards, school anthem and even the principal herself) was repackaged in novel ways by veteran Fallist Twitter users online. We explore how they created a new space for protest which was both multilingual and multimodal, and allowed for maximum engagement across the globe. Considering the vital role that tweets about the protest played online, we view the Fallist members as performing virtual 'acts of citizenship' (Isin, 2009, as cited in Stroud, 2015), a point expanded upon in the concluding section of this chapter.

First, we illustrate the wider context of decoloniality, the rise of Fallism and the timely protest at the school which together provide a multifaceted view of the pursuit of rights, agency and voice as it appeared on Twitter.

Decolonializing education

Decoloniality according to Ndlovu-Gatsheni (2015: 488) is a 'fairly modern concept built on the premise of dismantling power relations and conceptions of knowledge that foment the reproduction of racial, gender, and geo-political hierarchies and the ideologies imposed by white colonisers'. In South Africa it is specifically the marginalized children, who were 'born free', i.e. after the Apartheid era, who have thus had access to resources and knowledge systems (by attending ex-Model C schools) whom we explore. Already it has been noted that in situations where young black, coloured and Indian children have gained access to formerly white schools, these learners have been assimilated into the institution (as seen in the development of a 'white/European' accent for instance) while the school's educational policies and practices do not show any visible change (Carrim, 2003, 2006). While this practice of one-way assimilation has become commonplace, we wish to explore what happens when black learners who attend ex-Model C schools resist the hegemonic language and cultural practices at the school (compare Hiss & Peck, 2020).

Notably, decolonizing education was one of the primary aims laid forth in the newly drafted constitution of South Africa post-1994, with the inclusivity of African languages, and cultures part of Africanizing institutional policies. It is the perceived failure of the state to achieve this aim that was ferociously addressed by Fallist members during the period of 'MustFall' protests in South Africa. We draw on Linguistic Citizenship to explore how the protest was performed by Fallist members in what can be seen as the furthering of their pursuit for a decoloniality of the education sector in South Africa.

Fallism

The Fallism period initially began in 2015 when students at the University of Cape Town (UCT) protested against Cecil John Rhodes, a controversial colonial figure, whose statue was situated at the main entrance of the university. Students protested against what they saw as a daily reminder of reverence for the Apartheid and colonial regime and the continued institutional 'denial' of the black pain caused by the lauding of colonial figures such as Rhodes (compare Mpendukana & Stroud, 2018). This event made national headlines, and online platforms were soon buzzing with student-led decolonialization rhetoric. A distinct moment in this Rhodes saga was the throwing of human faeces at the statue – a clear sign of the disgust the statue and its continued status at the institution evoked. Facebook and Twitter were two important sites used to further the 'poo protest' against having Cecil John Rhodes's statue on campus and the hashtag #RhodesMustFall became a popular rallying cry for other young active individuals to show solidarity with the cause. In late 2015, when the University of Witwatersrand (Wits) announced an increase in student fees, Wit's students vocalized their concerns against this move using the hashtag #FeesMustFall. The MustFall suffix soon became used by political parties (to signal a vote of no confidence in the sitting president at the time Jacob Zuma), with #ZumaMustFall even gave rise to humorous comments by businesses calling for Zuma to stand down (#ZumaMustGo).

While the Wits protest served to index the economic burden felt by the students, it also laid bare white privilege at their institutions. The students bemoaned the fact that their cultures, languages and knowledge systems remained unrecognized and uncelebrated in the institutional environment – let alone in practice. In the same year, students at the University of the Western Cape (UWC) also took to social media using the hashtag #FreeEducation and #endoutsourcing. This was to place pressure on the government to finally put into practice the goals of trans-formation in education and improved economic structure as documented in the national constitution in 1994. While the Fallist context of online protest was sparked in 2015, it was not until the following year that schools in South Africa showed signs of unrest and protest. While the school that we studied is situated in Cape Town, there was a similar pro-test at another formerly white school in another province in South Africa two weeks earlier.

In August 2016, an all-girls ex-Model C high school in Pretoria made national headlines when black learners protested what they perceived as institutional racism. Learners spoke of having to comb their natural hair 'because it looked like a bird's nest' and were sternly discouraged from speaking their home languages (https://www.news24.com/news24/south-africa/news/black-girls-in-tears-at-pretoria-school-hair-protest-20160829).

Very soon, calls for decoloniality at the school emerged online with hashtags such as #StopRacismAtMilanGirlsHighSchool and #Zulaikha finding favour on Twitter. Milan Girls' High School, which was originally founded in 1902 and Winterberry Girls' High in 1960, have many common features, such as being located in an affluent area and catering for the children of middle to upper class parents. During Apartheid Winterberry Girls' High School primarily taught middle and upper class white English and Afrikaner girls. However, when Apartheid came to an end in 1994, Winterberry among other Model C[2] schools like Milan Girls High transi-tioned to being 'open schools'[3] allowing the admission of black, Indian and coloured learners. This change could be seen as a step forward in the bridging of separateness by offering institutional access to all racial groups in the country. At present, Winterberry is open to girls with different racial backgrounds; however, the majority of learners attending are black girls from middle-class-income households.

Despite Winterberry's explicitly outlining an institutional ethos pro-moting diversity and multilingualism in their school's Code of Conduct,[4] learners protested that school practices told quite a different story.

The September 2016 protest began after some learners laid extensive complaints in a letter of memorandum to the school authorities declaring the banning of African language(s) at the school and the stern (often humili-ating) and disparaging comments from educators regarding their natural African hairstyles as unconstitutional. Having had little success, these learners turned to the Western Cape Education Department to take the matter further, but reportedly were not offered an adequate response. The learners began physical protests on school grounds in September 2016 using placards with bold red and black writing on them, some of which read 'Africans fighting to be African in Africa' and 'My hair, my culture'. The learners also openly lamented what they saw as the hypocrisy of the school's anthem, entitled 'The truth we will proclaim'. The learners' posters revealed their disassociation with the anthem as they argued that they were not free to celebrate their culture and language. Their anger was also seen in the destruction of the school demerit book, where speaking isiXhosa, the language of the majority of learners was explicitly listed as a transgression. Learners caught speaking isiXhosa (even during breaks), had this 'transgression' dated, marked and signed in their demerit book and had to attend detention. Parallels between the Apartheid's passbook or dompas[5] and the demerit were drawn in the online protests. What's more, learners asserted their school principal, Catherine Brewster was the main enforcer of racialized practices at the school and insisted that she (the principal, who also happened to be a white female, step down from her position).

What we focus on in this study is what happened when self-identified Fallist members took on the protest on Twitter. We focus on trending hashtags that were supported by images and videos of learners holding placards, chanting and using their natural hair as a form of activism. Each of the trending hashtags at the time, which were #StopRacis mAtWBGHS, #thetruthwillproclaim and #BrewsterMustFall, played a symbolic role in creating an uproar online. We argue that the online performance of the learners' protest by Fallist members resulted in some marked change at the school: racial rules were removed from the school code of conduct, the school principal resigned at the end of the 2016 school year and isiXhosa was introduced a subject offered to black learners. However, despite the online exposure of the protest and all the changes it created at the school, as Hiss and Peck (2020) show in their analysis of the draft Code of Conduct post-1996, it is questionable just how much of a shift there was in the school's ethos as a result of the protest.

At the heart of the learners' protest was the desire to be accepted as rightful learners at the school. We use linguistic citizenship as the framework to unpack the contention by black learners that there was no equity across the race groups at the school. In particular, we are interested in the performance of the learners' identities by Fallist members in their bid to further the call to decolonize the curriculum on Twitter.

Twitter and hashtags

Twitter emerged in 2006 but established itself as socializing platform by 2011. It was mainly considered a microblogging site with users limited to a 140-character restriction when instant messaging, chatting, or posting a status, all of which are known as tweets. Later, smartphones made it possible to use 280 characters. Twitter was among the first platforms to provide a system that allowed users to follow people they were interested in and vice versa. In recent times, however, it has become a popular plat-form for users to express their life, activities, opinions, or give short status updates on what users are doing, where they are, how they are feeling, or provide links to other sites (Java *et al.*, 2007). More importantly, Twitter allows users to interact with events or people that they are not remotely close or learn about the world through another's eyes, making it an excel-lent platform for protest. One of the most innovating developments of Twitter due to growth in users since 2011 is the creation of new jargon with symbols. The @ symbol can be seen as a means to identify users, which users could use to communicate directly to each other or refer to each other in comments (MacArthur, 2019). The hashtag (#) symbol is used as a referencing label led by a combination of characters preceded by the hash (#) symbol. The function of a hashtag is meant to make it easier to find messages that carry a specific theme or content.

Moreover, the hashtag has 'developed into a "community building lin-guistic activity" fostering the creation of communities of people bound by their being interested in the same content and wishing to read and share information about it' (Callefi, 2015: 46). It has also made its appearance in the physical world as it is possible to see it on sweaters (e.g. #Selfie), mugs and other any printable space, such as placards as seen at WBGHS. People even use hashtags in everyday conversation, for example, 'life is #hectic'. Clearly, hashtags are popular as they have currency in a range of materials and spaces such as attire, in conversations or on social media. We are inter-ested here in the lives, communities and movements which the Fallist brought together when disseminating information about the protest through hashtags. It is for this reason that we analyse the use of three popular hashtags used in the study to uncover the issues raised at the school and their connection to global campaigns such as Black Lives Matter.

Theoretical Framework

This study operationalizes linguistic citizenship as a theoretical frame-work which allows for a fine-grained analysis of language and modalities used in Twitter posts by Fallist members online. We argue that various modalities are selected because of their own histories, multiplicities of uses and affordances. Linguistic Citizenship capturing these important distinctions. Stroud (2001: 4) explains that it is a 'fundamental means to understand language through the lens of citizenship and participatory democracy'. Later, he adds that '... if we are to engage seriously with the lives of others, an imperative is reconceptualising language in ways that can promote a diversity of voice and contribute to a mutuality and reci-procity of engagement across difference' (Stroud, 2018: 17).

The case in point is the practice of treating the use of African lan-guages, specifically isiXhosa, as a transgressive act on school grounds. It is this prohibition and other restrictive school rules regarding hair and comportment which led to the protest at the school. Considering the difference in the way the three main languages (English, Afrikaans and Xhosa) were used, lauded or denied, Linguistic Citizenship allows us to address the materiality of language in linguistic minority groups that suffer both structural and representational discrimination (Stroud, 2001). In the case of the school, language use is clearly an important element of the protest, with users on Twitter touting this 'transgression' to illustrate the need for decolonization of education. In this regard, we are interested in the variety of semiotic means in which Twitter users express their agency, voice and participation in their tweets during the protest (compare Williams & Stroud, 2015). Linguistic Citizenship is vital to our understanding of the online protest as it highlights 'how non-mainstream speakers wrestle control from political institutions of the state by using their language over many modalities and giving new meaning and repurposing to reflect the social and political issues that affect them' (Williams & Stroud, 2015: 6). In this regard, we use Linguistic Citizenship to rethink the relationships of power underlying language and modalities on Twitter.

The citizenship part of Linguistic Citizenship is also critical to our understanding of the protest and the role that the Fallist members played in its ultimate success. Stroud and Williams (2017) painstakingly clarifies that citizenship needs to be read in a wider, more nuanced manner. Just as 'Linguistic' does not only include language per se, 'Citizenship' refers to much more than geography and official status; it refers to the agency and voice that an individual may have in and of themselves. Drawing on Isin (2009, as cited in Stroud, 2015: 24) citizenship occurs when 'new actors articulate claims for justice through new sites that involve multiple and overlapping scales of rights and obligations (...). The manifold acts through which new actors as claimants emerge in new sites and scales are becoming the new objects of investigation'.

We argue that the protesting learners experienced less agency and voice on school grounds because of the restrictions placed on them by the institution. This is apparent as learners were forced to remain within school grounds, in effect 'diminishing the efficacy of the protest'. Thus, while the protest began on school grounds, it is the tweets posted by Fallist Twitter users that are explored as timely 'acts of citizenship' which Isin explains as 'deeds by which actors constitute themselves (and others) as subjects of rights' (Isin, 2009: 371). This clearly is the case with Fallist Twitter users furthering the cause of the learners online. In this study we focus primarily on multimodal strategies used by Fallist Twitter users as they disseminated information about the protest to a larger, more diverse audience online. We see their acts as mutually constitutive of their established stance regarding decoloniality, exclusion and agency in education. We particularly discuss the manner in which Fallist Twitter users refashion the learners protest through concepts such as resemiotization and recontextualization.

Iedema (2003: 41) describes resemiotization as a means of observing how meaning making shifts within different contexts and practices or from one stage of practice to another. Leppänen *et al.* (2014: 116) assert that resemiotization 'focuses on the examination of the unfolding and rearticulation of meaning across modes and modalities, and from some groups of people to others'. In addition, it emphasizes the need for socio-historical exploration and understanding of the complex processes which constitute and surround meaning-making. Iedema (2003: 49) emphasizes that resemiotization allows us to pose supra-logogenetic questions about how displays or representations come about as semiotic constructs through the deliberations of all actors involved, i.e. resemiotization is a 'kind of perspective which is important for revealing, describing and understanding representation as a truly multimodal construct, embodying not merely the sounds and images which we see, but also all the semiotics, the coincidences and the compromises which played a role in its inception'. In linking this to the protest of WBGH, we contend that Fallist intervention played a significant role in ensuring that the learners' grievances were given wider exposure. This was done by utilizing their own modes and modalities of articulating the learner's experiences and in turn recontextualizing the same use of semiotic resources (hashtags, images, posts etc.) to recreate the online representation of the WBGHS protest. Importantly, while the Fallist generally used their own modes and modalities to represent the learners' protest, they also draw the viewers' attention to their own activist cause. They can thus be said to have added to their decolonial vision through the WBGHS protest.

Recontextualization as Linell (1998: 116) states, occurs when 'words and concepts circulate, and are circulated, across domains of practice and knowledge; words and ideas wander from mouth to mouth, and across minds, texts, and discourses, in an intercrossing of contexts and positions'. Brannen (2004) echoes that recontextualization examines how meaning shifts and changes from one context to another, and how meanings are attached to the objects and processes involved when moving from one context to another. Therefore, this chapter explores the resemiotization and recontextualization practices of Fallist intervention in the learner's protest. In addition, the (re)contextualizing of black girls' bodies within a white institutional space contributes to the historicity of racialization in South Africa and constitutes the claim of institutional racism which Fallist activist highlight while at the same time drawing viewers in on the larger decolonial cause constructed through their previous representation of online activism. One example is that of the corporeal site of protest, i.e. the use of the body to act out the protest through chanting, dancing, carrying slogans and so forth. One way in which we draw in the body is through the notion of 'skinscapes'. Originating from linguistic landscape studies, Peck and Stroud (2015: 134) define skinscapes as 'the material stuff of identity and affect as a corporeal linguistic landscape ... a collection of inscriptions in place. Just as a linguistic landscape can be carried on placards and t-shirts, so can landscapes be carried on the surface of skin'. We observe how Fallists create online posts in tandem with multimodal representations of the learners chanting, singing and so on and how they are refashioned to draw viewers in on the historical suffering of black bodies in white spaces and black bodies within the education domain.

More specifically, we see how the Fallist members interrupt the status quo (Pinchevski, 2001) and where learners' sense of selves was refashioned and repackaged for an online audience. This leg of the protest was integral to the '... deconstruction of dominant voices and more equitable linguistic engagement ...' (Stroud & Williams, 2017: 18) at the school.

Methodology

The data collected for this paper are part of a larger qualitative study that draws on multimodal data sourced from Twitter. All of the data were located online without the need for passwords or registration, thus in online public space. In order to analyse how different modes are in fact resemiotized versions of the learners' protest at the school, we deliberately selected three different types of data: (1) semiotics of surveillance and punishment, (2) bodies in protest and (3) emergence and popularity of trending hashtags. Considering hashtags as an important semiotic resource of the protest, we draw on three of the most popular hashtags that were trending at the time of the protest that exemplified the themes above, specifically #thetruthwewillproclaim (referencing the school's anthem), #brewstermustfall (referencing the WBGHS principal, Ms Brewster) and #StopRacismAtWBGHS (referencing the school itself).

Twitter: A multimodal site of protest

This section overviews posts and images emerging on the hashtags that sparked the protest online. Of interest is the engagement with online users by self-identified Fallist members who used the hashtags to further the learners' protest, to serve their call for wider decolonization and to link the protests to larger global movements such as Black Lives Matter. The section also highlights how Fallist members exercised virtual 'acts of citizenship' on behalf of the learners.

What msunery is this?

In Figure 8.1, we see a tweet consisting of a text question, two hashtags and three images. The post itself had at the time been retweeted[6] 404 times and received 93 likes. What follows is an analysis that draws on how the school surveilled and punished learners through its 'demerit' system.

Figure 8.1 'What msunery is this?'

The post itself was uploaded by a self-identified Fallist[7] member, renamed LMWOW. The high number of retweets is arguably due to the large number of twitter followers that the user had at the time (approximately 2154 followers). The tone of the post seems both appalled and angry. The tweet reads 'A learner was punished for speaking Xhosa like what msunery is this?' The subject of the post is 'a learner', in this way constructing an image of a child of school going age. We can deduce that this faceless and nameless learner was someone that was denied the right to speak isiXhosa at the school. While the race of the learner is not explicitly mentioned, we can assume that the learner is black as she has isiXhosa in her repertoire.[8]

What LMWOW has highlighted is one of the most pressing issues that some learners were protesting, i.e. the ban on speaking their home languages on school grounds, a rule which extended beyond school if learners were in school uniform. Learners at the school were expressly instructed at school to watch out and listen for 'bad behaviour' as it was defined in the school's Code of Conduct. This tweet ends with the angry

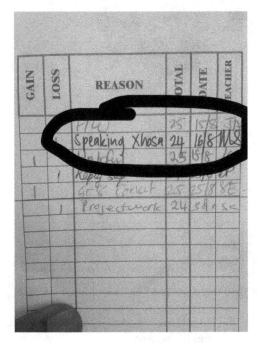

Figure 8.1(a) 'The isiXhosa "offence"'

Figure 8.1(b) 'Front cover of the demerit book'

Figure 8.1(c) 'Torn pages of demerit book'

red-face emoji at the end adding texture to the verbal message and show-ing that the user was angry.

The image labelled (Figure 8.1) shows the post as it appeared online with three composite pictures i.e. (8.1(a)) the Xhosa 'offence' (left), (8.1(b)) the cover of the demerit book (top, right) and (8.1(c)) torn pages of the demerit book (bottom, right). Circled in black (either by the learner or the Fallist Twitter user) is the offence – 'speaking Xhosa' – followed by three columns specifically for 'demerit' points, date of offence and signature of the teacher. As stated elsewhere, learners caught transgressing had to go to detention or submit to some other punitive measure imposed on them. Importantly, while the teachers would surveil the learners to identify any transgressions that occurred in class, it was learners' peers who policed them during school breaks, thereby performing a part of the school rules. Importantly, learners with English as their mother tongue were distinctly advantaged as their lack of competence in African languages meant that they were most unlikely to commit this 'offence'. Moreover, we see that the Code of Conduct accommodated Afrikaans speakers as well as it was a language taught as a subject at the school. In effect, this meant that only black learners who spoke African languages would be negatively impacted. The question 'What msunery is this?' was very effective as 'msunery' was used frequently at the time to mean 'nonsense'. Msnunery comes from the word 'msunu'[9] and when used online it indicates exasperation and incre-dulity at something or someone. Moreover, by using the word 'msunery', the user was able to tap into the trending hashtag #msunery, which first emerged as a response to all the corruption and race hatred in South Africa. This made the post both informative and 'on trend'.

The rhetorical question further acts to elicit online reactions. 'Like what msunery is this?' not only conveys anger but empathizes the plight of learners who were prohibited from speaking their own home language at school. The post clearly sees the prohibition of Xhosa as unconstitutional and unethical and implicitly points to the vulnerability of black learners in this formerly white school.

Reading the post in its entirety, i.e. the 'msunery' comment, the angry emoji face and the images of the demerit book, viewers of the tweet can quickly grasp the struggles faced by learners at the school. The Fallist were able to demonstrate the colonial power exercised through the school's language policy.

Apart from the page displaying the isiXhosa 'offence' – Figure 8.1(a) – there are two other smaller images in Figure 8.1. Figure 8.1(b) is a picture of the front cover of the book, with a finger strategically concealing the name of the learner. This was most likely done to ensure they did not suffer retribution or victimization. The dark skin colour of the finger covering the name of the learner is another subtle form solidarity among protesters of colour.

Figure 8.1(c) also shows the booklet, but here it has been torn to shreds. Placed in a white plastic bag, it appears to represent garbage, and may signal the learners' discarding the system of surveillance and punishment altogether. This representation of torn up pieces of the demerit book is also reminiscent of the tearing apart and burning of the 'dompas' (dumb pass) during the civil protests in the 1960s, a point discussed in more detail further on.

As the demerit book has the name of each learner and becomes the responsibility of the bearer, this book can be viewed as a legal document or contract signed by learners, indicating their acceptance of the document that learners had to carry with them all the time. In the next section we comment on the impact on the learners' identities.

Black hair matter

Figure 8.2 and Figure 8.3 show (a) how the protest was tied to well-known and successful campaigns such as Black Lives Matter and (b) how the learners' bodies were used as modes of protest.

In Figure 8.2, we see an initial post by Rhodes Must Fall. It reads, 'Photos of the placards are heart-breaking' followed by the name of the school and the popular #StopRacismAtWBGHS.[10] We also see three different signboards (placards) held up by learners. We know that the carriers of these signs are the learners themselves as their blue uniform can be seen in the image. The visible uniforms frame the sign thus contextualizing it both verbally and multimodally. While only the finger of the protestor was shown in Figure 8.1(b), here the whole body is constructed by the school uniform – semiotic of protest, which we argue enhances the contextual credibility of the protest.

Figure 8.2 'They must go drop off their culture in Europe...'

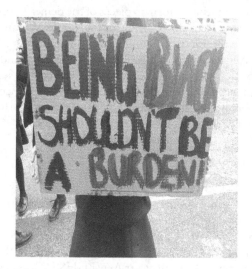

Figure 8.2(a) 'Being black shouldn't be a burden'

The initial post by Rhodes Must Fall consists of three images. The first (Figure 8.2(a)) uses the words 'Being black shouldn't be a burden' (written in capital letters), Figure 8.2(b) uses the words 'They tell us to leave our cultures at home' (in capital letters) and Figure 8.2(c) the words 'Black hair matter' (in capital letters). The signs in Figure 8.2(a) and Figure 8.2(c) seem

Figure 8.2(b) 'They tell us to leave our cultures at home'

Figure 8.2(c) 'Black Hair Matter'

to have been written in red and black paint while Figure 8.2(b) appears to have been written with a black board marker, thus making it more clearly a personal narrative of the learners' lived experiences at the school. While red paint has been used to write the words 'black' and 'burden', red paint has been used to write all the words in Figure 8.2(c). Significantly, black and red are colours strongly associated with Fallist protest movements (see Oliver, 2019) and the capitals indicate black pain.

Here we see the identity of the learners (as black) being clearly positioned as the problem at the school. Their identity as black is seen as an encumbrance that they have to carry with them. The idea that being black is a problem is reinforced by the image in Figure 8.2(b) in which the learners state that they were told to leave their (black) cultures at home. The act of protesting against this school is, therefore, seen as having multiple levels, not only is it against the strict prohibition on speaking African languages, but it is also the outright rejection of their identity, their culture and even their phenotype. This last point is clearly demonstrated by the sign 'Black Hair Matter' which highlights the plight of black learners who were said to be banned from wearing their hair naturally (see Hiss & Peck, 2020 for a discussion of grooming at WBGHS). It is clear that the RhodesMustFall Twitter user has skilfully resemiotized the protest in a manner that users can quickly ascertain what the protest was railing against. 'Black Hair Matter' also sounds very similar to the better-known movement, Black Lives Matter. It currently has 820,000 followers on Twitter and is a household campaign name in virtual space. The two movements also have the same acronym (BLM), which means that by using that acronym or by including the hashtag Black Lives Matter, Twitter users drive traffic to this specific protest.

When Sibongile retweeted this post, she added, 'They must go drop off their culture in Europe maybe bazobuya benenqondo [they will come back with some sense]'. The tone of this post appears angry. In it, Sibongile declares that 'they' – most likely referring to white school educators – should 'drop off their culture in Europe'. She then goes on to state in isiXhosa, 'they will come back with some sense'. Here, there is an implicit reference to the advent of colonialism as colonizers came from Europe. There is also a call by SibongileM for these white teachers to return to their homeland. It is clear that 'home' is referenced quite differently. On the one hand, learners are told to 'leave our culture at home' while white educates are told to go back home (to Europe). It is, therefore, white people that are constructed as out-of-place at the school.

The decision to mix English and isiXhosa is not uncommon on Twitter. However, in this post, it signals that the post is most likely meant for isiXhosa speakers – presumably Twitter users who identify as black. The inclusion of isiXhosa in the post may also be SibongileM's way of performing her agency as an individual who can use her African languages as a symbol of power and importance.

In Figure 8.3, there is an image of three happy WBGHS learners. The post, written entirely in capitals, states:

'WE MADE HISTORY (yellow power emoji hand sign followed by red heart sign)

WE DEMAND THAT SHE STEPS DOWN' (full stop)

Figure 8.3 'We Made History'

The use of only capital letters is akin to shouting in real life, so the LelethuS appear quite happy and unabashed. The 'she' that LelethuS refers to is the principal, a particularly contentious person who was summarily given her own hashtag #BrewsterMustFall, which is discussed later. Nevertheless, the user assumes that the reader would be aware of the unfolding protest and would by now already know who 'she' is. The use of deictic pronouns shows an investment in a continued narrative which the viewer has been drawn into, indicating the successful dissemination of the saga online. Moreover, the 'we', in tandem with the yellow emoji and red heart is symbolic of the multiplicity of actors involved in the MustFall movement and how the learners' distress has become part of the larger activist cause. Thus, the learners are no longer operating on their own but are backed by the entire Fallist community.

The use of the closed fist also has intertextual links with the anti-Apartheid struggle movement, which was also used by the Fallist during their nationwide protests. Before this, the closed raised fist was also an unequivocal sign of a call for emancipation during Apartheid. This became an icon when the first democratic President, Nelson Mandela, was freed from prison. Hence, the raised closed fist has a particularly significant role in the fight against racial injustice in the country. The heart emoji next to the fist denotes a deep commitment to this struggle, with the full stop at the end of the second line stylistically indexing the end of the saga for the learners.

The girl on the left in Figure 8.3 is holding a placard reading, 'My hair, my culture' and the other is holding a placard reading 'Africans fighting to be African in Africa'. These placards index the learners' need to be able to wear their hair naturally as it is part of who they are. Just as the placard is a semiotic of the protest, the learners' hair becomes a sign of the protest. Similar to Peck and Williams' (2018) argument that memories and trauma can reside in the tattooed skin of coloured men, we contend that natural black hair is layered with trauma as it was historically depicted as barbaric and uncivilized.

The second placard is also important as it indexes the struggle these learners faced in being who they are in their own country. We could also reframe this as the learners need to be students that are accepted as such by their own school. The #truthwewillproclaim is also quite significant here, as it is the learners' 'truth' of being African and Black and being able to wear their hair naturally that these learners are proclaiming. It there-fore serves as a double entendre, referencing both the school's anthem, on the one hand, and the protest, on the other.

At the time when 'The truth we will proclaim' was simply the school's anthem located in the learners' demerit book, it was seemingly infallible, and learners were unable to challenge this artefact of power at the school. However, we argue that the properties of the anthem were irrevocably disrupted when resemiotized as a hashtag as the reference to the anthem became a tool to reveal irony and evoke the ire of supporters. It points to the contradictions within it to highlight identity construction at the school and to interrogate it. The anthem is no longer a burden to the learners, but a tool which can enable learners to seek clarity and hold the school to account. It is also a means that learners' can use to declare the subjective 'truth' about their own identities while taking a jab at the school's institu-tional ideology.

The life of hashtags

In Figure 8.2, the hashtag #StopRacismAtWBGHS was one of three that highlighted the protest online. The hashtag #StopRacism mediatizes racial, political, economic and institutionalized debates rooted in South African society. This hashtag can be seen as an adaptable prefix, which when it is coupled with a cause, e.g. 'At WBGHS', immediately highlights a specific racial issue and draws public attention to it.

In this way, we see how hashtags have lives beyond their origins (i.e. the #StopRacism). This can also be viewed as the 'stickiness' and 'persistence' (Romero et al., 2011) of the modified hashtag, which, by joining two clauses constitutes a new life for the hashtag online. Romero et al. (2011: 695) describe 'stickiness' as '... the probability of adoption [of one hashtag] based on the number of "exposures" and "persistence" as the extent to which 'repeated exposures to a hashtag continue to have significant marginal effects' be aligned with the topic of the hashtag itself, with hashtags on politically controversial topics showing a particularly high degree of persistence (Romero *et al.*, 2011: 696). One way in which the hashtag #StopRacismAtWBGHS demonstrates a high degree of persistence is through Fallist intervention. Figure 8.1 shows LMWOW's post, the first ever post with the hashtag #StopRacismAtWBGHS. This hashtag marked the protest as not only as a cause for concern generally, but also as further enhancing the overarching mandate of the Fallist movement, i.e. to fight against discriminatory practices to effect change. A mutually beneficial synergistic relationship between the learners and the Fallist activists is shown clearly: both are seen as working towards a decoloniality of pedagogy in South Africa, albeit on a different scale. The post also suggests that the protest by the young learners can be viewed as another layer of crisis which Fallism intends to challenge. In Figure 8.2, SibongileM, who appears to be one of the members in the community following the #StopRacismAtWBGHS, retweets a post created by Rhodes Must Fall. This highlights the strategy used by Fallist activist to give voice to the protesting black learners. In this way, the cause grows through persistence (Romero *et al.*, 2011) in using #StopRacismAtWBGHS and its link to Fallism in South Africa.

Moreover, Figure 8.2 shows that the post created by SibongileM is supported by a collection of images of the learners in protest. The images show the learners holding up placards: 'Being black shouldn't be a burden', 'They tell us to leave our cultures at home' and 'Black Hair Matter'.

It can be argued that the image with the 'Black Hair Matter' placard on it draws on the global campaign, Black Lives Matter, although the use of characters is not preceded by the hashtag symbol: the use of 'black' and 'matter' links the placard to the Black Lives Matter campaign. This was clearly used to give additional exposure to the learners' protest through the extended social media networks that it had. In similar vein, Fallism in South Africa can be said to have gained its momentum by linking its cause to decoloniality within the South African context, while at the same time joining forces with the larger global movement Black Lives Matters. The fact that #StopRacismAtWBGHS had its own visibility and established community (both of existing community and incoming members) further mediatized the matter at the school and to some extent, allowed the protest to be viewed multimodally and apart from the mainstream national media, which had significant gatekeeper ability at the time. Here we see how the Fallist activists, by tapping into their pre-existing semiotics of online protest against increased tertiary tuition fees, were able to adopt, elevate and ultimately shape the successful end of the protest. The interwoven relationships between the many stakeholders in this protest will be discussed in the next section.

Discussion

The impetus that Twitter gave to swift, tangible and necessary change for learners at WBGHS showed its potential power. The learners' online protest was demonstrably assisted by self-identified Fallist who, by helping the learners, also furthered their campaign to decolonize education in South Africa. This type of synergist collaboration would not have been possible had the learners not created 'material' for their protest (videos, images, placards etc.) and became the material for the protest themselves (e.g. by wearing their hair naturally). Online exposure by Fallist users, who were key individuals of a greater online activist campaign, were able to provide the necessary exposure and pressure to ultimately influence the pedagogical practices at the school.

We argue that, had the protest continued to be centralized at the school, the voices of the learners may well have been drowned out through the channelling of larger (more mainstream) media outlets. In this case, we suggest that the learners' protest was successful because it was rese-miotized and refashioned by Fallists members to make it more effective, trendy and shareable online. We contend that the Fallist were able to mould conventional semiotics to fit into virtual space and hence provide it with more affordances. This stretching and reshaping of the learners' semiotics of protest changed the lifespan, look and appeal of the protest – hence we see that the Fallist were able to provide an important agentic force from outside of the institutional domain.

Some of the injustices suffered by black learners at the school were: (1) reminiscent of Apartheid language planning, a language, in this case English, became a language of prestige and the language of education; this was bolstered by the punitive measures set in place for speaking African languages at the school; (2) embodied/internalized exclusion, specifically when considering the manner in which black girls' bodies were viewed, judged, disparaged and ultimately deemed unacceptable in their natural form; and (3) the demerit book became an artefact of surveillance and exclusion. While the demerit book may not have been created to regulate black learners per se, it was nonetheless the perceived outcome. And some learners responded to it (by tearing it to shreds and placing it into a plastic bag), it has clear links to the fight against the 'dompas'. For instance, both the demerit book and the dompas were implemented in a white dominant space, both shared an authority asserted over black people, and the behaviours expected in white spaces. In this instance, the demerit book and the dompas set out clear instructions. This is evident in the way in which black individuals could use a white space provided they comport themselves correctly; thus, sustaining an ideal space in which the black people could not influence change, but only assimilate or suffer punitive consequences (compare Fanon, 2009).

Notwithstanding all the explicit injustices involved, perhaps the most sinister impact was that on their identity as women in a post-apartheid society, with structural racism still very much at play. In this case, the long-term impact of the demerit book and the institutional rules used to chastise, punish and reject black bodies at the school (Carrim, 2009;

Thompson, 2009). Clearly, this is an important period in young girls' lives when they develop into the type of adults they wish to become and gain a clearer picture of what their position in society will be and ultimately how they will raise their children (Thompson, 2009). We argue that the demerit book went a long way to pushing an agenda of assimilation with the dominant white English group, with little to no significant change to the structural legacy of Apartheid.

The #truthwewillproclaim was also an important cog in the semiotics of protest. In the first instance, the school claimed to build learners' confidence in being 'who they truly are'. However, the learners in question were simultaneously tasked with adopting the identity of the school to be accepted. This tension between the school's assertion that learners should be comfortable with who they are (their identity) while not being black is the challenge that the learners faced. In light of this contradiction, we argue that the academic space of WBGHS at that time had not made significant changes to integrate black learner's post-1994 and we argue that the school's policy indexed a greater plan of moulding a new middle-class black elite which could exist alongside their white counterparts. Soudien (2004: 111) explains this phenomenon by expressing the view that 'the story of education in South Africa is essentially, in these terms, a story of reconfiguration of dominance in relation to race, class, gender and language dominance. Dominant practices have adjusted to the contingencies, but *the presumptions upon which they have been premised have remained unchanged'* (original emphasis).

In this way, we see that learners with a black skin were accepted at the school, but at the same time were meticulously groomed to look and sound as white as possible. We argue that this is consistent with the assertion made by Harber and Mncube (2011: 233) that education can be harmful when '…learners are not protected [at the school] and the schools actually perpetrate symbolic violence on the learner'. Case in point, the use of isiXhosa, an official South African language as well as a home language/mother tongue for many of the learners is penalized. This we see as an example of the symbolic harm inflicted on the learners. In South Africa, the Apartheid government used hair tests to separate racial groups. The 'pencil test', i.e. involved placing a pencil in the person's hair to see if it got stuck there. If it did, they would not only be publicly shamed, but they would be placed in the 'undesirable' category of 'black'. To capture the present-day stigma of having hair that is 'thick' or 'wild' can be seen as conflict which black learners faced when they enter the school. The importance placed on learners' hair was made explicit in the sign (Figure 8.3) 'My hair, my culture'. We see how their struggle emanated from the Code of Conduct which meticulously detailed width, length and colour of braids, and placed restrictions on comportment and the use of cultural adornments. These corporeal norms for black girls can be seen as invisible shackles that these learners wore each day. So, when they started protesting, they did so in every unbraided hair follicle, loud voices and struggle songs. We cannot overstate how important the corporeal body was to this protest. These black learners were constrained by the school and, had it not been for the exposure online, the outcome may have been vastly different. In a very real sense then, the learners' decision to leave their hair uncombed and in its natural state was a corporeal semiotic of protest. This worked in tandem with the many other signs of protest – tweets by Fallist members, trending hashtags and emotive images.

Concluding Thoughts

In this chapter we have employed Linguistic Citizenship to explore agency, voice and other modes of participatory aid by Fallist members as they sought to rally support for the plight of black learners at WBGHS. We see that their tweets included anti-Apartheid symbolism, hashtags emanating from the Fallism movement itself, e.g. #MustFall, the refashioning of images of learners with natural hair, and code-switching between English and Xhosa. Following Isin (2009, as cited in Stroud 2015), we recognize that the Fallist tweets are in fact 'acts of citizenship' aimed at legitimizing black learners at the school. By doing so we can better understand the vulnerable position that the black learners found themselves in and the significance of timely intervention by Fallist members.

In many ways, the learners' struggles may have remained localized at the school with little recourse seen in the failure of their initial attempts at school, then at provincial level. The reason for these failures could be because the school was not guilty of doing anything unconstitutional. Two languages were offered and used at school (English and Afrikaans), and guidelines were provided for hair grooming and attire in keeping with a notion of an 'esteemed' school culture. From the outside looking in, the school was not in any way infringing on the learners' rights and this is what made the role of independent protesters vital. Unlike the pressure that incoming black middle-class parents may have endured to 'maintain' the character of the school and endure restrictions on their children's language use and culture in a bid to 'fit in', the Fallist refused to comply.

To conclude we argue that Linguistic Citizenship reveals the inadequacy of a liberal and inclusive education policy when white middle-class sensibilities (values) are systematically entrenched and resistant to transformation. At the same time, it indexes the need for an external, force on an online platform far away from the school, but close enough for public outcry to effect change. What we see is a perfect storm of tweets giving voice to young black learners who demanded more than just the recognition of their language and culture; they wanted their legitimacy as learners at the school to be recognized, inclusive of their languages, skin colour, and culture.

Notes

(1)   Reference to Winterberry Girls High School, WBGHS, #StopRacismAtWBGHS. and the principal's names are all pseudonyms created by the authors.

(2)   These refer to formerly whites only schools that were primarily funded by a body of parents and alumni. Winterberry is further presented as a former Model C school.

(3)   Refers to whites only schools that voted to have an open policy, admitting black, Indian and coloured learners. This was in line with transformative measures taken in education in 1990 as a step to creating a single non-racialized education system.

(4)   This is a school policy that provides guidelines to learners on how to behave, general discipline rules and appearance and dress code. The school policy claimed to be harnessing diversity and multilingualism, but instead banned the use of African languages and introduced strict monitoring of black girls' hair and bodily comportment.

(5)   The dompas was a reference book that controlled the mobility of black people in white areas. Failure to present this book to the police resulted in physical punishment or a hefty fine.

(6)   A retweet is when a post is shared by another twitter user. This information would then be shared with all their followers. When a twitter is shared many times over it is said to have gone 'viral'.

(7)   Details have been removed.

(8)   Language and race is still very much a thing in SA with blacks still speaking African languages, and coloured, English and Afrikaans and whites, English, and Afrikaans mainly. So, while there are some mixings, for the most part the language-race relationship has remain unchanged since apartheid ended.

(9)   It is a colloquial term used by isiXhosa and isiZulu speakers as an insult or to create humour of something ironic. It translates into 'anus'.

(10)   This post was retweeted 60 times and had 23 likes. Once it was retweeted by SibongileM, it then started its count of retweets again.

References

Brannen, M.Y. (2004) When Mickey loses face: Recontextualization, semantic fit, and the semiotics of foreignness. *Academy of Management Review* 29 (4), 593–616.

Carrim, N. (2003) Race and inclusion in South African education. *IDS Bulletin* 34 (1), 20–28.

Carrim, N. (2006) Human rights and the construction of identities in South African education. PhD thesis, University Witwatersrand, Johannesburg.

Carrim, N. (2009) Hair: Markings on the body and the logic of discrimination. *Perspectives in Education* 27 (4), 375–384.

Caleffi, P.M. (2015) The 'hashtag': A new word or a new rule? *SKASE Journal of Theoretical Linguistics* 12 (2), 48–69.

Fanon, F. (2009) The fact of blackness. *Theories of Race and Racism: A Reader* (pp. 257–266). London: Routledge.

Harber, C. and Mncube, V. (2011) Is schooling good for the development of society? The case of South Africa. *South African Journal of Education* 31 (2), 223–245.

Hiss, A. and Peck, A. (2020) 'Good schooling' in a race, gender, and class perspective: The reproduction of inequality at a former Model C school in South Africa. *International Journal of the Sociology of Language* 264, 25–47.

Iedema, R. (2003) Multimodality, resemiotization: Extending the analysis of discourse as multi-semiotic practice. *Visual Communication* 2 (1), 29–57.

Java, A., Song, X., Finin, T. and Tseng, B. (2007) Why we twitter – understanding microblogging: Usage and communities. In *Proceedings of the 9th WebKDD and 1st SNA-KDD 2007 workshop on Web Mining and Social Network Analysis* (56–65). New York: ACM.

Leppänen, S., Kytölä, S., Jousmäki, H., Peuronen, S. and Westinen, E. (2014) Entextualization and resemiotization as resources for identification in social media. In P. Seargeant and C. Tagg (eds) *The Language of Social Media* (pp. 112–136). London: Palgrave Macmillan.

Linell, P. (1998) Discourse across boundaries: On recontextualizations and the blending of voices in professional discourse. *Text-Interdisciplinary Journal for the Study of Discourse* 18 (2), 143–158.

MacArthur, A. (2019) The real history of Twitter, in brief. See https://www.lifewire.com/history-of-twitter-3288854 (accessed May 2019).

Mpendukana, S. and Stroud, C. (2018) Of monkeys, shacks and loos: Changing times, changing places. *Making Sense of People and Place in Linguistic Landscapes* (pp. 183–200). Bloomsbury Publishing.

Ndlovu-Gatsheni, S.J. (2015) Decoloniality as the future of Africa. *History Compass* 13 (10), 485–496.

Oliver, C.F. (2019) A platform to protest: A virtual ethnography of the UWC Fees WILL FALL Linguistic Landscape. Unpublished MA thesis, University of Western Cape.

Peck, A. and Stroud, C. (2015) Skinscapes. *Linguistic Landscape: An International Journal* 1 (1–2), 133–151.

Peck, A. and Williams, Q. (2018) Skinscapes and frictions: An analysis of Zef Hip-Hop 'Stoeka-style' tattoos. In A. Peck, C. Stroud and Q. Williams (eds) *People in Place: Making Sense of Linguistic Landscapes* (pp. 91–106). London: Bloomsbury.

Pinchevski, A. (2001) Freedom from speech (or the silent demand). *Diacritics* 31 (2), 71–84.

Romero, D.M., Meeder, B. and Kleinberg, J. (2011) Differences in the mechanics of information diffusion across topics: Idioms, political hashtags, and complex contagion on Twitter. Proceedings of the 20th International on World Wide Web (pp. 695–704). New York: ACM.

Soudien, C. (2004) Constituting the class': An analysis of the process of 'integration' in South African schools. In L. Chisholm (ed.) *Changing Class: Education and Social Change in Post-Apartheid South Africa* (pp. 89–114). Cape Town: HSRC Press

Stroud, C. (2001) African mother-tongue programmes and the politics of language: Linguistic citizenship versus linguistic human rights. *Journal of Multilingual and Multicultural Development* 22 (4), 339–355.

Stroud, C. (2015) Linguistic citizenship as utopia. *Multilingual Margins: A Journal of Multilingualism from the Periphery* 2 (2), 22–22.

Stroud, C. (2018) Linguistic Citizenship. In L. Lim, C. Stroud and L. Wee (eds) *The Multilingual Citizen: Towards a Politics of Language for Agency and Change* (pp. 17–39). Bristol: Multilingual Matters.

Stroud, C. and Williams, Q. (2017) Multilingualism as utopia: Fashioning non-racial selves. *AILA Review* 30 (1), 167–188.

Thompson, C. (2009) Black women, beauty, and hair as a matter of being. *Women's Studies* 38 (8), 831–856. doi:10.1080/00497870903238463.

University of Witwatersrand student protests 2015 timeline (2016) *South African History Online.* See http://www.sahistory.org.za/article/university-witwatersrand-student-protests-2015-timeline (accessed June 2018).

Williams, Q.E. and Stroud, C. (2015) Linguistic citizenship: Language and politics in postnational modernities. *Journal of Language and Politics* 14 (3), 406–430.

9 Remixing Linguistic Citizenship

Quentin Williams

Introduction

It took less than a decade to extend Linguistic Citizenship from a term usually applied to institutional contexts (e.g. language policy, schools, governments) to the realm of popular culture language and performance research in South Africa. The first to do so were Williams and Stroud (2010) who applied the term to an analysis of hip-hop culture and language. The term was then applied in a close study of stand-up comedy (Williams & Stroud, 2013) and later the term was extended to the co-production of race, gender and sexuality in performance (Williams & Stroud, 2014; Williams, 2017). The general thrust then, as it is today, is that Linguistic Citizenship is a term well suited for close attention to the way agency[1] and voice[2] is performed in popular cultural contexts, spaces and places.

Williams and Stroud (2013) and later Stroud and Williams (2017) proposed that Linguistic Citizenship be used as an important concept for redefining what we mean by language and multilingualism. Their concern was to demonstrate not only what complex and messy language use looked like, but also how historically marginalized speakers, those racialized multilingual speakers who spoke marginalized languages, required of languages to make sense of their agency and voice. A close study of hip-hop and other popular cultural performances, in this regard, indicated that some public and political institutions in South Africa promoted modernist, structural-functionalist understandings of language, bilingualism and multilingualism (following Heller, 2007). However, as Stroud (2018) argued, Linguistic Citizenship provided a rhetorical alternative that could advance new epistemologies of language, agency and voice, if we dared to explore the performances and practices that are found *outside* policy institutions.

This chapter reflects on the conceptual development of remixing Linguistic Citizenship. The term 'remixing' emerged from the ethos that underlies the rhetoric of Linguistic Citizenship, i.e. (1) 'the nurturing of new forms of human mutuality' (Stroud & Williams, 2017: 168); and (2) the creative practices of language or everyday multilingual forms and functions[3] that emphasize new forms of relationality in citizenship performances against forms of communication that seek 'to silence, invisibilize, and sort speakers and languages hierarchically' (Stroud & Williams, 2017: 168). A remixing of Linguistic Citizenship is related to the argument that in order to account for the emergence of new voices, it is necessary to demonstrate how multilingual speakers are engaged in, interact with Others, perform, practice, mix, mash and mesh an alternative politics of language whose point of departure is a linguistics of transgression[4] and entanglements; in other words, those 'key features of local enactments of citizenship' (Williams & Stroud, 2014: 308). A remixing of Linguistic Citizenship demonstrates to us that what multilingual speakers do with language and language varieties, outside the strictures of institutions defined by the nation-state, 'shift[s] the brief of a politics of language towards a focus on language as part of a broader, socially distributed semiotics' (Williams & Stroud, 2014: 308).

This chapter has four further sections. In the next section, I provide a brief overview of popular culture and language research in South Africa. This is followed by a discussion of the impetus behind the suggestion that Linguistic Citizenship be remixed. I outline the shift to the study of popular cultural forms, such as hip-hop culture, as a way to demonstrate the potential they have for enriching the analytical vocabulary of Linguistic Citizenship. Specifically, I begin by discussing the need to focus on the nooks and crannies where language, multilingualism, agency and voice are practised differently from institutional contexts. I also clearly define what is meant by remixing and how it came to be wedded to the term Linguistic Citizenship. I then move on to specifically discuss how we applied a remixed approach to Linguistic Citizenship to two foci or performances: hip-hop and stand-up comedy. This is then followed by a concluding section on the future trajectory of a remixed approach to Linguistic Citizenship.

Popular Culture and Language

Popular culture is an important context in which Linguistic Citizenship is practised convincingly. According to Harrington and Bielby (2001), popular culture is characterized by interactions and complex semiotic constructions mediated through popularized music, religion, sport and a range of other activities. But popular culture is not only about mass entertainment, it is also about 'the food we eat, the clothing we wear, the people we spend time with, the gossip we share, the roadways we travel, and so forth' (Harrington & Bielby, 2001: 2). In South Africa, popular culture is closely connected to the social and political imagination of the country (Kriger & Zegeye, 2001; Nuttall & Michael, 2000; Newell & Okome, 2014; Wasserman & Jacobs, 2003). Previously South Africa was considered 'a closed space', or, at the very least, as separate from the African continent. It is undergoing cultural and linguistic 'creolization' now, where there is arguably a new emphasis on the 'throwing together' of hybrid linguistic and cultural forms – creolization and bricolage. One of the predominant forms of popular culture has been music such as Kwaito (Livermon, 2020; Ndabeni & Mthembu, 2018) and hip-hop (Marci, Haupt, 1996). The latter, especially, has been seen as a transgressive culture practice that uses language as a powerful medium to (re)create the terms and conditions in the practice of agency and voice, especially among young multilingual speakers.

Hip-hop in Cape Town started at the turn of the 1980s during the most violent period of apartheid (compare Haupt, 1996, 2008; Nkonyeni, 2007; Warner, 2007; Watkins, 2000). Hip-hop artists had found in the global hip-hop nation a 'connective marginalization' (Osumare, 2007) which served as a common frame of reference for young black and coloured multilingual speakers in township spaces, who found solace and comfort in shared circumstances of poverty and discrimination. By 1982, a fledgling hip-hop community had formed and began to apprentice followers into the 'style community' (following Alim, 2009b) that came to define hip-hop across the greater peninsula of Cape Town (Nkonyeni, 2007: 156–157). With the emergence of sub-genres of rap such as Spaza Rap and Zef Rap, Cape Town hip-hop has grown its style community into one that is currently realizing its transformative potential by lifting marginalized voices into the spotlight through mainstreaming previously marginalized languages.

Since its inception, hip-hop in Cape Town has always had an interesting non-hegemonic relationship with transnational whiteness, and the use of colonial languages such as English and Afrikaans. From the heady days of the 1980s, coloured[5] hip-hop artists developed this relationship by cultivating a form of hip-hop authenticity that drew heavily on the anti-racism and anti-hegemonic transnational hip-hop nation established in the United States (rearticulating through lyrics the conscious philosophies of Public Enemy, KRS-One, among others, and the 'each-one-teach-one' philosophy that became part of the anti-racist movement, the Zulu Nation). In one sense (because not all hip-hop artists agree on this point), Cape Town hip-hop became the site where the recontextualization of a global struggle consciousness was inserted into local struggles against apartheid and the symbolic refiguring of local whiteness (Warner, 2007) and the resemiotizing of Afrikaans into Kaaps or Gamtaal. This took place at the same time as notions of 'colouredness' were undergoing refiguration (Haupt, 1996).

Now, almost 20 years after the first democratic government branded the unifying idea of multiracialism into the metaphor of the rainbow nation (Alexander, 2013), new forms of performance genre, such as Spaza Rap (pioneered by black Xhosa hip-hop heads) and Zef Rap (pioneered by white Afrikaans hip-hop heads), are showing that the rainbow nation seems to be, quite disconcertingly, 'an optical illusion' (Alexander, 2013). In particular, Zef culture has become a form of release for white Afrikaner youth amidst an assumed crisis of power, masculinity and sexuality (Kreuger, 2012). According to Marx and Milton (2011), Zef culture is reconfiguring Afrikaans whiteness, mediated through 'zef' cultural artefacts and performances, in a deliberate attempt to speak 'to the perceived sense of marginal and liminal experience of white Afrikaans youth in post-apartheid South Africa' (compare Marx & Milton, 2011: 723).

Spaza Rap, a mixture of isiXhosa, Afrikaans and Tsotsitaal, is the 'term used to describe rap in isiXhosa. It was invented in Cape Town and is a clear example of the different paths South African hip-hop has taken in diverging from the American model' (Pritchard, 2009: 54). In an interview published on the blog titled, *The UnderGround Angle*, Rattex, one of the leading pioneers of the Spaza Rap genre, reports that when they created it 'Spaza was small back in the day – it was all about English raps. English rappers used to call us Kwaito MCs'. Becker (2008: 10) notes that Spaza rappers 'have creatively appropriated hip-hop in their quest for alternative, fluid, consciously 'African' identities in contemporary South Africa' and that music, clothing and embodiment among young isiXhosa-speaking hip-hop artists in a Cape Town township 'did not necessarily entail the confirmation of old, or the construction of new [ethnicized/racialized] boundaries' (Becker, 2008: 11; Becker & Dastile, 2008).

Given the important role of popular culture on the African continent for the production of non-institutionalized voices (Dolby, 2006; Simone, 2008), the question arises as to how discourses of agency and voice, as Linguistic Citizenship, circulates in and across popular cultural practices such as hip-hop. Studies by Alastair Pennycook (2007) on transcultural flows and global English describes how young multilingual speakers invest in hip-hop remixed linguistic and non-linguistic resources to design new identities, and research by H. Samy Alim (2004, 2006), and most recently by Haupt *et al.* (2019) provide powerful insights into the importance of language, identity and gender as linked to agency and voice; evidence of Linguistic Citizenship. For a socially transformative context such as South Africa, Linguistic Citizenship understood and studied from within the context of popular cultural practices such as hip-hop can be 'both a facilitative and constraining factor in the exercise of democratic citizenship and voice' (Stroud, 2009: 208). Yet by combining the tenets of cosmopolitan citizenship and deliberative democracy, Stroud (2010) argues, Linguistic Citizenship sensitizes us to an understanding of language that could help prise open those modalities and contexts (such as hip-hop) where agency and voice is contested, and where language and multilingualism is used as a political resource.

Into Multilingual Nooks and Crannies: Remixing Linguistic Citizenship

A key empirical assumption sought in Williams and Stroud (2010) went something like this: If hip-hop as a culture, practice and performance cultivates an alternative politics of language in what Besnier (2009) referred to as 'the nooks and crannies of everyday life outside of institutionalized contexts', then an alternative conception of agency and voice is possible. In other words:

> Because interactions among marginalized, mobile and diverse, often (translocally) relocated, people take place in the context of the local, bars, streets, and other places of everyday encounter, the politics of the ordinary is increasingly a site where diversity and marginalization are constructed and deconstructed, negotiated and challenged. (Williams & Stroud, 2015: 407)

Besnier's (2009) conception of nooks and crannies redirected attention to multi-sited contexts of hip-hop in Cape Town, in particular the local (and global) performance of historically marginalized language varieties such as Kaaps (a historically marginalized variety of Afrikaans) and prison registers such as Sabela. The initial analysis was of ciphas or freestyle rap battles (a performance genre of rap) that formed the basis of linguistic competition among young multilingual speakers, and the emergence of what Williams and Stroud (2010) called an extreme locality that created the conditions for locally styled registers, which in turn created the semiotic space to exercise agency and voice.

Inspired by the groundbreaking hip-hop sociolinguistics research of Alim (2006) and Pennycook (2007), the following conclusions were possible: that because young multilingual speakers were proactively reworking what they meant by language, 'creating new norms and standards and revealing in stark clarity the micro-processes behind the formation of registers' (Williams & Stroud, 2010: 57) were possible. This suggested that they are exercising control over their own language(s), their own agency and voice, hence, their own Linguistic Citizenship. We concluded our analysis thus: (1), 'What we see here is precisely how a grassroots [that is, bottom up] and polycentric practice of multilingualism is simultaneously creating the conditions and contexts for multilingual citizenship' (Williams & Stroud, 2010: 57); and (2) that those were 'conditions of diversity' that 'are the preconditions for the exercise of youth agency and voice, that is, multilingual citizenship' (Williams & Stroud, 2010: 57).[6]

In hindsight, Stroud's (2001) initial proposal of Linguistic Citizenship was a catalyst not only in the reconceptualization of language, multilingualism, agency and voice for a transformative social context such as South Africa, but that, as soon became evident, other contexts would pick up the term as well (see Rampton, Cooke and Holmes' chapter in this book). Linguistic Citizenship also became important to sociolinguists and applied linguists who entered the cultural and sociological battleground of South Africa where redefining the nation (Jones & Dlamini, 2013), race, gender and identity politics (Erasmus, 2017; Mangcu, 2014), the routing and re-rooting of economic resources in aid of the revitalization of indigenous languages (Alexander, 2013), and the resurgent wave of recognizing minority languages, among other important issues, became key to how we centrally defined agency and voice for historically marginalized citizens (see Stroud & Heugh, 2003). Much later, Stroud (2010) argued that sustaining such momentum required a postliberal vision for a global world where we are soberly aware that the nation-state is still relevant, a system not in retreat, nor driven back by the creative use of multilingualism or marginalized languages (see Lim *et al.*, 2018; compare Cooke & Peutrell, 2019; Wee, 2011; Ramanathan, 2013).

For Stroud (2010, 2018), Linguistic Citizenship has always engaged with a global sociological battleground where those heard and seen are bringing about institutional change. Linguistic Citizenship, he maintains, offers an inroad to a 'process of engagement that opens doors for respectful and deconstructive negotiations around language forms and practices, (to) lay the groundwork for a mutuality and susceptibility to alternative forms of being-together-in-difference' (Stroud, 2018: 37). It is a notion that informs us about the formation of new socialities, their lifespan and futurity/utopic dimensions, but also the embodied transmodality of new registers of hope, relationality and interculturality (see Stroud & Williams, 2017).

According to Stroud (2018: 18), 'Linguistic Citizenship is fundamentally an invitation to rethink our understanding of language through the lens of citizenship and participatory democracy at the same time that we rethink understandings of citizenship through the lens of language' (compare Stroud & Heugh 2003). In other words, 'Linguistic Citizenship encourages us to critically rethink the notion of "linguistic" as practices that can be known through a variety of discourses and modalities' (Stroud, 2018: 23). The focus is always on acts of Linguistic Citizenship that bring to the fore what 'citizens' do with linguistic and non-linguistic resources as they chart a transformative understanding of their citizenship, ultimately shifting 'the location of agency and voice'. And Linguistic Citizenship is a notion that concomitantly offers a metalanguage to reconceptualize multilingualism differently from modernist conceptions of language, people and interaction (going beyond the structural-functional concerns raised in Heller, 2007). As Stroud (2018: 36) puts it:

> Rethinking 'multilingualism' through the lens of [Linguistic Citizenship] would offer some traction in thinking about new, future, orderings of speakers and languages that go beyond or sidestep the more familiar affirmative politics of recognition with its dangers of colonial replication. [Linguistic Citizenship] seeks to interrupt such colonial regimes of

language by building an inclusiveness of voice in ways that repair and rejuvenates relationships to self and others. Such rethinking would be cognizant of the historical particularities and context dependencies of different *multilingualisms*.

This conception, almost seven years after the publication of Stroud (2001), brings us closer to describing new multilingual relationalities as tied to acts of Linguistic Citizenship and the distribution of new (and utopian) relations of agency and voice, in a way that requires us to think where diversity resides in the linguistic of everyday encounters. And it is in thinking about *where* diversity resides in the everyday nooks and crannies of South African life that a remixed approached to Linguistic Citizenship was possible.

The elaboration and application of Linguistic Citizenship as a transformative term rather than an affirmative one to almost every language practice and multilingual form and function in selected nooks and crannies in South Africa has inspired endeavours towards remixing (see Williams [2017] for a full-length study). Packaged in the notion of remixing is not only the analytics of how to distinguish between what is local and global (linguistically) when a multilingual speaker uses language in place and space, but how deeply qualitative the norms of such use have become (compare Aronin & Singleton, 2008: 4). A remixed approach to Linguistic Citizenship considers that a stretching of global genres is at play whenever multilingual speakers perform and practise popular culture, and that there is almost always friction in the flows that multilingual speakers either receive or are part of when it comes to matters of race, gender and sexuality; an inescapable empirically proven fact (compare Milani, 2015).

Remarkably, the term 'remixing' complemented Linguistic Citizenship in such a way that the analysis of how multilingual speakers revisit and reinvent local meanings and values of language is enriched. This has led to important questions regarding the meaningfulness of Linguistic Citizenship for understanding *where* and *why* agency and voice are tied to the practice of citizenship in a world in flux and flow, especially in contexts of friction and immobility. Williams (2017: 1) defines remixing as a phenomenon that persuades a multilingual speaker '...to engage in the linguistic act of using, combining and manipulating multilingual forms and functions tied to histories, cultural acts and identities to create new ways of doing multilingualism'. In this regard, Linguistic Citizenship has become firmly wedded to research on multilingual hip-hop and other types of popular cultural performances in South Africa. On the one hand, the remixing of Linguistic Citizenship found inspiration in the hip-hop research of Alim (2006) and Pennycook (2007), in particular, building on the idea that the '...complex linguistic remixing across the globe...[and]... the multiplicity of indexicalities brought forth by ... multilayered uses of language ... demands that we develop a new approach to language and globalization that focuses on the agency and voice of young multilingual speakers' (Alim, 2009a: 7; compare Pennycook, 2007: 122). On the other hand, if 'remixing provides us with important questions about the supposed one-to-one relationship between language and identity' (Alim, 2009b: 117) then where it concerned the performance of identity, or agency and voice in hip-hop culture and other cultural forms, we see the lines and threads to apply a remixed Linguistic Citizenship analysis. Importantly, such an approach to Linguistic Citizenship implicitly and explicitly highlight: (1) the embodiment of language (and of course by extension multilingualism) in the performance of hip-hop genres such as 'body rap' (Williams, 2017); (2) the scale and variability of various linguistic regimes that popular cultural practices such as hip-hop challenge or reinforce in the context of multilingual hip-hop activism (Williams, 2018); and (3) the use of new speech forms (whether in online or offline contexts) that arise out of novel multilingual contact situations and the expansion (or shrinkage) of multilingual repertoires (see e.g. Williams, 2016). A discussion of what such an analysis would look like follows next.

Two Foci, Interactional Contexts for Remixing Linguistic Citizenship

In the following, I proceed to map out and discuss the development of a remixed Linguistic Citizenship analysis with a specific focus on (1) the performance of freestyle battle rap and race in Cape hip-hop culture, and (2) the performance of stand-up comedy.

Remixing Linguistic Citizenship as hip-hop genre and race

What can we learn from multilingual speakers' performance of voice and participation in everyday nooks and crannies than exclusively in institutional contexts? This is the question that we have tried to answer since 2010 by bringing together complementary theoretical concepts and a multi-sited approach to data collection, and an analysis of the sampling and performance of braggadocio as a hip-hop genre localized in the context of Cape Town hip-hop (Williams & Stroud, 2013).

Young multilingual speakers often introduce, transform and remix hip-hop genres, to such a degree that they provide 'intertextual metacommentaries on the politics of identity' (Williams & Stroud, 2013: 18) in the performance of braggadocio. As Sarkar (2009: 142) points out, often young multilingual speakers practising hip-hop (or who are fans of hip-hop) become those 'self-aware voices', 'poetic voices ... of a new multilingual, multiracial urban generation seemingly left out of language planners' calculations' (Sakar, 2009: 153). The same is true of young multilingual speakers in South Africa, especially those active in rap performances.

In Williams and Stroud (2013), we specifically analysed the sampling of local varieties in the braggadocio performance through a stylization of voice. The analysis comprised a single performance of braggadocio that saw several hip-hop artists perform the genre in Accented-African American English, mixed with a local form of South African English, Kaaps (a variety of Afrikaans), Sabela and isiXhosa. Each performer demonstrated how locally marginalized voices are stylized in the performance. Significantly, the findings demonstrate that braggadocio performances have been 'shaped by recent intensities of deepening diversities as well as the performance of new forms of entangled selves in South Africa' (Williams & Stroud, 2013: 33). This was also evident in the intertextual relations and rap personae that was remixed in the performance of braggadocio, leading to the following questions: 'Why should this sort of practice be subject to language political deliberation at all? In what way are (the artists) performance political? In what way can their performances be the seeds of social change?' (Williams & Stroud, 2013: 33).

Unfortunately, there were no clear answers at the time nor could we find a link explicitly made to Linguistic Citizenship. At the time it was settled knowledge that language was a resource through which education, employment and other formal institutions could realize social transformation, but that it would be deferred if we ignored the racial and linguistic history of the country by not recognizing the semiotic practices of multilingual speakers, especially in terms of how they 'transgress boundaries' and 'stylize and appropriate indexicalities of the Other'. The point here was directed to those responsible for designing, planning and developing multilingual policy to persuade them to consider how Cape hip-hop culture's language use could help us advance a broad, yet critical analysis of language practices in the nooks and crannies of a not-yet realized nonracial South Africa (society without racism). And to convince the designers, planners and developers of multilingualism that hip-hop culture offered a glimpse into the social life of language, post-Apartheid, and the semiotic efforts by historically marginalized speakers to bring new ways of speaking and being from the periphery to the centre.

Understanding the enduring nature of race and racism through language was one of *the* sociological and sociolinguistic challenges we have to meet to bring about a non-racial South Africa (Williams & Stroud, 2014). Research on popular culture in South Africa has documented the variability of racial classification (both structural, cultural and economic) and the stubbornness of racism that persist (over and above what I cited in the second part of this chapter). Such research has also shown that South African youth have always challenged the political and social imagination and reality of Apartheid and sought to make it known through popular culture (compare e.g. Dolby, 2006: 34).

A close study and analysis of stylizing language and the coproduction of 'whiteness' and 'colouredness' in Cape hip-hop's freestyle rap performances at the time demonstrated that race as a structural category endures in South Africa, and that in spite of this problem, the positioning of racial subjects, and the coproduction of such positioning in the performance of freestyle rap performances suggest that white supremacy, though still present, is contestable and can be 'figured semiotically' (Williams & Stroud, 2014). The analysis unpacked the blow-by-blow, moment-to-moment positioning of racial subjectivity of two hip-hop artists (a white emcee versus a coloured emcee) during a freestyle rap performance at the Annual African Hip Hop Indaba (Cape Town) in 2011. We concluded that the co-production of 'whiteness' and 'colouredness' and the performance of racial positioning are a reflection of how racial inequality is sustained, but also challenged in South African society at large. We also pointed out that though racialization is challenged in the performance it is also reinforced. On the one hand, the white emcee's performs his whiteness through tough masculinity, the use of African American English, fragments of Kaaps, and South African and British English. On the other hand, the coloured emcee's performance is wholly in Kaaps. We followed a summary of the analysis with concluding thoughts that focused mainly on the 'white-outing' of the white emcee: how the coloured emcee caused a 'racialized outing' outrage by explicitly pointing to the whiteness of his opponent, and how the white emcee performed an unmarked, transnational and transportable 'whiteness' that allowed the artist to protect himself and shift the location of his whiteness, among other things. We concluded that the coloured emcee explicitly highlighted the racial implications of the white emcee's performance, and, more devastatingly, called in question his masculinity, hip-hop authenticity and non-engagement with his opponent's racialized body and working-classness. It was clear that racism did not win the battle.

In *Remix Multilingualism* (2017), a full-length essay on the remixing of Linguistic Citizenship, the analysis points to the complex messiness of multilingualism through thick descriptions of the performance of several hip-hop genres, with a focus on the mixing of race, gender and space. There, the analysis also demonstrates how young multilingual speakers who practise hip-hop and invest their time in this culture do so to chart an alternative path out of their spatial and cultural circumstances. The terms of their Linguistic Citizenship, as they act it out, are determined by how they use language to make sense of their sociopolitical and socio-economic realities. The analysis supports Mohanty's (2010: 150) argument that 'when multilingualism is associated with inequality, it privileges few and disadvantages many'; an important observation for the context of South Africa where there is a 'pressing need to decouple multilingualism as inequality and focus on multilingualism for greater voice, that is, linguistic citizenship' (Williams, 2017: 195).

Remixing Multilingualism provides the possibility to see and understand the marginal voices of multilingual speakers in an intertextual, poetic way, which institutional settings will always misconstrue. It demonstrates how hip-hop culture and hip-hop language use have always been transgressive, and have also always provided young multilingual speakers with the semiotic and non-linguistic means to 'work' with an alternative sense of language and multilingual communication. This is accomplished at a level that makes it possible for young multilingual speakers to develop new norms and standards for the formation of new registers (see Goebel, 2008; Newell, 2009; and Roth-Gordon, 2009).

Over and above suggesting an alternative sense of language, the analysis of hip-hop performance genres – whether it is freestyle rap, body rap and braggadocio – gives legitimacy to young people's multilingual practices and creates favourable conditions for the expression of previously marginalized voices. This kind of analysis provides an alternative understanding of the named languages performed – English, Afrikaans, isiXhosa – and affirms to participants in the *Remix Multilingualism* study that they are indeed part of the larger democratic processes and structures in South Africa, in spite of the tenuous nature of their citizenship (see Chipkin, 2007). The young people in *Remixing Multilingualism* remixed voices, languages and combined those with non-linguistic resources to act out 'new discourses of citizenship' and to manage linguistic diversity in such a way that they are able to challenge linguistic prejudice.

Remixing Linguistic Citizenship as stand-up comedy

A remixed approach to Linguistic Citizenship does not offer a quick fix or a panacea for the problems of language, multilingual communication and citizenship in South Africa. Our position was that if we diversified our data on popular cultural performances, we could provide a better analysis of these problems. And stand-up comedy performances provided a welcome additional context for understanding the latter.

Stand-up comedy as a performance genre openly bore the struggles with diversity, dislocation, relocation and anomie in a country in transition. It is a type of popular culture genre that remixes our understanding how South African citizens, through messy forms of multilingualism, come to grips with what is often referred to as post-racial inequities (compare e.g. Stroud, 2017).

Intended for a language policy readership, Williams and Stroud (2014) highlight how language shaped by displacement, anomie and contact in a multilingual, yet superdiverse, South Africa could lead to 'the articulation of lifestyles and aspirations' that are qualitatively different from ones shaped during apartheid South Africa. On the one hand, the argument was that the latter holds significant implications for the design of language policies. On the other hand, the question was asked how everyday diversity formed by convivial interactions informs us more about how multilingual speakers reconfigured public spaces for broader, better democratic involvement. In this regard, Linguistic Citizenship was the lens and stand-up comedy the performance genre that captured the everyday multilingual conviviality found in the multilingual nooks and crannies of South Africa.

The point of departure was to argue against the essentialization of diversity within a liberal tradition that tends to affirm the rights of speakers rather than advocate for a transformative approach to the equal distribution and use of languages in public space. Of course, the contention was that the premise of a linguistic human rights framework undermines linguistic diversity through selective agency and the feigning of ignorance with regard to the material and economic constraints on historically marginalized speakers in South Africa. The linguistic human rights approach to language, as Stroud (2001, 2010) has argued convincingly over the years, romanticize linguistic and social order. It is also 'unable to deal with the quotidian mix and mesh of everyday politics in rapidly emerging, transnational and cosmopolitan encounters in speech communities that are increasingly complex, stratified and hybrid' (Williams & Stroud, 2014: 291). In other words, it is ill-equipped to deal with the remixing of language and multilingualism. To remedy this problematic, a focus on conviviality as a way to understand 'interactions and negotiated difference' in order to demonstrate how 'linguistic citizenship provides an inroad into the semiotic practices whereby convivial relationships are created and sustained' enriched a context-bound understanding of language, multilingualism, agency and voice (Williams & Stroud, 2014: 292). Thus the pair of terms 'conviviality' and 'Linguistic Citizenship' make for a powerful analytical combination to analyse the multilingual performances of the white-Xhosa-speaking-Jewish stand-up comedian, Nik Rabinowitz.

The example of stand-up comedy performance revealed not only the conviviality of everyday diversity but also how multilingual diversity is often misunderstood or misinterpreted. A line-by-line analysis of the performance by Rabinowitz revealed how he held a mirror up to South African society to show the potential for recognizing new voices and new acts of citizenry in a new democracy. In this regard, he also pitched the importance of stand-up comedy 'for not only understanding multilingualism, but also for understanding how multilingualism creates the conditions for everyday convivial acts of citizenship' (Williams & Stroud, 2014: 306). And here was the point on remixing: That the performance 'scripted the ways in which local everyday micro-interactions and non-authoritative and marginal discourses could become resemiotized into public displays and enactments of citizenship, linking the parochial realm of comedy with that of the wider community through audience engagement' (Williams & Stroud, 2014: 306).

Stand-up comedy is not only transgressive, heteroglossic, but demonstrates the entanglement of histories, cultures, languages and spaces. It speaks against censorious and authoritative voices in favour of those seeking greater articulation of their citizenship. Importantly, it provides us with the context to expand the remit of Linguistic Citizenship as a term (1) that 'offers alternative possibilities for understanding voice and agency on interlinked public arenas' (Williams & Stroud, 2014: 308); (2) in which 'practices of linguistic transgression and the entanglement of multiple voices are key features of local enactments of citizenship' (Williams & Stroud, 2014: 308); and (3) for which we need better theoretical tools to advance more 'research into the implications of non-standardness and non-fixedness for acts of citizenship – where language is policed by its users/speakers (non-experts) and subject to multiple, polycentric normativities' (Williams & Stroud, 2014: 308).

In Williams and Stroud (2015) the analysis was turned once again on the stand-up comedy performance of Rabinowitz to argue what it would mean to reconstruct a meaningful and inclusive notion of citizenship. Mindful that South African democracy has transitioned for more than a decade or so at the time but on unstable grounds, and in spite of a sterling constitution and institutions that seem to hold, we found ourselves once again drawing parallels to other postcolonial countries in Africa with fraught democracies. Like others, we (Williams & Stroud, 2015: 407) argued that you could not deny that 'engagement with diversity and marginalization is taking place across a range of institutional and informal political arenas'; and that if we explored acts of Linguistic Citizenship closely they would reveal what is obvious to many keen sociolinguistic observers today: for many people engaging diversity is about 'getting on with the neighbors, handling diversity or difference, and finding a good fit for themselves in what is happening around them – a subtle exercise of the *politics* of the ordinary, in other words' (2015: 407, emphasis in the original).

With regard to the latter, Engin Isin's (2009) research has become a fruitful source of making sense of how citizens themselves engage the semiotics of citizenship as actors. As he put it:

> new actors articulate claims for justice through new sites that involve multiple and overlapping scales of rights and obligations (...). The manifold acts through which new actors as claimants emerge in new sites and scales are becoming the new objects of investigation. (Isin, 2009: 370)

Here, Isin is arguing that the way we have defined citizenship has changed throughout the 20th century and that because of that we require a new way of talking and writing, a new vocabulary for describing citizenship. He also notes that citizenship is often enacted in fluid and dynamic spaces that are formed through contest and struggle, against nation-states. Isin (2009: 371) proposes the idea or notion of studying 'acts of citizenship' which he refers to as those 'deeds by which actors constitute themselves (and others) as subjects of rights' (or alternatively, as those with 'the right to claim rights'. For Isin then, those actors who claim the right to citizenship or the act of claiming rights in new sites today push us to rethink and retheorize what we mean by citizenship in our current global, social and political climate. In a similar vein, Stroud (2010: 213) argues that Linguistic Citizenship adjusts 'semiotic practices of citizenship away from a totalizing sense of language' because it is better 'attuned to the implications of [a] multitude of identities, subject positions and positions of interest'.

We infused a remixing of Linguistic Citizenship as acts to great effect in our analysis.

Conclusions

Linguistic Citizenship offers a useful means of gaining greater understanding and studying of language and multilingualism, and an inclusive idea of citizenship in a non-racial society. Its utility lies not only in advancing a critique of language, the intersectionality of race, or a description of agency and voice out of the messiness of multilingualism, but also in providing the rhetoric for emphasizing the importance of the dynamics and dimensions of emergent relationalities among multilingual citizens.

This paper provides reflections on a systematic effort to remix the analytical utility of Linguistic Citizenship, as a way of providing evidence from the nooks and crannies of hip-hop culture and stand-up comedy. For the better part of a decade, research on Linguistic Citizenship has been in dialogue with South African sociolinguists, adding value to the debate on linguistic agency and voice, and revealing what it would look like if we took the way multilingual speakers in a new democracy work towards their own conception of language and multilingual communication seriously. The remixing of Linguistic Citizenship is a recognition that there is a kind immediacy in describing diversity when multilingual speakers design their communication practices along intercultural and intertextual lines (much like barkers studied by Haviland, 2009). And that if applied to the future of multilingualism in South Africa, then we could ultimately realize Biko's utopia of a 'joint culture' in a non-racial society such as ours (see Mangcu, 2014: 15), ridding ourselves finally from the universalizing missionary zeal that was colonialism, the particularity of abstract and concrete violence wrought by the apartheid system, and, above all, that dastardly of all ills, racism.

The question we now face is this: Down which path will a continued remixing of Linguistic Citizenship lead us? The recent calls for decolonization advanced by the MustFall protests suggests the way. And to help the debate along this path, as Stroud and Williams (2017: 168) argue, Linguistic Citizenship is good for disrupting modernist understandings of language and to illuminate a path towards realizing how 'the potential for new empowering linguistic mediations of the mutualities of our common humanity with different others are worked out'; and, of course, the decolonization project in South Africa. We revised our definition of Linguistic Citizenship as '...the event/moment when representing languages in particular ways becomes crucial to, becomes the very dynamic through which, acts of agency and participation, and reconceptualizations of self in matrices of power occur' (Stroud & Williams, 2017: 184–1859) (compare Williams, forthcoming). And we concluded thus:

> We find instances of linguistic citizenship in many peripheral contexts where there is a groundswell of resistance to centrist and neoliberal/colonial replications of languages and selves. Such re-appropriations of language by communities of speakers on the periphery often involve (and evolve) understandings of language, authenticity and ownership that diverge significantly from more institutionalized discourses on language. (Stroud & Williams, 2017: 185)

In more ways than one, a remixed approach to Linguistic Citizenship has been useful in analysing centrist and neoliberal/colonial replications of languages and selves. Focusing on acts of Linguistic Citizenship in the remixing of the term has taught us that, in cases where there are re-appropriations of language by communities of speakers on the periphery to express better agency and voice, there is often an evolved understanding by the speakers themselves of language, authenticity and ownership that diverges significantly from institutionalized discourses on language.

In this regard, there is more remixing to be done, in more nooks and crannies, which can be achieved in the following ways:

- Firstly, Linguistic Citizenship studies have matured but still need to provide a comprehensive account of the struggle of agency and voice, as linked to the transformation of language and multilingualism, across the lifespan. While much of the research on the remixing of Linguistic Citizenship has focused on the language and multilingual practices of young speakers of youth ages, it could yield more empirical insight if research projects were developed that focused on the multilingual practices of speakers of prepubescent age, on adults and the elderly in socially and culturally defined nooks and crannies. Such a broad focus could generate significant insights into the dynamics of multilingualism, agency and voice, and a comprehensive insight into the present and future dynamics of citizenships.
- Secondly, there is a need to develop comparative research studies that investigate the intersection between racialized economies, bodies, languages and agency at the individual and speech community level. The aim would be to describe the various carnal regimes that model, frame and sustain social and sociolinguistic inequalities in nooks and crannies outside institutional settings that through activism have the potential to transform the latter. The latter is an under-researched area in Linguistic Citizenship studies, and as such there is an imperative to highlight those symbolic systems that fence in some and privilege certain bodies over others.

Notes

(1) Agency could be plainly understood here to have to do with the means to bring about institutional change.
(2) Voice, the means to make yourself heard.
(3) By everyday multilingual forms and functions I mean those communicative resources used by speakers to make meaning, however mundane or specific, as they navigate the ebbs, flows and frictions of from morning to noon.
(4) It is not of course always the case that Linguistic Citizenship is about transgression, it could also be highly normative (see Lim et al., 2018).
(5) 'Coloured' is a racial epithet created in colonial times, used during Apartheid to describe such citizens as not quite white nor strictly black or African.
(6) Stroud's influence here is significant because his suggestion was that the initial use of multilingual citizenship here was an attempt to rebrand Linguistic Citizenship for reception in the broader policy and planning context of South Africa. It was his hope that multilingual citizenship would be more palatable for Chapter 9 institutions such as the Pan South African Language Board (PANSALB) and Non-Governmental Organizations (NGOs) working towards a non-racial society.

References

Alexander, N. (2013) Thoughts on the New South Africa. Auckland Park: Jacana Media.
Alim, H.S. (2004) You Know My Steez: An Ethnographic and Sociolinguistic Study of Styleshifting in a Black African Speech Community. Durham, NC: Duke University Press.
Alim, H.S. (2006) Roc the Mic Right: The Language of Hip-Hop Culture. London: Routledge.
Alim, H.S. (2009a) Introduction. In H.S Alim, A. Ibrahim and A. Pennycook (eds) Global Linguistic Flows: Hip–Hop Cultures, Youth Identities and Politics of Language (pp. 1–24). London: Routledge.
Alim, H.S. (2009b) Translocal style communities: Hip Hop youth as cultural theorists of style language, and globalization. Pragmatics 19 (1), 103–127.
Aronin, L. and Singleton, D. (2008) Multilingualism as a new linguistic dispensation. International Journal of Multilingualism (5), 1.
Becker, H. (2008) Negotiating culture in contemporary South Africa: Photographic self-representations from the Cape Flats. Paper presented at CODESRIA, Yahaoundé, 7–11 December.
Becker, H. and Dastile, N. (2008) Global and African: Exploring hip hop artists in Philippi Township, Cape Town. Anthropology Southern Africa 31 (1&2), 20–30.
Besnier, N. (2009) Gossip and the Everyday Production of Politics. Honolulu: University of Hawai'i Press.
Chipkin, I. (2007) Do South Africans Exist? Nationalism, Democracy, and the Identity of a People. Johannesburg: Wits University Press.
Cooke, M. and Peutrell, R. (eds) (2019) Brokering Britain, Educating Citizens: Exploring ESOL and Citizenship. Bristol: Multilingual Matters.
Dolby, N. (2006) Popular culture and public space: The possibilities of cultural citizenship. African Studies Review 49 (3), 31–47.
Erasmus, Z. (2017) Race Otherwise: Forging a New Humanism for South Africa. Johannesburg: Wits University Press.
Goebel, Z. (2008) Enregistering, authorizing and denaturalizing identity in Indonesia. Journal of Linguistic Anthropology 18 (1), 46–61.
Harrington, L. and Bielby, D. (ed.) (2001) Popular Culture: Production and Consumption. Hoboken, NJ: Wiley-Blackwell Publishers.

Haupt, A. (1996) Rap and the articulation of resistance: An exploration of subversive cultural production during the early 90s, with particular reference to Prophets of da City. Unpublished MA mini-thesis, University of the Western Cape.

Haupt, A. (2008) *Stealing Empire: P2P, Intellectual Property and Hip Hop Subversion.* Cape Town: HSRC Press.

Haupt, A., Williams, Q.E., Alim, H.S. and Janse, E. (eds) (2019) *Neva Again: Hip Hop Art, Activism and Education in Post-apartheid South Africa.* Cape Town: HSRC Press.

Haviland, J.B. (2009) Little rituals. In G. Senft and E.B. Basso (eds) *Ritual Communication* (pp. 21–50). Oxford: Berg.

Heller, M. (ed.) (2007) *Bilingualism: A Social Approach.* New York: Palgrave McMillan.

Isin, E.F. (2009) Citizenship in flux: The figure of the activist citizen. *Subjectivity* 29, 367–388.

Jones, M. and Dlamini, J. (eds) (2013) *Categories of Persons: Rethinking Ourselves and Others.* Johannesburg: Picador Africa.

Kreuger, A. (2012) Part II: Zef/poor white kitsch chique: Die Antwoord's comedy of degradation. *Safundi* 13 (4), 399–408.

Kriger, R. and Zegeye, A. (eds) (2001) *Culture in the New South Africa.* Cape Town: Kwela Books.

Lim, L., Stroud, C. and Wee, L. (eds) (2018) *The Multilingual Citizen: Towards a Politics of Language for Agency and Change.* Bristol: Multilingual Matters.

Livermon, X. (2020) *Kwaito Bodies: Remastering Space and Subjectivity in Post–apartheid South Africa.* Durham, NC: Duke University Press.

Mangcu, X. (ed.) (2014) *The Colour of our Future: Does Race Matter in Post-Apartheid South Africa?* Johannesburg: Wits University Press.

Marx, H. and Milton, V.C. (2011) Bastardised whiteness: 'Zef'-culture, Die Antwoord and the reconfiguration of contemporary Afrikaans identities. *Social Identities* 17 (6), 723–745.

Milani, T. (2015) Language and citizenship: Broadening the agenda. *Journal of Language and Politics* 14 (3), 319–334

Mohanty, A.K. (2010) Language, inequality and marginalization: Implications for the double divide in Indian multilingualism. *International Journal of the Sociology of Language* 205, 131–154.

Ndabeni, E. and Mthembu, S. (2018) *Born to Kwaito.* South Africa: Blackbird Books.

Newell, S. and Okome, O. (eds) (2014) *Popular Culture in Africa: The Episteme of the Everyday.* London: Routledge.

Newell, S. (2009) Enregistering modernity, Bluffing criminality: How Nouchi speech reinvented (and fractured) the nation. *Journal of Linguistic Anthropology* 19 (2), 157–184.

Nkonyeni, N. (2007) Da struggle kontinues into the 21st century: Two decades of nation conscious rap in Cape Town. In S. Field, R. Meyer and F. Swanson (eds) *Imagining the City: Memories and Cultures in Cape Town* (pp. 151–172). Cape Town: HSRC Press.

Nuttall, S. and Michael, C.A. (eds) (2000) *Senses of Culture: South African Culture Studies.* Oxford: Oxford University Press.

Osumare, H. (2007) *The Africanist Aesthetic in Global Hip-Hop: How Power Moves.* New York: Palgrave Macmillan.

Pennycook, A. (2007) *Global Englishes and Transcultural Flows.* London: Routledge.

Pritchard, G. (2009) Cultural imperialism, Americanisation and Cape Town hip–hop culture: A discussion piece. *Social Dynamics* 35 (1), 51–55.

Ramanathan, V. (ed.) (2013) *Language Policies and (Dis)Citizenship: Rights, Access, Pedagogies.* Bristol: Multilingual Matters.

Roth-Gordon, J. (2009) The language that came down the hill: Slang, crime, and citizenship in Rio de Janeiro. *American Anthropologist* 111 (1), 57–68.

Sarkar, M. (2009) 'Still Reppin Por Mi Gente': The transformative power of language Mixing in quebec hip-hop. In H.S. Alim, A. Ibrahim and A. Pennycook (eds) *Global Linguistic Flows: Hip-hop Cultures, Youth Identities, and the Politics of Language* (pp. 139–158). London: Routledge.

Simone, A. (2008) Some reflections on making popular culture in urban Africa. *African Studies Review* 51 (3), 75–89.

Stroud, C. (2001) African mother tongue programs and the politics of language: Linguistic citizenship versus linguistic human rights. *Journal of Multilingual and Multicultural Development* 22 (4), 339–355.

Stroud, C. (2010) Towards a postliberal theory of citizenship. In J.E. Petrovic (ed.) *International Perspectives on Bilingual Education: Policy, Practice and Controversy* (pp. 191–218). New York: Information Age Publishing.

Stroud, C. (2017) A postscript on the post-racial. In C. Kerfoot and K. Hyltenstam (eds) *Entangled Discourses: South–North Orders of Visibility* (pp. 230–238). London: Routledge.

Stroud, C. (2018) Linguistic Citizenship. In L. Lim, C. Stroud and L. Wee (eds) *The Multilingual Citizen: Towards a Politics of Language for Agency and Change* (pp. 17–39). Bristol: Multilingual Matters.

Stroud, C. and Heugh, K. (2003) Linguistic human rights and linguistic citizenship. In D. Patrick and J. Freeland (eds) *Language Rights and Language Survival: A Sociolinguistic Exploration* (pp. 191–128). Manchester: St Jerome.

Stroud, C. and Williams, Q.E. (2017) Multilingualism as utopia: Fashioning non-racial selves. *AILA Review* 30, 165–186.

Warner, R. (2007) Battles over borders: Hip Hop and the politics and poetics of race and place in the new South Africa. Unpublished PhD dissertation, York University.

Wasserman, H. and Jacobs, S. (eds) (2003) *Shifting Selves: Post–Apartheid Essays on Mass Media, Culture, and Identity*. Cape Town: Kwela Books.

Watkins, L. (2000) Tracking the narrative: The poetics of identity in the rap music and Hip Hop culture of Cape Town. Unpublished MA dissertation, University of KwaZulu Natal.

Williams, Q. (2016) Rastafarian-herbalists' enregisterment of multilingual voices in an informal marketplace. *Stellenbosch Papers in Linguistics* 49, 279–299.

Williams, Q. (2017) *Remix Multilingualism: Ethnography, Hip Hop and the Performance of Marginalized Voice*. London: Bloomsbury Press.

Williams, Q. (2018) Multilingual activism in South African Hip Hop. *Journal of World Popular Music* 5 (1), 31–49.

Williams, Q.E. and Stroud, C. (2010) performing rap ciphas in late-modern Cape Town: Extreme locality and multilingual citizenship. *Afrika Focus* 23 (2), 39–59.

Williams, Q. and Stroud, C. (2013) Multilingualism in transformative spaces: Contact and conviviality. *Language Policy* 12, 289–311.

Williams, Q.E. and Stroud, C. (2014) Multilingualism remixed: Sampling texts, braggadocio and the politics of voice in Cape Town Hip-Hop. *African Studies* 73 (1), 1–22.

Williams, Q. and Stroud, C. (2015) Linguistic Citizenship: Language and politics in post-national modernities. In T. Milani (ed.) *Language and Citizenship: Broadening the Agenda* (pp. 89–112). Amsterdam: Johns Benjamins Publishing Company.

Wee, L. (2011) *Language without Rights*. Oxford: Oxford University Press.

Part 4

Postscripts: Taking Linguistic Citizenship towards New Directions

10 WEIRD Psycholinguistics

Emanuel Bylund

Language is arguably the most defining trait of humans. In no other species has a semiotic system emerged that is as complex and, at the same time, as diverse as human language, evading centuries of attempts by linguists to successfully capture its inherent complexities. The uniqueness of human language raises several questions regarding the human mind: How do we acquire, process, store and produce language? And, how does language, once acquired, influence our actions and thoughts? Since its emergence in the late 1800s, the field of psycholinguistics has investigated these questions with ever-increasing vigour. Researchers in the field of the psychology of language have made – and are still making – considerable progress in conceptual development and technology. However, a potentially problematic aspect of this development is that the knowledge generated thus far mainly stems from a so-called WEIRD (Western Educated Industrialized Rich Democratic) context (Henrich *et al.*, 2010a, 2010b). This means that significant aspects of the rich variety of cultural and social contexts in which humans acquire and use language, or the diversity of human languages, have not been captured and may thus leave epistemological and methodological watermarks on knowledge production. Since psycholinguistics is essentially an empirically based endeavour, which relies on experimental and quasi-experimental paradigms to gain insights into the psychology of language, there is an urgent need for diversification.

This chapter sets out to analyse the WEIRD bias in psycholinguistics, with a particular focus on research on the multilingual mind. In doing so, the chapter makes use of the notion of utopia (e.g. Stroud, 2015; Stroud & Williams, 2017). This was recently introduced as part of the theoretical complex of Linguistic Citizenship (Stroud, 2001, 2009, 2018; Stroud & Heugh, 2004) as a means of denoting 'a better world' that is 'foreshadowed in the present but as yet unrealized' (Stroud, 2015: 25). While utopia has proved a useful tool for analysing expressions of alternative representations of language(s), for instance, it is not only a means of examining a given state-of-affairs, but also a means of conceptualizing an unrealized alternative prefigured in that state. In this chapter, the unrealized alternative is a psycholinguistic research endeavour where the agenda is not dictated by WEIRD biases.

The chapter is divided into two main sections. The first section, 'The WEIRD', deals with both research on the notion of WEIRD as well as WEIRD research (that is, research availing itself of WEIRD subjects and contexts), and serves to illustrate the properties of the WEIRD bias in extant research. The concept of WEIRD is introduced, followed by a brief bibliometric analysis and a selective overview of WEIRD assumptions in psycholinguistic research on the multilingual mind. Attention is also given to the representation of the non-WEIRD in psycholinguistic studies. The second section of the chapter, 'A Psycholinguistic Utopia', outlines the potential of a psycholinguistic paradigm that is not WEIRD, using South Africa as a starting point. Here, the South African multilingual situation is outlined, followed by an overview of the current status of psycholinguistics in research and tertiary education in South Africa. Against this backdrop, a psycholinguistic utopia is discussed.

Throughout the chapter, I make use of the following conceptual distinctions: the notions such as first language (L1) and second language (L2) are defined in accordance with their original meaning making function, namely the order of acquisition, regardless of language dominance. In other words, an L2 is a language acquired after the onset of the acquisition of the L1. The term 'non-WEIRD' serves as an umbrella term for anything that is not WEIRD. This does not by any means imply that all that is not WEIRD is uniform or similar in any way; instead, non-WEIRD is defined in opposition to WEIRD. While the term WEIRD was initially taken to denote participant characteristics (Henrich *et al.*, 2010a), it has come to function as an umbrella term for contexts and even assumptions of a certain nature (see commentaries and response in Henrich *et al.*, 2010b). Moreover, the study of psycholinguistics (or psychology of language) is conceptualized in broad terms, to represent the study of how the mind processes language, how language interacts with other aspects of the mind, as well as how the mind can accommodate the acquisition of languages of very different kinds (e.g. Rueschemeyer & Gaskell, 2018). The psycholinguistic phenomena and research directions covered in the chapter are not meant to be exhaustive, but to illustrate applications and manifestations of the concept of WEIRD.

The WEIRD

The concept of WEIRD

The tendency to draw data from Western participants and Western settings is not unique to psycholinguistics, but it is part of a general trend in the cognitive sciences. Over the past few decades, the cognitive sciences have seen several calls for diversification of research participants and contexts (e.g. Bender & Beller, 2013; Bender *et al.*, 2012; Medin & Atran, 2004; Norenzayan & Heine, 2005; Rozin, 2001, 2009). In their paper published in *Nature* in 2010, Henrich *et al.* (2010a) introduce the concept of WEIRD as a means to highlight the Western bias in research on the human mind. They argue that the notion of human cognitive and perceptual universals is inherently flawed, as its evidentiary basis mainly consists of data drawn from American undergraduate students (of Psychology, even). To this end, they review evidence from a variety of domains showing that processes such as visual perception, numerical cognition, cooperation and analytic reasoning may indeed vary across languages and cultures. They conclude that the commonly studied WEIRD subjects (undergraduate students) may be the 'worst population on which to base our understanding of Homo sapiens' (2010a: 22), simply because these subjects far from constitute a representative sample of the world's population. To overcome the WEIRD bias, Henrich *et al.* (2010a) suggest a number of short-term and long-term solutions, including stricter reviewing and publishing guidelines regarding claims for universality, and interdisciplinary networks of behavioural scientists and ethnographers.

The WEIRD argument was generally well-received, with some scholars even suggesting that stronger measures than those identified by Henrich *et al.* (2010a) are necessary if the WEIRD bias is to be properly overcome (e.g. Downey, 2010). However, a decade later, things are more or less business as usual, testifying either to the slow wheels of academia, to the conceptual and methodological difficulties in actually addressing the bias, and/or to a faded interest.[1]

WEIRDNESS in psycholinguistics: Bibliometrics and studied phenomena

While the concept of WEIRD targets the cognitive sciences at large, and relates to issues of language and the mind, it is yet to be properly applied to the field of psycholinguistics. The keynote article by Henrich and colleagues that introduced the concept of WEIRD and the accompanying commentaries made some important observations about language in general, but seldom explicitly related to psycholinguistic problems, and no remark was made concerning the topics of multilingualism. This is not to say that there have not been other publications addressing the WEIRD bias, for instance by analysing speech processing phenomena in languages that are typologically different from those commonly studied (see contributions in Norcliffe *et al.*, 2015), by examining less commonly studied – though not less commonly occurring – language acquisition situations (Bylund & Athanasopoulos, 2014, 2015), or by drawing attention to Western assumptions about the architecture of language (and its underlying mental mechanisms) (Evans & Levinson, 2009). However, despite these valuable contributions, the WEIRD bias is very much a reality of the field, as the overwhelming majority of studies is still being produced in WEIRD settings.

Bibliometric figures

A numerical demonstration of the WEIRD bias may be obtained by means of a bibliometric analysis that examines author affiliations of articles published in journals central to the field. This was done for a number of journals, which belong to the top tiers of the Thomson-Reuter ISI lists of journal rankings based on citations, where psycholinguistic research on multilingualism is usually published (e.g. *Bilingualism: Language and Cognition, Cognition, Journal of Experimental Psychology: General, Journal of Memory and Language, Psychological Science*). The period covered is the past 11 years available, from 2006 to 2016.[2] The selected journals, largely published studies from the United States, the United Kingdom and Canada, which taken together top the lists (see Table 10.1 in the appendix). These numbers clearly illustrate the Western concentration of author bases, and by extension, the Western concentration of knowledge production on these topics. It should be acknowledged that some journals (e.g. the *Journal of Experimental Psychology* franchise) are run by the American Psychological Association, and thus likely to attract America-based authors or topics pertinent to the American context. However, this does not detract from the argument that the most influential journals in the field publish research on mainly WEIRD subjects from WEIRD contexts.

In addition to the bibliometric data, it is also possible to adopt a critical perspective on central psycholinguistic research themes, in order to tease out a number of assumptions about language and the mind that are likely rooted in the WEIRD bias. In what follows, we will look at such assumptions with particular attention to the areas of language development and emotive language.

Additional language learning

The study of how an additional language is acquired is central to answering important questions regarding the human language learning ability. Some of these are: Is this ability largely expended with the acquisition of the first language, does it operate within a sensitive period. Traditionally, two different situations of additional language learning have been covered in the psycholinguistic literature. The first concerns the acquisition of a second language (L2) in the setting where it is the main medium of communication. This situation is associated with international migration such as that of a speaker of one language settles down in a new country and acquires the language spoken in that country.

The second situation concerns so-called foreign language learning, whereby an additional language is acquired through formal classroom instruction. Here, contact with the language to be learnt is mainly confined to the classroom context. While these types of learning situations are far from uncommon, they are not the only ones by which an additional language is acquired (cf. Canagarajah, 2007).

Another situation is, for instance, when additional language learning occurs in a multilingual context, and the target language is a *lingua franca* that is not necessarily the L1 of the individuals who use it. In these instances, the learner does not need to relocate to a new country, nor do they need to enrol in classes, in order to acquire the language. Instead, exposure to it, and subsequent acquisition, occurs through natural – and often inevitable – encounters with the language, be it through family members, peers, schooling or so. These kinds of situations are different from the ones commonly studied, crucially because the input is predominantly provided by other L2 speakers,[3] with the implication that what constitutes the 'target language' may in fact be multiple systems with both convergent and idiosyncratic lexico-grammatical rules. In such situations, the traditional concept of nativelike attainment is significantly blurred.

Language attrition

The phenomenon of language attrition is commonly defined as a non-pathological loss or restructuring of language skills that were once possessed (e.g. Schmid, 2013). While being a relatively young field of research, the study of attrition has generated important insights into language development, documenting the (non)stability of linguistic processing and representation. Similar to research on additional language learning, attrition research has tended to focus on situations in which an individual suffers from attrition as he/she moves to another country where another language is the main medium of communication, and exposure to the L1 is thus reduced. Again, while this is not an uncommon situation, it is not the only one in which attrition phenomena may occur. In a multilingual setting, where different languages are used in different contexts and for different purposes, circumstances (e.g. schooling or work-related) may mean that speakers experience reduced L1 input and use, and as a consequence their L1 knowledge is restructured.

In such multilingual settings, instances of L1 restructuring may actually occur without there necessarily being any reduction in L1 input. A less commonly studied situation concerns processing and representation in native speakers of a lingua franca who are constantly exposed to L2 speech. While linguistic input is often assumed to be central for L1 retention, the properties of that input are less studied. If the input contains linguistic features that are different from the ones the speaker once acquired (e.g. different patterns or grammar, and information structure), the speaker's sensitivity to certain linguistic distinctions may be restructured.

Common to the situations of additional language learning and language attrition is the centrality of the notion of nativeness. The native speaker construct has been subject to intense debate within the field of applied linguistics (e.g. Afendras *et al.*, 1995; Birdsong & Gertken, 2013; Cook, 1999; Davies, 2003). This debate has led to considerable criticism of the use of the native speaker's (i.e. the L1 speaker's) behaviour as a benchmark for L2 attainment and L1 retention. The main argument is that language representation and processing in a bi-/multilingual individual can never be expected to be identical to that of a monolingual individual, because of crosslinguistic influence (compare the notion of 'multicompetence').

Emotional language

In research on language and emotions, a long-held view has been that the individual's language of emotions is the L1, and that an L2 does not carry the same emotive loading – if any at all (for a recent discussion, see Caldwell-Harris, 2014). Again, this view clearly stems from (and might hold true for) a predominantly monolingual setting where the L1 is the primary language of communication, but it disregards other potential constellations, which might ultimately reject the alleged privileged status of the L1. As pointed out by Pavlenko (e.g. 2008), sufficient socialization in the L2 may very well turn this language into a primary means of expressing and experiencing emotions. There are other situations in which a language other than the L1 would be used to express emotive language. For instance, in a multilingual setting, a certain language (or languages) may be more strongly associated with or preferred for emotive expression, without that language necessarily being the L1 of the speakers concerned. Instead, societal perceptions of a given language's emotional potential and appropriateness may be what ultimately determines this outcome (Oostendorp & Bylund, 2012). Such a situation would serve to show that factors other than initial exposure or socialization may come into play in determining emotional linguistic behaviour.

While the phenomena outlined above are intensely studied in current psycholinguistic research, they are also specific research topics with specific research questions attached to them. To move beyond this specific agenda and gain a better perspective of the conceptual frames that guide the field, one has to take a step back. In these frames, the phenomena of monolingualism and multilingualism have quite different statuses. Even though current statistics shows that, from a global viewpoint, the number of individuals who use more than one language in their everyday communication far exceeds those who use only one (Aronin & Singleton, 2012), multilingualism is still construed as the exception and monolingualism as the default (for a similar point, see Bak & Mehmedbegovic, 2017). Seeing multilingualism as the exception is not necessarily negative; the way multilingualism is viewed has changed radically over the past century. Initially, linguistic and psychological research conceived of multilingualism as something that was cognitively harmful (e.g. Goodenough, 1926; Saer, 1923), a view that was possibly driven by ideologies of 'one nation, one language' in which the diversity represented by multilingualism had no place (Pavlenko, 2014). In an attempt to change this view, modern-day approaches focus on the potential cognitive advantages afforded by multilingualism.[4] However, what these views have in common is the conception of multilingualism as an exception, as they both pose the question: 'how does multilingualism influence x or z?' (as opposed to 'how does monolingualism influence x or z?').

Non-WEIRD as weird in psycholinguistics

While the overwhelming majority of psycholinguistic research is produced in and centred on WEIRD settings, as seen in the previous section, there is a non-negligible number of studies that focus on language and conceptualization in non-WEIRD participants and contexts (e.g. Brown, 2011; Bylund & Athanasopoulos, 2014; Haun & Rapold, 2009; Hobson, 1999; Levinson, 1997; Levinson et al., 2002; Lucy, 1992; Majid & Burenhult, 2014). These studies naturally have great potential to contribute with unique data for testing, for example, allegedly universal behavioural patterns. More often than not, the non-WEIRD evidence serves to reject such alleged universality.[5]

In some instances, however, the non-WEIRD evidence is framed or presented in a somewhat noteworthy way. For instance, a study on colour categorization in a Melanesian community was published in *Nature* as *Colour categories in a* **stone-age tribe** (emphasis added) (Davidoff et al., 1999). While the epithet 'stone-age tribe' might have been a useful rhetorical take to draw attention to the – by WEIRD standards – atypical sample, and thus boost the visibility of the study, it is also an epithet that could be perceived of as less than flattering. In fact, the phrasing is reminiscent of early cultural-anthropological work on pre-modern societies, which were often characterized in pejorative terms (e.g. 'primitive', 'savage' and 'wild'; see discussion in Lévi-Strauss, 1962). In that literature, these terms too served to underscore the studied population's divergence from the WEIRD standards.

Another example of a noteworthy engagement with non-WEIRD evidence is found in a study on metaphors for musical pitch (e.g. a *high/low* note) published in *Cognition* (Eitan & Timmers, 2010). Here, typological patterns for expressing pitch are reviewed for a number of different languages with the intention of uncovering potentially universal mappings. Among the typologically very distinct pitch metaphors we find examples relating to 'the Shona mbira (Zimbabwe)' (2010: 406), with low pitch expressed as 'crocodile', and high pitch as 'those who follow crocodiles'. What is implicit in the text, however, is the fact that *mbira* is a musical instrument (a type of lamellophone, sometimes called a 'thumb piano'), and not a language community, as one might think. Evidence of actual usage patterns of crocodile metaphors among Shona speakers is not reported, and the reader is referred to another study for further treatment (Ashley, 2004), which in turn refers to a study on the mbira (Berliner, 1981 [1978]). Even so, later in the study, crocodile terms are compared to metaphors that are not distinct musical-instrument terms, but language-specific metaphors in common use. The risk of misunderstanding is thus strong, and some studies citing Eitan and Timmers (2010) indeed describe the crocodile expressions as if they were the typical pitch metaphors used by Shona speakers : 'crocodile – which, *among the Shona of Zimbabwe*, corresponds with low pitch' (Zbikowski, 2017: 508, italics added).[6] The fact that the crocodile expression are part of the title of Eitan and Timmers' study, 'Beethoven's last piano sonata and those who follow crocodiles', may further increase the likelihood of misunderstanding. The misunderstanding is likely the result of gaps in or even complete absence of research on the Shona language.

Taken together, these examples illustrate that while non-WEIRD evidence might serve to advance scientific progress around a particular question, it is also sometimes couched in such a way that it seems to represent unusual or atypical instances of human behaviour. Such framing runs the risk of exoticizing the studied behaviour, and ultimately the participants enacting it. In fact, the use of non-WEIRD data in WEIRD research has been criticized for its utilitarian tendencies, whereby non-WEIRD contexts are often simply conceived of as untapped potentials of 'exotic' data (e.g. Comaroff & Comaroff, 2011).

A Psycholinguistic Utopia

Having outlined WEIRD traits of current psycholinguistic research, I will now in a more explicit way engage with the topic of psycholinguistic utopia. This I will do using as a starting point the case of South Africa, which, as the sections below will show, is characterized by societal multilingualism and, at the same time, a relative absence of psycholinguistic research.

Multilingualism in South Africa

The current South African constitution states that the official languages of the Republic of South Africa are (in alphabetical order) Afrikaans, English, isiNdebele, isiXhosa, isiZulu, Sepedi, Sesotho, Setswana, siSwati, Tshivenda and Xitsonga. According to the constitution, the provincial governments must promote, regulate and monitor the use of these languages, and use of at least two of them in communication with their citizens. The language diversity of modern-day South Africa is largely a result of the country's political past, which saw, among other things, the arrival of the colonial Germanic languages, an almost complete extinction of the Khoe and San languages, demarcation of national borders with little regard to indigenous groups, and laws that enforced social separation of different ethnolinguistic groups. In addition to its 11 official languages, South Africa also recognizes a number of languages that are either historically indigenous minority languages (e.g. the Khoi, Nama and San languages) or languages brought to the country through immigration, indentured labour, or the slave trade (e.g. German, Greek, Gujarati, Hindi, Portuguese and Tamil). According to the constitution, these languages must be promoted (see Mesthrie, 2002).

From a legislative point of view, its 11 official languages make South Africa one of the world's most multilingual countries. The country also ranks fairly high in terms of linguistic diversity, as measured by Greenberg's (1956) Linguistic Diversity Index (LDI), which represents the probability that any two random people from the same region (or, in this case, country) will have different L1s. For South Africa, the LDI is 0.87, meaning that the likelihood that two randomly chosen individuals from the population speak the same L1 is 13%. The LDI, along with the multilingual constitution, obviously does not mean that each South African citizen speaks all 11 languages, but according to census data and large-scale studies, the overwhelming majority of the South African population is multilingual (Coetzee-Van Rooy, 2012).

The multilingual situation in South Africa is dynamic in the sense that various studies have documented that the linguistic repertoires of speakers are undergoing a shift, with the English language increasingly gaining ground, often at the expense of other languages. Specifically, it has been observed that there is a tendency in coloured and black[7] communities to use English in private domains, as opposed to Afrikaans or Bantu languages, reflecting either increased bilingualism or language shift (Anthonissen, 2009; Bylund, 2014; de Kadt, 2005; de Klerk, 2000; Deumert, 2010; Dyers, 2008; Kamwangamalu, 2003; Posel & Zeller, 2016). There is also considerable diversity of dialectal and stylized varieties, prompting research into the question of mixed codes (McCormick, 2002; Mesthrie, 2002).

The South African education system to some extent caters for their students of varying linguistic backgrounds. In primary education, schooling might proceed through one or several of the local languages. In secondary education, English is the predominant medium of instruction, independently of the student's L1 or previous language of instruction. In tertiary education, English is the primary medium of instruction. Up until recently, some universities offered dual medium instruction (in languages such as Afrikaans), and other universities may offer interpreting, podcasts, and even tutorials to some extent in local languages.

Psycholinguistics in South African tertiary education and research

Currently, the psychology of language is a most under-represented research area in South Africa. Sociolinguistic research, on the other hand, is well-represented in the country: several scholars based in South Africa carry out frontline research on sociolinguistic issues, publishing their findings in high-impact outlets. These differences in disciplinary representation are also reflected in the academic offerings at tertiary education institutions. For instance, up until the year 2017, no South African university offered more than an introductory course (if at all) to psycholinguistics/psychology of language (judging from online programme guides).[8] Of course, this is not at all odd, as it is both natural and strategic that departments choose to build student capacities around their existing strengths.

Another consequence of the scarcity of South African psycholinguistic research is that several psycholinguistic aspects of Southern Bantu languages and Afrikaans are unknown (such as the processing and representation of noun classes or double adpositions). This has also influenced the teaching of psycholinguistics at tertiary level, since teaching materials to a great extent need to rely on WEIRD textbooks and/or WEIRD studies, which may not only have limited ecological validity in the (South) African context, but also South African students may not be familiar with them. Taken together, limited programme offerings and low levels of exposure to local psycholinguistic research reduce the likelihood that students will pursue post-graduate specializations in psycholinguistics. This, in turn, perpetuates the scarcity of psycholinguistic research in the country, and at a more general level, contributes to the slow growth of our knowledge about the psychology of language in non-WEIRD contexts.

At the same time, however, it is of course also legitimate to ask whether there is any need, beyond that of basic research, for South African psycholinguistic research. The answer to such question is a simple yes. Obvious areas of practical application concern acquired and developmental language disorders in multilingual populations, or, more specifically, (1) correctly assessing, diagnosing and remediating language problems in children; (2) addressing problems with the acquisition of literacy in multilingual contexts; or (3) detecting early signs of dementia in elderly people. Similarly, studying conceptual development and cognitive processing in interaction with language acquisition is important to gain a better understanding of the benefits afforded by linguistic diversity and multilingualism, and how these may be productively harnessed in education.

In addition to these more traditional applications are those that concern the psycholinguistics of everyday behaviour. Recent research shows that decisions taken in a L2 may be different from those taken in the L1 (e.g. Geipel *et al.*, 2015, 2016; Hayakawa *et al.*, 2017; Vives *et al.*, 2018). This evidence suggests that individuals whose dominant language is their L1 exhibit greater risk-taking in the L2, are more rational in the L2, and have less-nuanced mental imagery in the L2. These phenomena are often subsumed under the umbrella term 'the foreign language effect'. Clearly, in a country where a significant part of the population operates in a language that is not their L1, it is important to know the extent to which, for example, political decisions may be influenced by said foreign language effect. Another aspect concerns public notices and communications, and the influence of linguistic categories on their reception. For instance, due to the historical drought that recently hit (and is still affecting) parts of the country, the provincial governments circulate information about water-saving measures. Here, knowledge about the potential influence of spatio-temporal metaphors and tense categories on the perception of temporal proximity of the day the water runs out (so-called Day Zero) can serve to inform the linguistic framing of these notices so that they are optimally designed, and yield the greatest possible effect on water-saving behaviour (e.g. 'Day Zero has been moved *forward/backward* by two weeks').

The utopia: A non-WEIRD psycholinguistics

Against the backdrop of the WEIRD bias, as well as the potential for psycholinguistics in South Africa, I now discuss a utopia of non-WEIRD psycholinguistics. Utopian expressions for an alternative psycholinguistics may be found on the pages of academic exploration such as the present one, which seek to move beyond the WEIRD bias. This type of evidence is more of the kind that Ernst Bloch (discussed in detail by Levitas, 1990: 15) labels *abstract utopia*, which expresses desire and is compared to 'wishful thinking'. Another kind of utopia is found in actual attempts at, in this case, expanding existing South African research on psycholinguistics, such as the establishment of a professional association, the African Psycholinguistics Association (APsA, www.apsa.africa), which seeks to bring together researchers on the African continent working on psycholinguistic topics. Another example along these lines is the construction of a dedicated space, the Multilingualism and Cognition Lab at Stellenbosch University, which seeks to function as a hub for local research on the multilingual mind (https://www.sun.ac.za/english/faculty/arts/linguistics). Following Bloch's taxonomy, these endeavours (see also Norcliffe *et al.*, 2015) are better labelled 'concrete utopia', since they simultaneously anticipate and effect the future.

The starting point for these expressions is the notion of absence: the lack of something which is not WEIRD (publications, textbooks, associations etc.), which in the end can be traced back to the absence of non-WEIRD psycholinguistic research. In this state of absence, the prefiguration of utopia then resides in the matter that can fill the void. Taking the South African situation as a point of departure, one can envisage a psycholinguistic research enterprise that is not dictated by WEIRD biases. Concretely, in this research, pre-conceived ideas about the relationship between order of acquisition of a language and proficiency and emotionality with that language would be few. Instead, linguistic behaviour would be viewed as a dynamic outcome of a combination of experiential factors. As a consequence, the traditional view of native-speaker competence would be untenable, as the conditions underlying such competence would largely be absent. It is important to note here that unlike critiques of the native speaker construct that target concerning multicompetence, this critique is concerned with societal configurations of language use. Moreover, the creative use of multiple linguistic resources in urban varieties, for example, would pose a challenge not only to linguistic classification but also assumptions about what should be regarded as a language/variety and its psycholinguistic status.

It is also possible to take the reasoning one step further, so as to imagine what biases might be produced in a multilingual setting instead. Here, questions asked about multilingualism in current WEIRD psycholinguistics would be completely flipped. What the brain can do with only one language is what would attract interest. This, then, would give rise to questions such as how is the brain affected by using only one language? How malleable is the monolingual mind? Is there something different about monolingual repertoires? Research on these questions would be published in journals such as *Monolingualism: Language and Cognition*, the *International Journal of Monolingualism* and the *Journal of Monolingual Development*. While an interesting thought experiment, replacing one set of biases with another is not necessarily an improvement of the situation. It does not readily find a place in any version of utopia, as this concept has at its core the notion of 'something better'.

Concluding Remarks

In the reasoning above, the notion of utopia is used as a tool to construe an alternative reality of knowledge production. The phenomenon treated here (i.e. research) might seem distant from the issues dealt with by previous studies on language and utopia, which have focused on everyday aspects of (linguistic) citizenship as they relate to fields and issues of contestation. While psycholinguistic research might be less present in a direct way in people's everyday lives, the findings it generates can have a massive impact on life choices and opportunities (e.g. education). For this reason, the WEIRD bias relates not only to the academic enterprise, but also to people's everyday life. As such, the psycholinguistic utopia is ultimately connected to participation (or the lack thereof) in knowledge production and an epistemological reorientation to be affected by a next generation of scholars.

Notes

(1) A few years after WEIRD was introduced, the so-called replicability crisis hit the cognitive sciences (Open Science Collaboration, 2015), with an unusually large number of studies failing to replicate. As this has become an increasing concern of the field, it may also have contributed to pushing the concept of WEIRD into the periphery.

(2) I am thankful to Robyn Berghoff for helping me access these data.

(3) It could be argued that this kind of situation is also found in certain linguistically diverse urban settings in the west, where there are few native speakers of the majority language. While this is true, it should also be recalled that in WEIRD contexts, those situations are experienced by a rather small part of the population, making them the exception rather than the rule. Studying such less typical WEIRD subjects may thus be informative.

(4) Note, however, that this view is currently being questioned, in view of recent evidence suggesting that the influence of multilingualism on cognitive and linguistic abilities is either inconsistent, negligible, or confounded with other factors (Bylund *et al.*, 2019; Lehtonen *et al.*, 2018).

(5) An example would be the assumption that space is the only concrete domain used for temporal expressions. This was disproved in Sinha *et al.*'s (2011) study on the Amondawa language.

(6) While I myself do not have systematic evidence of how speakers of Shona express pitch, the 10 or so Shona speakers I have run the crocodile metaphors past have reacted with laughter and/or incredulity, saying that they have never heard of it.

(7) These terms denote ethnic origin and were established during the apartheid era. Though not uncontested in contemporary South African society, they are widely used in official statistics, mass media, academia, etc.

(8) It should be noted that other courses/modules (e.g. on L1 development, L2 acquisition may of course bring in psycholinguistic issues, but they are not solely dedicated to psycholinguistics.

References

Afendras, E.A., Millar, S., Aogáin, E.M., Bamgboše, A., Kachru, Y., Saleemi, A.P., Dasgupta, P. (1995) On 'new/non-native' Englishes: A gameplan. *Journal of Pragmatics* 24 (3), 295–321. https://doi.org/10.1016/0378-2166(95)00030-V

Anthonissen, C. (2009) Bilingualism and language shift in Western Cape communities. *Stellenbosch Papers in Linguistics* 38 (2), 61–76. https://doi.org/10.5842/38-0-48

Aronin, L. and Singleton, D. (2012) *Multilingualism*. Amsterdam: John Benjamins Publishing.

Ashley, R. (2004) Musical pitch space across modalities: Spatial and other mappings through language and culture. In S. Lipscomb, R. Ashley, R. Gjerdingen and P. Webster (eds) *Proceedings of the International Conference on Music Perception and Cognition* (p. 8). Adelaide: Causal Productions.

Bak, T.H. and Mehmedbegovic, D. (2017) Healthy linguistic diet: The value of linguistic diversity and language learning across the lifespan. *Languages, Society and Policy.* https://doi.org/10.17863/CAM.9854

Bender, A. and Beller, S. (2013) Cognition is ... fundamentally cultural. *Behavioral Sciences* 3 (1), 42–54. https://doi.org/10.3390/bs3010042

Bender, A., Beller, S. and Medin, D.L. (2012) Turning tides: Prospects for more diversity in cognitive science. *Topics in Cognitive Science* 4 (3), 462–466. https://doi.org/10.1111/j.1756–8765.2012.01202.x

Berliner, P. (1981 [1978]) *The Soul of Mbira: Music and Traditions of the Shona People of Zimbabwe.* Berkeley: University of California Press.

Birdsong, D. and Gertken, L.M. (2013) In faint praise of folly: A critical review of native/non-native speaker comparisons, with examples from native and bilingual processing of French complex syntax. *Language, Interaction and Acquisition / Language, Interaction et Acquisition* 4 (2), 107–133. https://doi.org/10.1075/lia.4.2.01bir

Brown, P. (2011) Color Me bitter: Crossmodal compounding in Tzeltal perception words. *The Senses and Society* 6 (1), 106–116. https://doi.org/10.2752/174589311X1289 3982233957

Bylund, E. (2014) Unomathotholo or i-radio? Factors predicting the use of English loan-words among L1 isiXhosa–L2 English bilinguals. *Journal of Multilingual and Multicultural Development* 35 (2), 105–120. https://doi.org/10.1080/01434632.2013.849714

Bylund, E., Abrahamsson, N., Hyltenstam, K. and Norrman, G. (2019) Revisiting the bilingual lexical deficit: The impact of age of acquisition. *Cognition* 182, 45–49. https://doi.org/10.1016/j.cognition.2018.08.020

Bylund, E. and Athanasopoulos, P. (2014) Language and thought in a multilingual context: The case of isiXhosa. *Bilingualism: Language and Cognition* 17, 431–443.

Bylund, E. and Athanasopoulos, P. (2015) Motion event categorisation in a nativised variety of South African English. *International Journal of Bilingual Education and Bilingualism* 18 (5), 588–601. https://doi.org/10.1080/13670050.2015.1027145

Caldwell-Harris, C.L. (2014) Emotionality differences between a native and foreign language: Theoretical implications. *Frontiers in Psychology* 5. https://doi.org/10.3389/fpsyg.2014.01055

Canagarajah, S. (2007) Lingua franca English, multilingual communities, and language acquisition. *The Modern Language Journal* 91, 923–939. https://doi.org/10.1111/j.1540-4781.2007.00678.x

Coetzee-Van Rooy, S. (2012) Flourishing functional multilingualism: Evidence from language repertoires in the Vaal Triangle region. *International Journal of the Sociology of Language* 2012 (218), 87–119. https://doi.org/10.1515/ijsl-2012-0060

Comaroff, J. and Comaroff, J.L. (2011) *Theory From the South: Or, How Euro-America is Evolving Toward Africa.* Boulder, CO: Paradigm Publishers.

Cook, V. (1999) Going Beyond the native speaker in language teaching. *TESOL Quarterly* 33 (2), 185–209. https://doi.org/10.2307/3587717

Davidoff, J., Davies, I. and Roberson, D. (1999) Colour categories in a stone-age tribe. *Nature* 398 (6724), 203–204. https://doi.org/10.1038/18335

Davies, A. (2003) *The Native Speaker: Myth and Reality.* Clevedon: Multilingual Matters.

de Kadt, E. (2005) English, language shift and identities: A comparison between 'Zulu-dominant' and 'multicultural' students on a South African university campus. *Southern African Linguistics and Applied Language Studies* 23 (1), 19–37.

de Klerk, V. (2000) Language shift in Grahamstown: A case study of selected Xhosa-speakers. *International Journal of the Sociology of Language* 2000 (146), 87–110.

Deumert, A. (2010) Tracking the demographics of (urban) language shift – an analysis of South African census data. *Journal of Multilingual and Multicultural Development* 31 (1), 13–35.

Downey, G. (2010) We agree it's WEIRD, but is it WEIRD enough?, 10 July 2010. https://neuroanthropology.net/2010/07/10/we-agree-its-weird-but-is-it-weird-enough/ (accessed October 2018).

Dyers, C. (2008) Truncated multilingualism or language shift? An examination of language use in intimate domains in a new non-racial working class township in South Africa. *Journal of Multilingual and Multicultural Development* 29 (2), 110–126. https://doi.org/10.2167/jmmd533.0

Eitan, Z. and Timmers, R. (2010) Beethoven's last piano sonata and those who follow crocodiles: Cross-domain mappings of auditory pitch in a musical context. *Cognition* 114 (3), 405–422. https://doi.org/10.1016/j.cognition.2009.10.013

Evans, N. and Levinson, S.C. (2009) The myth of language universals: Language diversity and its importance for cognitive science. *Behavioral and Brain Sciences* 32 (5), 429–448; discussion 448–494. https://doi.org/10.1017/S0140525X0999094X

Geipel, J., Hadjichristidis, C. and Surian, L. (2015) How foreign language shapes moral judgment. *Journal of Experimental Social Psychology* 59, 8–17. https://doi.org/10.1016/j.jesp.2015.02.001

Geipel, J., Hadjichristidis, C. and Surian, L. (2016) Foreign language affects the contribution of intentions and outcomes to moral judgment. *Cognition* 154, 34–39. https://doi.org/10.1016/j.cognition.2016.05.010

Goodenough, F. (1926) Racial differences in the intelligence of school children. *Journal of Experimental Psychology* 9, 388–397.

Greenberg, J.H. (1956) The measurement of linguistic diversity. *Language* 32 (1), 109–115. https://doi.org/10.2307/410659.

Haun, D.B.M. and Rapold, C.J. (2009) Variation in memory for body movements across cultures. *Current Biology: CB* 19 (23), R1068–1069. https://doi.org/10.1016/j.cub.2009.10.041

Hayakawa, S., Tannenbaum, D., Costa, A., Corey, J.D. and Keysar, B. (2017) Thinking more or feeling less? Explaining the foreign-language effect on moral judgment. *Psychological Science* 28 (10), 1387–1397. https://doi.org/10.1177/ 0956797617720944

Henrich, J., Heine, S.J. and Norenzayan, A. (2010a) Most people are not WEIRD. *Nature* 466 (7302), 29–29. https://doi.org/ 10.1038/466029a

Henrich, J., Heine, S.J. and Norenzayan, A. (2010b) The weirdest people in the world? *Behavioral and Brain Sciences* 33 (2–3), 6183; discussion 83–135. https://doi.org/10.1017/S0140525X0999152X

Hobson, C. (1999) Morphological development in the interlanguage of English learners of Xhosa. Unpublished doctoral dissertation, Rhodes University.

Kamwangamalu, N.M. (2003) Social change and language shift: South Africa. *Annual Review of Applied Linguistics* 23, 225–242.

Lehtonen, M., Soveri, A., Laine, A., Järvenpää, J., de Bruin, A. and Antfolk, J. (2018) Is bilingualism associated with enhanced executive functioning in adults? A meta-analytic review. *Psychological Bulletin* 144 (4), 394–425. https://doi.org/10.1037/bul0000142

Levinson, S.C. (1997) Language and cognition: The cognitive consequences of spatial description in Guugu Yimithirr. *Journal of Linguistic Anthropology* 7 (1), 98–131. https://doi.org/10.1525/jlin.1997.7.1.98

Levinson, S.C., Kita, S., Haun, D.B.M. and Rasch, B.H. (2002) Returning the tables: Language affects spatial reasoning. *Cognition* 84 (2), 155–188. https://doi.org/10.1016/S0010-0277(02)00045-8.

Lévi-Strauss, C. (1962) *La Pensée Sauvage*. Chicago: University of Chicago Press.

Levitas, R. (1990) Educated hope: Ernst Bloch on abstract and concrete utopia. *Utopian Studies*, 1 (2), 13–26.

Lucy, J.A. (1992) *Grammatical Categories and Cognition*. Cambridge: Cambridge University Press.

Majid, A. and Burenhult, N. (2014) Odors are expressible in language, as long as you speak the right language. *Cognition* 130 (2), 266–270. https://doi.org/10.1016/j.cognition.2013.11.004

McCormick, K. (2002) Code-switching, code-mixing and convergence in Cape Town. In R. Mesthrie (ed.) *Language in South Africa* (pp. 216–234). Cape Town: Cambridge University Press.

Medin, D.L. and Atran, S. (2004) The native mind: Biological categorization and reasoning in development and across cultures. *Psychological Review* 111 (4), 960–983. https://doi.org/10.1037/0033-295X.111.4.960

Mesthrie, R. (2002) *Language in South Africa*. Cambridge: Cambridge University Press.

Norcliffe, E., Harris, A.C. and Jaeger, T. F. (2015) Cross-linguistic psycholinguistics and its critical role in theory development: Early beginnings and recent advances. *Special Issue of Language, Cognition and Neuroscience* 30 (9), 1009–1032. https://doi.org/1 0.1080/23273798.2015.1080373

Norenzayan, A. and Heine, S.J. (2005) Psychological universals: What are they and how can we know? *Psychological Bulletin* 131 (5), 763–784. https://doi.org/10.1037/0033-2909.131.5.763

Oostendorp, M. and Bylund, E. (2012) Emotions and HIV/AIDS in South Africa: A multilingual perspective. *Stellenbosch Papers in Linguistics* 41 (0), 77–89. https://doi.org/10.5842/41-0-84

Open Science Collaboration (2015) Estimating the reproducibility of psychological science. *Science* 349 (6251), aac4716. https://doi.org/10.1126/science.aac4716

Pavlenko, A. (2008) Emotion and emotion-laden words in the bilingual lexicon. *Bilingualism: Language and Cognition* 11 (02), 147–164. See https://doi.org/10.1017/S1366728908003283

Pavlenko, A. (2014) *The Bilingual Mind*. Cambridge: Cambridge University Press.

Posel, D. and Zeller, J. (2016) Language shift or increased bilingualism in South Africa: Evidence from census data. *Journal of Multilingual and Multicultural Development* 37 (4), 357–370. https://doi.org/10.1080/01434632.2015.1072206

Rozin, P. (2001) Social psychology and science: some lessons From Solomon Asch. *Personality and Social Psychology Review* 5 (1), 2–14. https://doi.org/10.1207/S15327957PSPR0501_1

Rozin, P. (2009) What kind of empirical research should we publish, fund, and reward? A different perspective. *Perspectives on Psychological Science* 4 (4), 435–439. https://doi.org/10.1111/j.1745-6924.2009.01151.x

Rueschemeyer, S.-A. and Gaskell, M.G. (eds) (2018) *The Oxford Handbook of Psycholinguistics*. Oxford: Oxford University Press.

Saer, D. (1923) The effects of bilingualism on intelligence. *British Journal of Psychology* 14, 25–38.

Schmid, M.S. (2013) First language attrition. *Wiley Interdisciplinary Reviews: Cognitive Science* 4 (2), 117–123. https://doi.org/10.1002/wcs.1218

Sinha, C., Sinha, V.D.S., Zinken, J. and Sampaio, W. (2011) When time is not space: The social and linguistic construction of time intervals and temporal event relations in an Amazonian culture. *Language and Cognition* 3 (01), 137–169. https://doi.org/10.1515/langcog.2011.0.

Stroud, C. (2001) African mother-tongue programmes and the politics of language: Linguistic citizenship versus linguistic human rights. *Journal of Multilingual and Multicultural Development* 22 (4), 339–355. https://doi.org/10.1080/01434630108666440.

Stroud, C. (2009) A postliberal critique of language rights: Toward a politics of language for a linguistics of contact. In J. Petrovic (ed.) *International Perspectives on Bilingual Education: Policy, Practice, and Controversy*. Charlotte, NC: Information Age Publishing.

Stroud, C. (2015) Linguistic citizenship as utopia. *Multilingual Margins: A Journal of Multilingualism from the Periphery* 2 (2), 20–37.

Stroud, C. (2018) Linguistic citizenship. In L. Lim, C. Stroud and L. Wee (eds) *The Multilingual Citizen: Towards a Politics of Language for Agency and Change* (pp. 17–39). Bristol: Multilingual Matters.

Stroud, C. and Heugh, K. (2004) Linguistic human rights and linguistic citizens. In J. Farland and D. Patrick (eds) *Language Rights and Language Survival: Sociolinguistic and Sociocultural Perspectives* (pp. 191–218). Manchester: St Jerome.

Stroud, C. and Williams, Q. (2017) Multilingualism as utopia. *AILA Review* 30 (1), 167–188. https://doi.org/10.1075/aila.00008.str.

Vives, M.L., Aparici, M. and Costa, A. (2018) The limits of the foreign language effect on decision-making: The case of the outcome bias and the representativeness heuristic. *PLoS ONE* 13 (9). https://doi.org/10.1371/journal.pone.0203528.

Zbikowski, L. (2017) Music, analogy, and metaphor. In R. Ashley and R. Timmers (eds) *The Routledge Companion to Music Cognition* (pp. 501–512). New York: Routledge.

Appendix

Table 10.1 Figures of author affiliations 2006–2016 of selected journals for articles containing the keywords 'bilingualism', 'multilingualism' and 'second language'. (The left column under each journal indicates country of author affiliation; the right column indicates number of authors with an affiliation in that country.) Source: SCOPUS.

Applied Psycholinguistics		Bilingualism: Language and Cognition		Cognition		Journal of Experimental Psychology: General	
United States	77	United States	198	United States	58	United States	14
Canada	34	United Kingdom	86	United Kingdom	25	United Kingdom	10
United Kingdom	29	Canada	61	Canada	12	Canada	8
Netherlands	15	Netherlands	52	Spain	10	Belgium	6
Germany	12	Germany	40	France	9	France	4
Australia	6	Spain	28	Germany	8	Germany	4
Japan	5	Australia	16	Israel	7	Netherlands	3
Turkey	5	Belgium	15	Japan	7	Spain	3
Greece	4	Hong Kong	13	Netherlands	7	China	2
China	3	Italy	12	Italy	5	Portugal	2
Israel	3	France	11	Australia	3	Italy	1
Singapore	3	China	10	Belgium	3	Japan	1
France	2	Sweden	10	Singapore	3	Turkey	1
Hong Kong	2	Israel	9	Argentina	2		
Italy	2	Japan	8	Greece	2		
Norway	2	Singapore	6	Hong Kong	2		
South Korea	2	Switzerland	6	Austria	1		
Spain	2	Norway	5	Chile	1		
Argentina	1	Finland	4	China	1		
Belgium	1	Portugal	4	Colombia	1		
Finland	1	Taiwan	4	Cyprus	1		
India	1	Saudi Arabia	3	Denmark	1		
Mexico	1	South Korea	3	Finland	1		
Qatar	1	Brazil	2	Luxembourg	1		
Slovakia	1	Denmark	2	Mexico	1		
Sweden	1	Hungary	2	Poland	1		
Taiwan	1	India	2	Portugal	1		
United Arab Emirates	1	Mexico	2	Switzerland	1		
		Poland	2	Taiwan	1		
		Russian Federation	2				
		South Africa	2				
		Turkey	2				
		United Arab Emirates	2				
		Argentina	1				
		Cyprus	1				
		Czech Republic	1				
		Greece	1				
		Iran	1				
		Macao	1				
		Malta	1				
		New Zealand	1				
		Serbia	1				
		Thailand	1				
		Uruguay	1				

Journal of Memory and Language		Psychological Science		Studies in Second Language Acquisition	
United States	30	United States	14	United States	104
United Kingdom	14	Spain	6	United Kingdom	29
Netherlands	13	United Kingdom	5	Canada	27
Spain	10	Canada	4	Sweden	12
Belgium	8	France	3	Netherlands	11
Canada	4	Belgium	2	Germany	10
China	4	Germany	1	Japan	8
France	3	Israel	1	New Zealand	7
Australia	2	Italy	1	South Korea	6
Germany	2	Luxembourg	1	Australia	5
Finland	1	Portugal	1	China	4
Hong Kong	1	Sweden	1	France	4
Israel	1	Switzerland	1	Belgium	3
Japan	1			Hong Kong	3
Switzerland	1			South Africa	2
				Spain	2
				Taiwan	2
				Brazil	1
				Chile	1
				Denmark	1
				Finland	1
				Italy	1
				Malaysia	1
				Mexico	1
				Poland	1
				Puerto Rico	1
				Thailand	1
				Turkey	1

11 The Sociolinguistics of Responsibility

Don Kulick

In discussions of social justice there is a subtle but important difference between talk about 'rights' and talk about 'entitlements'. 'Rights' are things (e.g. freedom, participation, equity and benefits) that people claim. 'Entitlements' are things (freedom, etc.) that people are owed by others. The difference turns on focus: in talk or analysis that concerns itself with rights, attention is on the demands made by individuals or groups who stake claims to rights. In thinking about entitlements, on the other hand, the spotlight is on those people, institutions and structures responsible for providing individuals with services, liberties and welfare that are their due as fellow human beings deserving of justice.

Historians have documented how the idea of human rights was critiqued practically from the moment it was first declared at the end of the 18th century (Hunt, 2007; Moyne, 2010). A year after the French National Assembly's Declaration of the Rights of Man and Citizen in 1789, the British essayist Edmund Burke published one of the best-known criticisms: an indignant, dismissive response that ridiculed the idea of universal human rights. Burke insisted that liberties could only be delivered by a government anchored in history.

Burke is cited approvingly by philosopher Hannah Arendt in her book *The Origins of Totalitarianism* (Arendt, 1973). In a chapter titled 'The decline of the nation state and the end of the rights of man', Arendt discusses how human rights, which are supposed to be inalienable, irreducible, and universal, in fact, are the exact opposite. Far from being universal and independent of all governments, human rights are utterly dependent for their recognition and fulfilment on the very nation-states that they are supposed to transcend.

The place one sees this with absolute clarity is in the plight of refugees and stateless persons. Arendt points out that historically, and, she says, not coincidentally, the numbers of denationalized and stateless people began to expand exponentially at precisely the time in history – the aftermath of the First World War – when talk of human rights began to gain international currency as a way of thinking about entitlements. But those supposedly fundamental human rights have no meaning for the vast majority of people they are meant to protect.

'The paradox involved in the loss of human rights is that such loss coincides with the instant when a person becomes a human being in general,' Arendt (1973: 302) writes. In other words, one loses one's human rights when one is stripped (because one is a stateless person or a refugee) of one's profession, citizenship, community and ability to act. When one loses all that, one becomes, precisely, nothing but a human – nothing but, Arendt says, '[one's] own absolutely unique individuality which, deprived of expression within and action upon a common world, loses all significance'. Arendt's point is that talk about rights – especially talk about theoretical, supposedly universal rights that are not anchored in civic structures and concrete legal protections that can hold individuals and institutions accountable to blame – can actually facilitate people's degradation, not their empowerment. And labelling an entitlement a 'human right' can be a way of depoliticizing it by making it supposedly inalienable and unquestionable – the responsibility, in other words, of everyone. But making everybody responsible, Arendt argues, ends up amounting to the same thing as making nobody responsible.

How might scholars of language in social life think about questions of entitlements and responsibility? This chapter briefly presents the work of two theoreticians whose work may provide some traction to do that. The two are the Italian philosopher Giorgio Agamben and the French philosopher Emmanuel Levinas. As far as I am able to tell, the work of these two philosophers does not feature much in discussions about language by sociolinguistics (but see Stroud, 2014). But it could, and perhaps it should. Agamben and Levinas address the social world and social relations from different perspectives and in different registers. Agamben focuses on the condition of modernity and what he, following Michel Foucault, calls 'biopolitics', which is a form of power that manages individuals by attaching them to particular subjectivities that are 'for their own good' – like when we are told that we should be happy that the government is reading our emails, listening to our cell phone conversations and watching our every move on CCTV security cameras because this is to protect us, it is 'for our own good'. Levinas is more explicitly metaphysical than Agamben, and his work is about how we are called into being by the address of another who appeals to us for recognition and engagement.

I became acquainted with these philosophers in the course of my research on the question of vulnerability; of how we might approach vulnerability in a way that does not inevitably see it as a deplorable condition from which people ought to be defended, rescued or liberated. In reading Agamben and Levinas to help me think about that, I came to realize that these two philosophers are also relevant to sociolinguists. The reason for that is because Agamben proposes a framework for perceiving how power works in the current state of our world, and Levinas, who insists that ethics precedes ontology – i.e. that relationships of responsibility to others are in place before we come to know ourselves as individuals – offers a highly original way of thinking about social relations outside or beyond the language of rights.

Agamben and Bare Life

Agamben has written books about a wide range of topics, from aesthetics to Biblical textual criticism. He has written extensively on language, in highly arcane terms that focus on how language secures its reference to the world through the possibility of its own suspension, in other words, by the possibility of its being destroyed, for example through torture. This kind of focus on extreme cases, on exceptions, is what characterizes the work for which he is most known internationally, namely his 1998 book titled *Homo Sacer: Sovereign Power and Bare Life*.

Homo sacer is about the power of the state to make people into outcasts. Agamben claims that the entire Western political tradition, from the Greek city states of Plato's time onwards to today, rests on a fundamental opposition between what he calls, using the Greek words, '*zoē*' and '*bios*'. The first of these concepts, *zoē*, means existence, biological life, life in the most basic sense of the word – the kind of existence in the world that non-human animals also have. Think, when you hear the word, of 'zoos' or 'zoology' and it is easy to remember this.

The second concept, *bios*, means life in the realm of the social and the political. It means a particular kind of life, a qualified life. Think of 'biography', of a life that has a meaningful trajectory, as a mnemonic for the word.

Agamben argues that this distinction between natural life and political life generated a third kind of life, one he calls 'bare life'. Bare life is politicized *zoē*. It is a life that is reduced to nothing but existence, but that is not, therefore, outside or beyond the political realm – it is, instead, a form of life that is *produced by* the political realm. The *homo sacer* – the 'sacred man' – of Agamben's book's title is the concrete figure of this bare life, the bearer, if you will, of bare life. In Roman law, a *homo sacer* was someone who, as Agamben explains, could be killed but not sacrificed. In other words, it was someone who was banned – someone whose life mattered enough to be banished from the community, but not enough to mourn if he was killed (note, not 'murdered' – killed. A *homo sacer*, by definition, could not be murdered – rather like a pig slaughtered at an abattoir is not generally held to be have been 'murdered', or an Iraqi civilian killed by an American drone is not generally held to be 'murdered', at least not by the United States government.

The paradigmatic modern exemplar of bare life, according to Agamben, is the prisoner in a Nazi concentration camp – a person who is reduced to mere existence by the actions of a calculating totalitarian state, and able to be killed without impunity.

Agamben's work has been enthusiastically received by many social scientists. The reason for this is that he insists that Nazi death camps are not an aberration. On the contrary, he insists that 'the birth of the camp in our time appears as an event the decisively signals the political space of modernity itself' (1998: 174).

The events of the past few decades have shown this to be a perceptive and accurate observation. The name Agamben (1998) gives to 'the political space of modernity itself' is the 'state of exception'. This phrase has two meanings. The first refers to the condition of being the exception; the second is a reference to the power that Agamben says is exercised by modern states, namely the power to govern by means of exception. Take the concentration camp, or its contemporary cousin, the American prisons of Guantánamo and Abu Ghraib as examples. The prisoners detained in these camps are exceptions, but the mechanisms that made them exceptions can be turned on anyone. The still, very much ongoing NSA scandal that I alluded to earlier is perhaps the most glaring example of how this not only can happen, but actually *is happening* right now.

Edward Snowden's 2013 revelations included the disclosure that the American National Security Agency, since 2006, has been collecting records on every phone call every American makes, has vacuumed the content of emails, Internet searches and chat rooms (partly by hacking into the servers of Google and Yahoo), has tapped the phones and emails of leaders like Angela Merkel, and has collected the cell-phone location data and email address lists of vast numbers of non-US citizens around the world. The justification for this massive covert intrusion of privacy is not that the state wants to penalize us or infringe upon our rights, or to punish us. It wants to protect us. The state gathers this information for our own good. The NSA has argued that it must be able to collect the information it does, regardless of any connection to terrorism, because the records might become 'relevant' to a terrorism investigation in the future.

This kind of interweaving of politics and life – where a good, safe life itself becomes the preoccupation of State power and where that good, safe life becomes a means of repression and control: this is biopolitics. And biopolitics, in Agamben's view, is the vector of power that is working today to bind our subjectivities to the state in such a way that we have all become virtual *homines sacri* (Agamben, 1998: 111, 115).

What may be useful for sociolinguists working with issues of diversity and power is that Agamben suggests a framework in which the state produces outcasts in the guise of protecting and furthering everyone's own good. His insistence that modern mechanisms of governance rely on biopolitical technologies that interlace our constitution of ourselves as subjects with the external control of the state – this conceptualization of life in 'the political space of modernity' can provide us with a kind of map or grid that we can use to help us think about things like discourse, subjectification, identification, diversity and scale.

Furthermore, there is a deficiency or a lack in Agamben's writing that makes it attractive to intervention from sociolinguists. That deficiency is the philosopher's solid disinterest in sociolinguistics and language practice. Agamben's copious writings on language are concerned with philosophy. His interlocutors are Heidegger, Benjamin and Wittgenstein; not Labov, Schegloff or Rampton. His interest is *'langue'*, not *'parole'*. Almost nowhere does Agamben connect the state of exception with actual language practice.

In fact, he seems happier thinking about this whole issue more in terms of the absence of language. For example, throughout the *Homo Sacer* book, Agamben proposes a cast of characters whom he sees as exemplifying bare life. A list of some of these appears in part three of the book, right at the very end (and indeed, to read the *Homo Sacer* book, I always suggest beginning with part three first and then going back to read the beginning). Two figures in particular stand out as the epitome of *homo sacer.*

The first is a literary figure, Bartelby the scrivener. Bartelby is a character in a short story of that name by Herman Melville, the American author, who wrote *Moby Dick* in 1851. Bartelby is a scribe hired by a lawyer to copy out legal texts. He is proficient at his job, but when the lawyer asks him to do anything other than copy out texts, he always responds, 'I would prefer not to'. Eventually Bartelby declines even to copy, saying that he would 'prefer not to'. His employer can't get him to leave because he would 'prefer not to', and finally, feeling sorry for him but desperate to get rid of him, the employer himself moves out of his offices into another building. The new tenants find Bartelby still inhabiting the offices, and when they ask him to leave, he responds 'I would prefer not to'. He is arrested and taken to prison, where he 'prefers not to' eat, and in the end, he dies.

The second epitome of *homo sacer* is a real person, or a real kind of person, described for example by the Italian author Primo Levi in *If This is a Man*, his 1947 memoir about the 11 months he spent as a prisoner in the Auschwitz concentration camp. This *homo sacer* is *der Muselmann*, 'the Muslim', as the camp inmates called him. 'The Muslim' was, of course, a Jew. The name denoted a person, a Jewish prisoner, who was near death due to exhaustion, starvation and hopelessness. 'Muslims' were shell-shocked, lethargic, unable to stand, unable to react to threats and violence, and mute. Other prisoners avoided them, and they were sent to the gas chambers as soon as their condition was observed by the camp guards.

What is striking, from a linguistic perspective, about both of Agamben's prime examples of *homo sacer*, is that neither of them has language. The only words Bartelby ever utters are 'I would prefer not to'. Agamben finds this compelling as an example of what he calls 'potentiality' – the ability to disrupt the working of power by refusing to either obey it or reject it. And in the *Muselmann*, Agamben sees someone who has passed beyond the reach of power.

By presenting these speechless figures as epitomes of *homo sacer*, Agamben appears to equate bare life at its barest with the absence of language. Like literary scholar Elaine Scarry's well-known analysis of physical pain and torture as forces that actively pulverize language (Scarry, 1988), Agamben seems to be suggesting that in its purest form, the bare life produced by the state of exception squeezes language from people like a grape and divests them of the possibility of expressive elaboration.

This would not be a problem if Agamben did not also see both Bartleby and the *Muselmann* as subjects of resistance who thwart power by rendering it inoperable. Bartelby, says Agamben (1998: 48), carries the promise of liberation from the state of exception. And the *Muselmann*, 'mute and absolutely alone', Agamben (1998: 185) writes, '*threatens* the *lex animata* [the living law] of the camp'.

Both figures, of course, die.

Now if the icons of resistance to the contemporary workings of power are speechless figures, who, in addition, are dying or dead, then one might perhaps be forgiven for having a bit of a hard time perceiving the emancipatory potential of Agamben's thinking. Another example is babies who died before they were baptized: they escape the Law, explains Agamben (1993 [1990]: 5–6). God's judgment doesn't touch them.

On the other hand, however, this idiosyncratic attention to the way language does not operate in the state of exception (in his book on witnessing and the holocaust, he calls this 'non-language' (Agamben, 2002 [1999]: 38), and the notion of 'potentiality' as a means of stoppage or rendering power inoperable – these are features of the theory that could be precisely what might make Agamben's work fruitful for linguists looking for new ways to approach or frame discursive or interactional data. The attenuated role Agamben accords actual linguistic practice in his framework of biopolitics and modernity opens a space for sociolinguists to challenge him with empirical material that inevitably must nuance any account of the state of exception and bare life.

To the extent that we accept Agamben's description that our current world is increasingly coming to be characterized by a state of exception that is turning us into *homines sacri*, the question becomes: What are the linguistic manifestations of that dimension of biopolitical existence? How does language work to produce, maintain – and contest or subvert – the state of exception? How is language differentially distributed in ways that interpellate and subjectivize different people as different kinds of *homo sacer*?

Levinas on Responsibility

The Lithuanian-French philosopher Emmanuel Levinas, who died at age 89 in 1995, is recognized as being a philosopher of ethics and alterity, which is to say that he theorizes difference between people and what that means for respectful engagement. This is importantly different from the classical liberal argument about ethics that bases engagement with others on empathy and a recognition of similarity. Classic liberalism holds that I should treat others in the way I would wish to be treated because my actions will affect others the same way they would affect me, and I can empathize because of the characteristics we have in common.

Levinas says something quite different. Rather than suggest that we are obligated to others because they are similar to us, Levinas argues that we are obligated to others because they are *different* from us, and from this position of difference, they make demands on us that enmesh us in a relationship – whether we like it or not (Levinas, 1969, 1991).

Levinas's argument goes something like this: people are different because each individual has a specific history, a specific place in social networks, a specific singularity. This singularity emerges through relations with others, whose existence, whose address and whose behaviour towards me is what determines a place for me and, thus, in a fundamental sense, is what makes me *me*. This relationship of susceptibility to others binds me to other people – since my existence as a subject depends on them. It also obligates me to them, both as an object of other people's actions and as an agent in relation to others. Levinas insists that the obligation is an ethical one, in that it is both a response to others and entails a response towards others.

Social life consists of encounters with other people who remind us, through their presence in the world, that we are not completely free and independent agents who can do whatever we want. These encounters make demands on us. The demands may sometimes be punitive and oppressive, but before they are anything else, Levinas maintains, they are first and foremost appeals for acknowledgement. These appeals emerge out of the inescapable vulnerability that each person has in relation to another, and they testify to that vulnerability: they rouse it and remind one of it.

Therefore, the fundamental modality of the calls that other people address to us is one that expresses passivity. They are appeals from the position of susceptibility; appeals to provide support, to offer kindness, to accept accountability, to share the world. And because they are formulated from a position of passivity, they are calls that do not imply any reciprocity. They ask us to act without any expectation of reward or even gratitude.

Levinas says that we can ignore these solicitations from others. We can evade them and act irresponsibly in relation to them. But what we cannot do is avoid them altogether. Attempting to do so – for example by asking a question like, 'Why should I care about refugees or stateless people?' – doesn't dispense with or annul a relationship so much as it affirms one. The fact that the question can be asked at all acknowledges that however one answers it, one *already* has a relation to refugees and stateless people. And it avows that the relationship entails responsibility – in the dual senses of both of 'the ability to respond' and 'the impossibility of indifference'.

Philosophical arguments for ethical obligation like those developed by Levinas are important because they offer a vantage point from which we can contemplate respectful engagement with others without requiring similarity or insisting on empathy. Levinas maintains that we are responsible for others not because they are similar to us or because we necessarily understand them, or because we can hope or expect to get something back from them (a returned favour, gratitude, love). Instead, he says, we are responsible for them because they are living beings who exist in our world and who *therefore* deserve to be accorded dignity and the opportunity to flourish.

This kind of understanding of responsibility – not as something one can choose, or something that is extraneous to social interactions, but, rather, as something that is a foundational feature inherent in and constitutive of all identities, social relationships and every social interaction – is a perspective that opens up a range of possibilities for sociolinguists. We have become so used to, and so vastly comfortable, seeing language in voluntaristic, individualistic terms of identity or agency or resistance that we have a hard time imagining how language also expresses ethical engagement. Even approaches to language that highlight mutual engagement, such as Howard Giles's Communication Accommodation Theory (Giles & Ogay, 2007), sees speakers' engagement with others in terms of psychology and structure, not in terms of ethics.

But Levinas's insistence that ethics precedes ontology invites us to ask ourselves what would happen to our understandings and analyses of language if we viewed interactions not just in terms of response, but also in terms of *responsibility*. If we asked how speakers' linguistic practices are not just actions that stake a claim in social space, but are also appeals for recognition and engagement, are calls to share the world? That to engage in language is to enact and express dimensions of the vulnerability and mutual susceptibility that are constitutive of human existence?

All this could easily tie into and extend the biopolitical concerns of Agamben outlined earlier, because the question of how we engage ethically one another is necessarily embedded in sociopolitical life. Ethics may precede ontology, as Levinas suggests. But any sociolinguist worth his or her salt will tell you that both ontology and ethics are achievements. They are manifested, enacted, and experienced through interactions, many of them involving language in the social world. How, for example, is responsibility both acknowledged and disavowed in how people talk about or talk to *homines sacri* such as refugees, or homeless people? In how individuals use language to negotiate national identities in what may be developing into a post-EU Europe?

Disability and Ethics in Sweden and Denmark

At this point in the discussion, an example might be helpful. Let me provide a brief one, not concerning the refugees or homeless people I have been mentioning throughout this essay, but, instead, taken from the research I conducted on the sexual lives of adults with significant disabilities. That work, which is detailed in the book *Loneliness and Its Opposite*, contrasts two Scandinavian countries, Sweden and Denmark (Kulick & Rydström, 2015). Those two countries share a history and many similarities when it comes to social and political structure, cultural orientations and language.

When it comes to the issue of sexuality in the lives of adults who have significant disabilities, however, the two countries diverge dramatically.

In Sweden, the idea that an adult with significant congenital impairments such as some forms of cerebral palsy, autism or Down syndrome, should be provided with information about sex, or any form of hands-on assistance with sex, is roundly rejected. That significantly disabled adults have any sexual feelings at all is repressed, denied and dismissed. The issue of sexuality is not discussed, and whenever it arises (for example, when a man's penis becomes erect when he is bathed by a support person), the default response is to actively intercede to prevent erotic awareness, and, above all, erotic activity, from ever arising.

In Denmark there is a different attitude. There, during the 1970s and ongoing today, people who work with adults with disabilities, as well as activists and family members who advocate for them, developed policies and practices for acknowledging and supporting the erotic lives of people with significant disabilities. The policies include national guidelines that inform support workers what they are permitted to do in regard to sexuality, what they are *not* permitted to do, and what they *must* do.

The first category – what support workers are permitted to do – involves providing information to adults regardless of whether or not they explicitly request it. This is in recognition of the fact that many people with congenital disabilities have received no sexual education and have often spent many years living in family homes, where their sex lives have usually not been topics of affirmative concern.

The second category – those activities which are not permitted – include insisting on talking about sex to anyone who clearly signals an unwillingness to participate in conversations about it. Crucially, it also means that support workers are forbidden to actually have sex with the disabled person that they support. A helper can assist the disabled person with activities like masturbation (for example by preparing, placing and turning on mechanical sex aids, and then leaving the room, returning at an agreed upon time, and cleaning up afterwards), or making it possible for two disabled lovers to have sex, e.g. by inflating an air mattress, undressing the couple, arranging them on the mattress, leaving the room and returning whenever they ring a buzzer for assistance to assume new positions.

But individuals who help someone with a disability have sex are prohibited from having sex in any form with the person they help.

The third category is in many ways the most important in terms of providing access to affirmative erotic knowledge and experiences. What support workers *must* do is this: if a person with a disability requests information about sex or assistance with it, the support worker they ask must assume the responsibility of finding someone who is able to provide the information or assistance. The support worker who is asked is under no obligation, him or herself, to engage in the erotic life of the person requesting help. But that worker does have a responsibility to find someone who will. This guideline protects the person with a disability from the humiliation of having to go from person to person to mention their need for information about or help with sex until she or he perhaps finally finds someone who might be willing to help (see Kulick & Rydström, 2015: 258–261).

Adults with significant disabilities who live in group homes in Sweden and Denmark are not exactly examples of the kinds of bare life that Giorgio Agamben has in mind in his writings on the topic. But because many of them have no verbal language and are dependent on others to be able to perform their most basic everyday needs, they are constantly at risk of being denied a *bios* and treated more or less as *zoë*.

Perhaps no one needs to be reminded that the gas chambers at death camps like Auschwitz were first rehearsed on people with intellectual and physical disabilities. Nor do we need to go particularly far back in European history to see cases of disabled people being treated appallingly. In Kulick and Rydström (2015: 67), for example, we cite a ghastly case from Denmark that was reported by reformers who advocated for change: a 39-year-old 'mentally retarded' (*psykisk udviklingshæmmet*) man who began to try to masturbate at age 16 was dealt with at the institution in which he lived first by restraining him, then by injecting him with female hormones. Then, when none of that worked, doctors performed a lobotomy on him. When he continued to show interest in his genitals, a second lobotomy was performed. Then electroshock treatment, then a third lobotomy.

This occurred *in the late 1960s.*

In many places in the world, people with significant physical and/or intellectual disabilities continue to be institutionalized and treated with intolerable cruelty (see e.g. Klepikova, 2017). Citing sociologist Erving Goffman's classic study of stigma, Martha Nussbaum (2006: 191) observes that:

> a central feature of the operation of stigma, especially toward people with impairments and disabilities, is the denial of individuality: the entire encounter with such a person is articulated in terms of the stigmatized trait, and we come to believe that the person with the stigma is not fully or really human.

People with disabilities, especially people with significant congenital impairments, teeter constantly and perilously on the brink of being regarded and treated as less than human.

In the *Loneliness and its Opposite* book, my co-author and I (Kulick & Rydström, 2015) interpret Danish support workers' engagement with the disabled adults with whom they work in affirmative terms. We argue that Swedish engagement, which involves refusals, disavowals and denials – which also are forms of engagement: doing 'nothing' (which is what Swedish support workers say they do in relation to sex and disability) is in fact always doing 'something', e.g. rejecting an appeal to inform or assist – is amoral and unjust. We evaluate the two countries in relation to the capabilities approach to social justice elaborated by Martha Nussbaum (2006), and using that approach as our metric, we concluded that Denmark clearly is a more just society for people with significant disabilities than is its neighbour Sweden (Sweden is the 'Loneliness' of the book's title; Denmark is 'Its Opposite').

What would happen if we looked at the material we discuss in terms of language, and in terms of the ideas of Agamben and Levinas that I outlined above? Many of the adults with disabilities I worked with during my ethnographic research had no verbal language. This was challenging to a linguistic anthropologist such as myself. The silences produced by the people I worked with were not so much interactional in the way Conversation Analysts like to analyse them (e.g. Hepburn & Bolden, 2013; Pomerantz & Heritage, 2013), as they were ontological. They demanded that caring others actively engage with them and interpret them. This was time consuming and demanding.

One young man who resided in one of the group homes for people with cerebral palsy I lived in, was born with a neurological problem that resulted in paralysis from the neck down. This man, Steen, was also spastic, on the autism spectrum, and he was deaf. He had no verbal language and could not use sign language either, since he couldn't move his hands. However, Steen understood sign language, and he communicated his desires by making sounds that were modulations of the syllable, 'uh.'

Caregivers and staff members in the group home where Steen has lived for many years interpreted these sounds by asking him yes/no questions, either through sign language, if they knew it, or by pointing to a small square of paper taped to the arm of Steen's wheelchair.

The paper, about half the size of a postcard, was divided into five rows, each of which contained eight squares. Inside each square was a letter, or, in the bottom row, a number from 1 to 10. The first row read A, B, C, D and so on, to H. Below that, the next row started with I, J, K and so on. When Steen made it clear by uttering an 'uh' sound that he had something he wanted to communicate, helpers would put their finger on the 'A' and move it, letter by letter, down the row and onto the next, until Steen made another sound. This indicated that the helper had chosen the correct first letter of the word Steen was thinking of. Then that person went back to 'A' and started over again, until she or he got the second letter. This went on until the helper successfully said the word that Steen had in mind. At that point, the helper would start to ask more yes/no questions, hoping to discover what it was that Steen wanted to communicate, going back to the square for more spelling out, in case it was still not clear what it is that Steen wanted to say.

This laborious system of communication was extremely successful. The people who worked in Steen's group home felt confident that they understood Steen, and Steen seemed content as well. One result of this communication was that Steen made it clear that he had a girlfriend whom he had met at the activity centre where he spent his weekdays. That girlfriend was deaf, like him, but she also had an intellectual disability and was virtually blind. Steen let it be known that he would like to invite his girlfriend over to spend the night. When the staff at Steen's group home determined that his girlfriend wanted this as well, they accommodated the couple once every six weeks by arranging work schedules such that the girlfriend could leave the group home where she lived and spend a romantic evening and night with Steen.

A situation like this is unthinkable in Sweden.

Now, in invoking philosophers such as Levinas or Agamben to make sense of engagement like that which the staff in Steen's group home extended to him, there is a risk of trivializing both the philosophers' thought and the empirical cases it gets applied to. Philosophers – Continental philosophers, especially – generally offer critical observations about life, not practical recipes for living. And as far as the empirical case is concerned, it certainly is possible to discuss the relationship between Steen and his support workers in terms other than those proposed by scholars like Levinas and Agamben.

Nevertheless, I believe that both philosophers have something to offer here that allows us to go beyond simply remarking that Danish support workers are more accommodating and progressive than their Swedish counterparts.

Levinas, to take him first, argues, as I noted above, that ethics precedes ontology. What this actually might mean is a topic dissected and debated by entire libraries of secondary literature on the eminent philosopher's writings. For our purposes, it is perhaps enough to note that Steen's support workers responded to Steen's appeal for recognition and respect, even though he has no verbal language to express it in, and they responded to it affirmatively and in a register of generosity and welcome. In responding in such a manner, the helpers became subjectified as ethically aware, responsible agents.

The opposite is true for Swedish support workers. In refusing a call from somebody like Steen – which, if the topic were sex, they unquestionably would do – they constitute themselves as ethically *un*aware agents, as agents who are both unresponsive and irresponsible, lacking morality and respect for a fellow human being worthy of dignity. The point is that thinking through this difference in Levinas's framework allows us to see that the contrast between Danish support workers and their Swedish counterparts runs deeper than just being a case of prejudice and discrimination (even though the contrast indisputably *is* animated by prejudice and discrimination). The point is that for non-disabled people to recognize not only that people with significant physical and intellectual impairments may have erotic desires, but also that they require assistance to be able to understand and explore those desires is to recognize both a fundamental sameness, but also, just as important, a crucial, irreducible difference.

The space between that familiar sameness and the in many ways unknowable difference is the space of ethics. And the response of the Danish support workers is an example of *responsibility* in its dual senses of both of 'the ability to respond' and 'the impossibility of indifference'.

As for Agamben, in addition to the situation I mentioned above – that people with disabilities are vulnerable to being stripped of *bios* and regarded solely as *zoë* – there is also the observation that the adults with disabilities I worked with are biopolitical subjects par excellence. The state is vigorously engaged in managing the most minute aspects of their existence. One of the reasons why Swedish support workers actively discourage disabled adults from engaging in erotic relations is that they worry about exploitation and abuse. They present their silences, dismissals and obstructions as benevolent protections. 'Don't wake the sleeping bear' (*Väck inte den björn som sover*), they say, meaning: don't draw attention to something that isn't seeking it (in English, the expression is 'Let sleeping dogs lie'). Even if it becomes evident that a person with a disability may have erotic feelings (because that person gets erections, for example, or emits sounds of pleasure when her genital area is being rinsed with a shower-head), such responses get resolutely framed as being non-sexual: the disabled person either doesn't understand that he or she has erotic desire, Swedish support workers tell one another, or desire can be satisfied in ways that do not involve genital eroticism, such as hugging, holding hands, or through the bestowal of grandmotherly kisses on the cheek.

Swedish support workers insist that adults with significant disabilities are fundamentally different from non-disabled adults in the realm of sexuality. To raise the issue of sexuality with them – for example, in educational programmes, group discussions, or private conversations – would be to project one's own eroticism onto a sexually innocent individual. This would risk awakening in that person an unasked-for desire that can manifest itself in unforeseen, unhappy, and possibly uncontrollable ways. It is an act of abuse. What this means is that, in Sweden, the erotic lives of a whole population of people are actively suppressed by the same individuals the welfare state employs to care for them under the guise of facilitating a life with dignity.

This is biopower in one of its most egregious manifestations.

What about language? I have already observed that Agamben almost nowhere connects his reflections on biopower and the state of exception with actual language practice. One place where he does do this, however, is in his 2002 [1999] book, *Remnants of Auschwitz*. In that book, Agamben's fascination with the muteness of the *Muselmann* continues, but here he discusses it in the context of bearing witness. Referring to accounts of the 'Muslims' narrated by survivors of the Nazi death camps such as Primo Levi, Bruno Bettelheim or Jean Améry, Agamben argues that the value of their testimony:

> lies essentially in what it lacks: at its center, it contains something that cannot be borne witness to.... The 'true' witnesses, the 'complete witnesses,' are those who did not bear witness and could not bear witness. They are those who 'touched bottom': the Muslims, the drowned. The survivors speak in their stead, by proxy, as pseudo-witnesses; they bear witness to a missing testimony ... Whoever assumes the charge of bearing witness in their name knows that he or she must bear witness in the name of the impossibility of bearing witness. (Agamben, 2002 [1999]: 34)

I read this observation to mean that ethical engagement with others necessarily involves awareness that one embarks on an impossible task. It is not possible to completely speak for another person, and that impossibility, for Agamben, represents a potentiality: one that 'becomes actual through an impotentiality of speech; it is, moreover, an impossibility that gives itself existence through a possibility of speaking' (Agamben, 2002 [1999]: 146).

In this sense, the 'lack' that Agamben refers to in the quote above does not refer to a 'lack' of language – something that, at least in the context of people with disabilities, we should object to (people like the adults I worked with do not 'lack' anything. They can communicate; it is just that they do it in ways that do not involve spoken language). What is 'lacking' – the centre that 'contains something that cannot be borne witness to' – is complete access to the individual experience of other people. This impossibility, it seems, is the potentiality that facilitates ethical engagement. As is his wont, Agamben (2002 [1999]: 69) goes to what he calls the most 'extreme expression' – the *Muselmann* and the Holocaust that brought the *Muselmann* into being and subsequently murdered him – to illustrate his point.

But clearly Agamben's argument is intended to be more than just a meditation on a monstrous historical event. It seems possible to apply the ethics of witnessing he discusses to anybody who takes the risk of attempting to speak for another being – especially another being who communicates in ways other than through spoken language.

The risk involved in bearing witness is a feature of engagement that, once again, differentiates Danish support workers from their Swedish counterparts. Unlike Swedish support workers, who refuse to engage with the sexuality of the disabled adults they assist, Danes are willing to take the risk of extending themselves to engage with others – others whom they know they will never fully understand, but whom they nevertheless are able to recognize and acknowledge as fellow adults deserving of attention and dignity.

Besides citizenship

In a book in which a running theme is 'citizenship' – especially 'Linguistic Citizenship' – the invitation that I have proposed in this paper to engage with the work of Agamben and Levinas may seem a bit jarring, and out of place.

In some ways, I can readily agree that it is. I began the chapter by pointing out the subtle yet important difference between 'rights' and 'entitlements'. Discourses of citizenship take both into account, of course. But inevitably, talk about citizenship is formulated in relation to the state and on how various groups establish what political scientist Engin Isin (2009: 371) has labelled 'the right to claim rights' in particular polities. The right to claim rights is crucial, since, as Edmund Burke and Hannah Arendt so powerfully argued (and, as Rawlsian philosophers of political liberalism such as Martha Nussbaum, and as critics of the Linguistic Human Rights approach like Christopher Stroud have continued to argue), 'rights' cannot be 'human rights', free-floating and universal. To have any meaning, rights have to be anchored somewhere, and the state, for all its many deficiencies and insufficiencies, is, at least at present and for the foreseeable future, the most secure anchor we have.

However, a limitation of a framework that highlights citizenship and rights is that the focus of attention and research tends implacably to drift towards people and groups who are articulate: people who protest, who challenge, who subvert, who resist in various ways, and whose practices of defiance researchers can identify, analyse and (to the extent that they are politically palatable to the liberal, largely left-leaning academics who write about them) identify *with*, bask in the progressiveness of, and advocate on behalf of.

People like the significantly disabled adults I have worked with – who, far from being the kind of multilingual subject discussed in other papers in this book, are non-lingual, or a-lingual – get forgotten. They get left out, partly because they stage no protests, create no performances, engage in no 'back-talk', make no political claims. The idea of linguistic citizenship discussed throughout this volume is a fine approach to language used by people who can wield it. But what about those who do not, or cannot?

Linguistic citizenship follows agents. In his concise recent definition, Stroud (2018: 4) explains the concept by noting that linguistic citizenship is 'what people do with and around language in order to position themselves agentively, and to craft new emergent subjectivities of political speakerhood'. The concern, in other words, as it is in most work in citizenship studies, is with documenting and understanding how people formulate needs and make demands on the state and its institutions (at least this is how I understand 'political speakerhood').

It is clearly critical to highlight such processes. But the point I am suggesting here is that doing so cannot exhaust the range of relations, commitments, obligations and responsibilities that human beings have with other beings with whom we share the world (both other human beings, and non-human beings as well).

In order for people like the ones I worked with in Denmark and Sweden to enter our awareness and our research frameworks, we need approaches besides those that focus on agentive rights-claiming. We need to explore how people come to acknowledge others as entitled subjects worthy of dignity. We need to consider how people respond responsibly (or not) to appeals from others, in particular situated contexts.

I have suggested that perspectives offered in the work of two Continental philosophers might help us think productively about how we might do that: how we might examine ethics and responsibility as interactional practices; how we might think about them as achievements. And I offered a concrete example of two contrasting modes of engagement with others: one, the Swedish case, denying responsibility; the other, the Danish case, affirming it. If this example has any value in a context like this, it is perhaps as a reminder that ethical engagement and responsibility are not just qualities or dimensions of social interaction that can be hoped for or inferred – they can be empirically documented, if one only knows how to look, and what to look for.

References

Agamben, G. (1993 [1990]) *The Coming Community*. (Michael Hardt, trans.). Minneapolis: University of Minnesota Press.

Agamben, G. (1998) *Homo Sacer: Sovereign Power and Bare Life*. (Daniel Heller-Roazen, trans.). Stanford, CA: Stanford University Press.

Agamben, G. (2002 [1999]) *Remnants of Auschwitz: The Witness and the Archive*. (Daniel Heller-Roazen, trans.). New York: Zone Books.

Arendt, H. (1973 [1968]) *The Origins of Totalitarianism*. New York: Harcourt, Brace, Jovanovich.

Giles, H. and Ogay, T. (2007) Communication Accommodation Theory. In B.B. Whaley and W. Samter (eds) *Explaining Communication: Contemporary Theories and Exemplars* (pp. 293–310). Mahwah, NJ: Lawrence Erlbaum,

Hepburn, A. and Bolden, G. (2013) The conversation analytic approach to transcription. In J. Sidnell and T. Stivers (eds) *The Handbook of Conversation Analysis* (pp. 57–66). Oxford: Wiley-Blackwell.

Hunt, L. (2007) *Inventing Human Rights: A History*. New York: W.W. Norton & Company.

Isin, E. (2009) Citizenship in flux: The figure of the activist citizen. *Subjectivity* 29, 367–388.

Klepikova, A. (2017) Social construction of mental disabilities in Russian residential care institutions. *Public Health Panorama* 3 (1), 22–30.

Kulick, D. and Rydström, J. (2015) *Loneliness and its Opposite: Sex, Disability and the Ethics of Engagement*. Durham, SC: Duke University Press.

Levi, P. (1959 [1947]) *If This is a Man*. (Stuart Woolf, trans.). New York: Orion Press.

Levinas, E. (1969) *Totality and Infinity: An Essay on Exteriority*. (Alphonso Lingis, trans.). Pittsburgh: Duquesne University Press.

Levinas, E. (1991) *Otherwise than Being: Or, Beyond Essence*. (A. Lingis, trans.). Dordrecht: Kluwer Academic Publishers.

Moyne, S. (2010) *The Last Utopia: Human Rights in History*. Cambridge, MA: Belknap Press.

Nussbaum, M. (2006) *Frontiers of Justice: Disability, Nationality, Species Membership*. Cambridge, MA: Belknap Press.

Pomerantz, A. and Heritage, J. (2013) Preference. In J. Sidnell and T. Stivers (eds) *The Handbook of Conversation Analysis* (pp. 210–299). Oxford: Wiley-Blackwell.

Scarry, E. (1988) *The Body in Pain: The Making and Unmaking of the World*. Oxford: Oxford University Press.

Stroud, C. (2014) Afterword. In Luiz Paulo Moita-Lopes (ed.) *Global Portuguese: Linguistic Ideologies in Late Modernity* (pp. 222–230). London: Routledge.

Stroud, C. (2018) Introduction. In L. Lim, C. Stroud and L. Wee (eds) *The Multilingual Citizen: Towards a Politics of Language for Agency and Change* (pp. 1–14). Bristol: Multilingual Matters.

12 Afterword: Seeding(ceding) Linguistically – New Roots for New Routes

Christopher Stroud

In the story 'Speech Sounds', Octavia Butler tells of an apocalyptic incident on a world scale where humanity suffers a devastating loss of language in a worldwide aphasic incident resulting in an ensuing chaos of violence and societal disruption/destruction (Butler, 2008). The story ostensibly offers a fundamental insight – that language is foundational for a co-habiting humanity through the political, economic structures we inhabit; that without language, social discord, disarray and ultimately the collapse of society will inevitably follow. What the story 'neglects' to tell, however, is how language, seemingly a foundation stone for the integrity of society, is itself a root cause of abusive and dysfunctional social relations. In fact, language is a mechanism *par excellence*, in depriving people of voice and agency, sorting individuals into hierarchical racial groupings, and mobilizing xenophobic misery against those who have been labelled 'different'. 'Othering' or 'closure' is part of the fundamental dynamic of language – of its normativity, constructed over centuries through metadiscursive regimes that shaped and tied language 'to schemes of social inequality, modes of imagining and controlling Others, and efforts to naturalize inequality' (Bauman & Briggs, 2003: 313).

Linguistic Closure

The chapters in this volume are awash with examples of how language sorts and discriminates, hierarchizes, boxes and excludes individuals and groups. Marcelyn Oostendorp, for example, notes in her chapter on utopia/dystopia how African migrants to South Africa are 'trapped' in 'in-between spaces', caught up in a 'wrong-kind' of multilingualism on the wrong kind of body, a multilingualism of coloniality. The 'utopian' promise of English acquisition to bring about a better, more hopeful, life proves instead to be a shibboleth, and African migrants' repertoire is an audible marker that they do not belong, and are likely victims of future xenophobic upset.

Hostages to repertoires of (multilingual) coloniality, they inhabit a multi-lingual dystopia forever remaining othered by language.

Multilingual Othering is also the theme of Salo and Karlander's chapter on semilingualism in Sweden, which is a detailed account of how the idea of 'semilingualism' became a driving force in policies on Swedish Mother Tongue Instruction. Emerging in the 1970s, co-temporaneously with a growing multi-party consensus on pluralism as political principle, semilingualism revealed an idea of multilingualism rooted in the fantasy of monoglossia, a belief in the existence of a 'whole' language, and the primacy of Swedish. Not surprisingly, the main legacy of what has become known as 'the semilingual debate' was to create a space for debating the pros and cons of mother tongue instruction in the acquisition of Swedish. In other words, linguistic pluralism was always a pluralism of Swedish primacy, of (near-)native acquisition of the State-bearing language, falling just that little bit short (Fanon, 1987), in a *lagom* sort of way. And, whereas Oostendorp, and Salo and Karlander reveal the insidious powers of language to Other by granting only specifically tailored 'voices' and agencies legitimacy, Kulick in his chapter turns the gaze to those who simply have no voice at all, who are *denied* 'voice', not only partially, but wholly. For Kulick, these are the disabled, institutionalized, and mentally impaired. But there are many more victims of the silencing of voice, such as those labelled autistic (inarticulate), demented (disarticulate), psychotic (the polyarticulate); indigenous (trans-articulate) or 'raced' (non-articulate) (compare Hyltenstam & Kerfoot, this volume).

These three examples of linguistic dystopia are textbook cases of what Lionel Wee in his chapter dissects as the myth of orderly multilingualism. He points to a core feature of language most visible in multilingualism, which is often relegated to the sidelines, made marginal, as noise, something to be rid of: this is *ambivalence*, the uncertainties that accompany all human engagements with others, brought to the fore in the interactions across difference that comprise multilingual encounters, but sanitized out of monoglossia, and kept at bay through the myth of order where 'disorder, contingency and unpredictability of multilingualism are problems that need to be managed if not altogether eliminated' (this volume: 20). He notes in particular how disorderly multilingualism is revealed in increased social complexity – a hallmark of social change (and even resilience). Orderly multilingualism is a multilingualism of heavily policed boundaries, regulated and compartmentalized, controlled and normative. It is this normativity that undergirds a liberal idea of voice, of what can be said, and the constraints on its saying in order to be audible.

In each case, orderly, normative, language offers the rationale for not having to listen, for not hearing, for not paying attention, for labelling something as 'noise' and for tu(r)ning a deaf ear (Brooks, 2020). Language is Santos's abyssal line, separating silenced monsters, unnamed, that reside on one side, from humanity on the other; it is what divides those barely existing in the zone of non-being from the human 'living' (see Fanon, 1987). The 'limiting instance' of the coupling of voice to a normative idea of language is total silencing, total closure. Indeed, to be cast out is just as much part of languaging as is being heard, and loneliness is an equally fundamental accompaniment of speaking as conviviality and community (compare Shuster, 2012). As Kulick notes by way of reference to the philosopher Agamben, 'language secures its reference to the world through the possibility of its own suspension' (p. 203). This is the ontology of language-as-we-know-it: the language of regulated genres and accepted speech, language as shibboleth.

Not surprisingly, it is the capability of (normative) language to silence or amplify voice that provides the centring for the construct of a nation-state, and its communicative institutional bedrock of Habermasian public space (see Wee, this volume). Language as shibboleth is the foundation on which 'an inherently exclusive mode of political subjectivity' (Turner, 2016: 142) is constructed, a citizenship of capture and closure (cf. also Brooks, 2020). Machineries of (nation-state) citizenship open up and close down spaces of participation and belonging by recognizing certain voices as worthy of rights, and according these right(s)-ful voices, agency and participation in the social contract. Habermasian public spaces manufacture marginality as much as they acknowledge voice. The production of marginality, of closure, takes on other extreme forms in, what Rae (2002) calls, 'pathological homogenizations' of society (see Agamben's 'states of exception'); racism, xenophobia and ultimately genocide that are the logical (if horrendous) and extreme, possibilities inherent in social systems built around a construct of language as shibboleth (recall the dehumanizing registers of 1994 genocidal Rwanda, the 'cockroaches' and 'tall trees' [Ndhahiro, 2019]). Derrida (1985: 292) reminds that '...there's no racism without language. The point is not that acts of racial violence are only words, but rather that they have to have a word.' No wonder then that Kulick despairs of a politics of voice to ever better the lot of the excluded, silenced and dispossessed.

Thus, in language, we have forged a tool through which we take form as a particular sort of Human as MAN (Wynter, 2003). This is a creature historically scripted as 'a liberal, white, bourgeois, heterosexual, man' (Turner, 2016: 142), what Maturana and Varelas (1980) might call *homo arrogans*. If we were able to 'rethink' language, we might find a way into other genres of the human (Bylund, this volume; Kulick, this volume; Wynter, 2003), other stories and other ways of language-ing ourselves for a better and more just society; in other words, how to 'think' a (political) construct of language that could be leveraged to go beyond the lived, historical shackles of citizenships of capture, and open up for new futures. Given the claustrophobic closure of institutional politics, it would mean attending to how 'political' subjectivities emerge on the margins of the linguistically normative, and developing an alternate concept of voice through serious listening to its manifold articulations, e.g. the remixing of voice in hip-hop or other performance arts (Williams, this volume). The notion of Linguistic Citizenship (Stroud, 2001) has been an attempt to begin such an exploration of a linguistically driven re-politization of citizenship (Stroud, 2001, 2015).

Linguistic Citizenship

Kulick notes how much of the politics of voice and agency attend only to those that 'articulate', to the detriment of the 'non-lingual' or 'a-lingual' who are left out and forgotten in political theories of voice because they 'stage no protests, create no performances, engage in no back-talk, make no political claims' (p. 215). However, there are many ways in which forms of diversity are contained and legislated as institutionally 'out of bounds' and their speaker-hoods made inaudible. Acts of Linguistic Citizenship like other forms of insurgent citizenships seek to interrupt these silencings. Linguistic Citizenship is about 'language' (broadly conceived in all its queerness/trans/intersemioticity) that may help reshape and re-conceptualize the political (again broadly conceived) beyond citizenships of closure and capture, one that can articulate 'a diversity and heterogeneity of the political …' (Turner, 2016: 142) and perceive voice and agency in those customarily silenced, ignored and banished to various forms of politically constructed non-existence. We are always both more or less than the words we utter. Linguistic Citizenship is about speaking/listening between the lines, finding sense in noise and salvaging subterranean selves, exorcized through liberal logics of (semiotic) exclusion. It refers to those acts of semiosis that people use to articulate (other) selves, configure alternate political subjectivities and knowledges, and engage in different ways of relating to others through what Williams (this volume) calls 'remixing', the diverse semiotic figures (poetic re-translation, theatre, performance (hip-hop), graffiti, linguistic landscapes of protest; the small squares of paper Kulick describes as taped to a chair or the complexities of the many forms of silence) (compare Bock & Stroud, 2021; Heugh et al., 2021).

From a southern and decolonial vantage point, Kathleen Heugh (this volume) sees Linguistic Citizenship as a way of counteracting the predation of the colonial habitus that has historically ignored local voice. She emphasizes the silenced voices of the many 'local' scholars of African linguistics whose work has been 'written out' of the academy in 'scholarly' wieldings of epistemic violence, noting that silencing and invisibilization (cf. Kerfoot & Hyltenstam, 2017) of linguistic heterogeneity is as much a feature of postcolonial and post-Apartheid contexts as it was of the high table of colonialism itself. I read Heugh as underscoring the ethical responsibilities that Linguistic Citizenship is responding to in acknowledging an interlocutor role for the forgotten/abandoned speakers and 'commentators' on southern multilingualisms (see also, in this volume,

Kulick on 'witnessing' and Williams on witnessing/testimonial through rap as acts of Linguistic Citizenship).

Aspects of Linguistic Citizenship are at work in articulating non-institutionalized (political) subjectivities in the chapter by van Niekerk, Jansen and Bock and the one by Hiss and Peck. Both attend to the officially subdued 'other selves' of speakers who feel themselves caught within the dystopian, inherited identity categories of an old Apartheid typology, while fully cognizant of the promise of other lives and sensibilities in the post-Apartheid contemporary. Both chapters draw attention to the lived ambivalence and contradiction in the everyday lives of their participants, and how their subjects use small stories (van Niekerk *et al.*) or a spectrum of social media (Hiss & Peck) to momentarily create a space of otherwise where they can refigure themselves against the grain of these lived historical categories ('I am my own coloured'). The felt contradiction initiates a process of *becoming*, of moving beyond, potentially providing the groundwork for a more resolute anti-racial political subjectivity (see Williams, this volume for further examples of racialized ambivalence).

In both cases, the crafting of alternative political subjectivities in these chapters emerges from the way the participants' counter-narratives build on a chronotopical structure that connects present sensibilities and perceived injustices to prototypical Apartheid violations. Each of the two cases represents an Oostendorp-ian dystopia where invasive past miseries produce a sense of personal disjunct with a lived present. This chronotopical framing is also what carries the language complaint in each chapter – the felt imposition of Afrikaans as a 'necessary' attribute of colouredness in van Niekerk *et al.* and the upset at the disciplinary downgrading of public isiXhosa in Hiss and Peck. Oostendorp reminds us that 'language activism alone is never sufficient, must be combined with social and political and economic activism' (p. 103) (see also Rampton *et al.*, this volume). In both cases, language, and talk about language was couched in, and co-substantial with, the social and political injustices of race that is at the forefront of concern.

The chapters are examples of an everyday engagement with diversity and marginalization that regularly takes place across a range of non-institutional and informal political arenas. They illustrate the many ways of thinking knowing and feeling around 'mundane ontologies of everyday life' (Papadopoulos, 2018: 58, 213), and are highly personal and intimate modes of *affectful* engagement with large-scale processes (compare Williams & Stroud, 2015, on some of the practices whereby intimate acts and feelings become public and political; Williams, this volume for 'remixing' in 'nooks and crannies'). Wee's chapter suggests that the ambiguity, ambivalence, and uncertainty so visible in van Niekerk *et al.* sit at the very core of Linguistic Citizenship.

One of the issues raised by the chapter by Rampton, Cooke and Holmes, in particular, is to what extent the 'becomings' in acts of

Linguistic Citizenship, articulated in unconventional, non-institutionalized uses of language and other semiotic practices, may carry into more formal structures and moments. Acts of Linguistic Citizenship are fundamentally interdiscursive, emergent and unfolding accomplishments, rather than bounded, conclusive events and that resemiotizations and entextualizations play a major role in end-point politics. (Rampton *et al.* note this explicitly in reference to 'text trajectories' across 'trans-contextual and multi-scalar frameworks' (p. 63); see also Williams, this volume, on the transnational scalarity of hip-hop, as well as Hiss and Peck's transnational #; Kulick on witnessing – which in many ways comprises chains of entextualizations and (re)wordings that distribute voice and agency out of opaque and into more transparent, receptive contexts, and Heugh who sees Linguistic Citizenship as a *mestizo* notion.)

Relatedly, Rampton *et al.* wonder to what extent traditional state-based institutions can host acts of Linguistic Citizenship that are otherwise often more likely to occur in 'grassroots activity at some distance from the centres of power' (p. 73). They suggest that Linguistic Citizenship has manifested successfully, at least momentarily, in highly institutionalized environments, such as the UK state school system from 1960 to 1980s. As Shilliam (2011) has pointed out, even thoroughbred colonial, neoliberal structures of patriarchy are seldom completely totalitarian, but comprise projects with openings, apertures of (relative) democracy where we might expect against-the-grain workings of Linguistic Citizenship to take root'.[1]

This was likely the case with the UK school reforms; Rampton and colleagues note that the window of opportunity for Linguistic Citizenship to enter UK educational institutions was ultimately closed off by 'a series of events which should not have occurred in a democratic society' (p. 74). Established structures work to accommodate and defuse the potentiality for radical structural transformation, and this appears to be what happened post-1990 in the UK educational establishment (and in many other education systems across the West), where democratic initiatives were coopted and accommodated in extant workings of a system without fundamental transformation. Such capture is also illustrated in Salo and Karlander's example, where formal policy structures succeeded in coopting a more inclusive plural political philosophy to a monoglossic ideology of semilingualism. Even with the apparent demise of semilingualism, a sense of monoglossic crisis remains: the emphasis on 'diversity' and multiculturalism (that in some measure counteracted discourses of semilingualism) has *itself* been coopted, even revitalized, in the notion of Rinkeby Swedish – semilingualism has merely changed its spots, morphed from leopard to hyena.

As I suggested earlier, capture and enclosure are how language as normativity and fixity works. We need to be wary of the very real risks in 'institutionalized entextualizations' and exercise vigilance with regard to how voice is 're-cited'; Heugh warns, for example, of 'a colonial habitus of speaking over…', denying local voices and their linguistic citizenship, predation, and erasure and misinterpretation; and Kulick references Agamben's *Muselman* who only finds 'freedom' in relinquishing language altogether; and, of course, there are many risks attendant on 'calling' out and 'naming languages' (see Stroud, 2001).

This said, we ought not to confuse 'capture' of voice, re-subordinated to dominant institutional prerogatives, with 'failure' or 'surrender'. The ambivalence we saw in the chapters by van Niekerk *et al.* and Hiss and Peck show the resilience of hopes for non/anti-racialism even in the face of its institutional distortions. And the 'experiments' in Linguistic Citizenship in formal institutions, although not 'sustainable' *per se* surely opened up options and possibilities, offered blueprints of sorts, for alternative futures – futures to be aspired to, of possibilities sensed but unfulfilled. This captures a kernel of Linguistic Citizenship, namely 'struggle', visible in a sense of 'becoming', of life trajectories, not an end-point that would invariably mean 'closure', but an opening up to visions of one day living differently (through language).

Political Ontologies of Language

Language-as-we-know-it, language as shibboleth and closure, is an idea of language among many, and one that is an artefact of a *double disarticulation* that abstracts language from its speakers, on the one hand, and from the relationalities of speakers to each other and the world, on the other. Being able to communicate and interact through language at all is seen more as a felicitous accident, a convenient by-product of how language is organized by a disembodied brain, than the very essence of language itself. Acts of Linguistic Citizenship as a semiotics of 'struggle', of possibility, and relationality, imply a different stance on language as ontology (Wynter, 2003) – one yet to be fully explored. Developing a stance on language from the horizon of Linguistic Citizenship entails thinking carefully about important aspects of relationality such as power, in particular the power to decide what (a) language is, which speakers are considered legitimate interlocutors. Above all, it requires thinking an ontology of language from the primacy of ethics, of how we as speakers relate to each other. Kulick, referencing Levinas, for example, asks 'what would happen to our understandings and analyses of language if we viewed interactions not just in terms of response, but also in terms of responsibility?' (p. 208). From a southern perspective, Heugh argues a similar point in her emphasis that understanding of southern multilingualism requires a gaze refracted through 'the agency and voice of southern people and communities' (p. 52). And, of course, an ethics of relationality is perfectly congruent with the centrality of ambivalence and unpredictability, openness and opaqueness in language that resists premature foreclosures of meaning (see Wee's chapter).

A number of chapters in this volume illustrate ways in which relationalities between the silenced find constituency and voice in language and 'beyond'. For example, Williams in this volume remarks on performance as comprising 'acts of Linguistic Citizenship', as they redefine and reposition people in relation to each other, and mediate how 'citizens, strangers, outsiders, aliens emerge not as actors already defined but as ways of being with others' (Isin, 2009: 383). Performances do not only mimic the political processes of the everyday, but comprise salient moments in themselves, as political issues unfold, unravel and develop across different genres, media and publics.

The learners in Hiss and Peck garner support and amplify their voices through the hashtag in a 'politics of affinity' with many other interests to bring pressure to bear on school authorities. Hashtags are 'sticky' (Ahmed, 2004); they mobilize large political affinities and create a transnational constituency across causes (#FeesMustFall, #RhodesMustFall, #BlackLivesMatter) linking them in a meshwork of complaint across institutions. In both van Niekerk *et al.* and Hiss and Peck, metalinguistic discourses of language as a target of change are played out in 'registers' beyond the linguistic, in terms of racialized body aesthetics or semiotic landscapes of the school. This a language of 'aesthetics' and viscerality (comfort in the linguistic landscape) rather than the language of policy documents. Thus, Linguistic Citizenship is about a variety of semiotic means through which speakers express agency, voice and participation in an everyday politics of language by using/spreading/situating their language over many modalities, giving new meaning to and repurposing language to reflect the social and political issues that affect them. In this sense, Linguistic Citizenship encourages a reframing of 'citizenship' (relationality) 'away from a totalizing sense of language...to incorporate a wider berth of' semiotic practices in order to become better 'attuned to the implications of a multitude of identities, subject positions, and positions of interest' (Stroud, 2010: 213).

Linguistic Citizenship: More than WEIRD

In his chapter on WEIRD psycholinguistics in the concluding section of the volume, Emmanuel Bylund reflects on how language as 'arguably the most defining trait of humans' (p. 183) requires a revamped 'utopic psycholinguistics', reaching beyond WEIRD. In the light of the idea of Linguistic Citizenship, a more than WEIRD psycholinguistics surely ought to be looking at the processing of relationality, fluidity and ambivalence in human language. Much contemporary psycholinguistics remains pre-occupied with countables and compartmentalization (first and second language; native-non-native) and distinct modularities (cognition, affect, body) and media (signs, written, sound bytes). By giving serious consideration to the messiness of language, the unpredictability of how meanings evolve across modalities and media, psycholinguistics could offer fascinating insights into different genres of the human (Wynter, 2003). Taking relationality, ethics, and responsibility as core design features of a political ontology of language could develop Maturana and Varela's (1980) idea of *homo amans*, and the principle of 'love' as a founding dynamic of language. In a recent paper on Fanon as a sociolinguist, Stroud and Mpendukana (forthcoming) argue that his idea of 'love' is consequential for a theory of self, citing the psychoanalyst Lazali (2011: 156) who sees how to give 'the unfamiliar within the self a status of interlocutor'; that is, 'how can conditions be created for a benevolent Other within the Self that is no longer a threat or a persecutor' as one of the most important questions? In other words, what is the psycholinguistics of acts of Linguistic Citizenship that can assist to re-surture the seams that divide to accommodate a more 'expansive' body of humanity? This is an issue that abandons 'modularity' (see also Williams, this volume) and that deliberately attempts to work across compartmentalizations (linguistic, social, personal). It is surely a fitting question to ask of a utopian psycholinguistics relevant to Linguistic Citizenship. In other words, where do we find the locus of Linguistic Citizenship in the neurological, plugs, sockets and chemistries of the mind? Maturana and Varela (1980) based their theory of language on studies of the optic nerve of the dove. There must be opportunities for envisioning a new psycholinguistics of language through an optics of the utopian.

In Lieu of a Conclusion

Rampton and colleagues raise a question on the portability of Linguistic Citizenship; given that the notion originated in a Southern African context, how easily transferrable is it to Western, Northern, clines, 'with a relatively high degree of political continuity' and 'where the idea of transformation' may lack 'the currency in public discourse that it has in a country like South Africa'? In the many of the chapters in the volume, acts of Linguistic Citizenship are found predominantly in situations of institutional capture, in contexts of marginality and vulnerability of speakers, where predation on the human is rampant and the collapse of ethical engagements with others imminent. Clearly, these contexts will differ from situation to situation as Linguistic Citizenship is not an *immutable mobile* (Law & Mol, 2001) traveling across an ever-expanding network of nodes and users. It is rather better seen as a *mutable mobile* (Law & Mol, 2001) akin to the Zimbabwean bush pump. The bush pump exhibits a 'liquid' mode of topological travel, the slow, imperceptible change and adaptation to context and circumstance, the tweaking of a screw and the adjustment of a valve, that ensure its smooth continued functioning as it moves from village to village (e.g. as 'sociolinguistic citizenship' in Rampton *et al.*, this volume).

The root of our evils, however, is not to be found *only* in the contingent political structures of the day. Might not the very structure of language as a normative system, that through which our humanity is constituted, lay both claims to and limit what we can imagine as alternative and more ethical futures. Perhaps it is not that language has been *coopted* (discursively or otherwise) to (nation-state) citizenships of capture and closure; perhaps societies have been *captured by language*, and that language, far from being a tool in politics, *is* the politics it seemingly is merely a corollary to. It is by means of 'Language–as-we-know-it' that we construe our humanity and our ethical engagements with others and our world; language provides the design features of our political institutions and discourses; as such, it is also a tool of societal and institutional abuse. It is this idea of language that ultimately underlies practices of closure and that forms our humanity, leads to closed societies, and drives techniques of control and homogenization. And it is this fact of a linguistics of closure that gives Linguistic Citizenship portability. We see this not least in Octavia Butler's story. As she tells it, language is suspended, ostensibly lost to all, and with this loss comes the collapse of normative institutions. However, in the final lines of 'Speech Sounds', humanity, tottering on the brink of complete destruction, begins to find new footing. Valerie Rye, the heroine of the story, saves the lives of two young children caught up in a horrible act of violence, and finds to her amazement that the 'illness' that erased language for all humanity has by some miracle left them untouched. Fearful of being discovered to have speech, they have remained silent until now, but in their moment of shock, they let slip some language. In an act worthy of a true *homo amans*, Valrie Rye decides to take care of the children. In Octavia Butler's words:

> *She had been a teacher. A good one. She had been a protector, too, though only of herself. She had kept herself alive when she had no reason to live. If the illness let these children alone, she could keep them alive.*

> *… The children began to cry, but she knelt on the broken pavement and whispered to them, fearful of frightening them with the harshness of her long unused voice.*

> *'It's all right,' she told them. 'You're going with us, too. Come on.' She lifted them both, one in each arm. They were so light. Had they been getting enough to eat? The boy covered her mouth with his hand, but she moved her face away. 'It's all right for me to talk,' she told him. 'As long as no one's around, it's all right.'*

> *… 'I'm Valerie Rye,', she said, savoring the words. 'It's all right for you to talk to me.*

In this moment of care and empathy, there is a rebirth of language. The ethical and loving relationship between Valerie Rye and the children kindles a new hope for humanity in what is clearly a powerful act of Linguistic Citizenship.

Note

(1) These would quite likely take different forms in different sites due to the many ways in which marginality and exclusion are determined in particularities of institutional and historical particularities context (Turner, 2016).

References

Ahmed, S. (2004) *The Cultural Politics of Emotion.* Edinburgh: Edinburgh University Press.

Bauman, R. and Briggs, C. (2003) *Voices of Modernity: Language Ideologies and the Politics of Inequality.* Cambridge: Cambridge University Press.

Bock, Z. and Stroud, C. (eds) (2021) *Language and Decoloniality in Higher Education: Reclaiming Voices from the South.* London: Bloomsbury Academic.

Brooks, A. (2020) Fugitive listenings: Sounds from the undercommons. *Theory, Culture and Society* 37 (6), 25–52.

Butler, O.E. (2008) Speech sounds. In O.E. Butler (ed.) *Wastelands: Stories of the Apocalypse* (pp. 245–255). San Francisco: Nightshade Books.

Derrida, J. (1985) Racism's last word. *Critical Inquiry* 12 (1), 290–299.

Fanon, F. (1987) *The Wretched of the Earth.* London: Penguin Books.

Heugh, K., Stroud, C., Taylor-Leech, K. and de Costa, P. (eds) (2021) *A Sociolinguistics of the South.* London: Routledge.

Isin, E. (2009) Citizenship in flux: The figure of the activist citizen. *Subjectivity* 29, 367–388

Kerfoot, C. and Hyltenstam, K. (eds) (2017) *Entangled Discourses: South-North Orders of Visibility.* London: Routledge.

Law, J. and Mol, A. (2001) Situating technoscience: an inquiry into spatialities. *Environment and Planning D: Society and Space* 19, 609–621.

Lazali, K. (2003) The emergence of the subject in politics: Some reflections on the Algerian situation and on the the work o Frantz Fanon. In N.C. Gibson (ed) *Living Fanon* (pp. 149–157). New York: Palgrave Macmillan.

Maturana, H.R. and Varela, F.G. (1980) *Autopoiesis and Cognition: The Realization of the Living.* Dordrecht: Reidel.

Ndhahiro, K. (2019) In Rwanda, we know all about dehumanizing language: Years of cultivated hatred led to death on a horrifying scale. See https://www.theatlantic.com/ideas/archive/2019/04/rwanda-shows-how-hateful-speech-leads-violence/587041 (accessed September 2020).

Papadopoulos, D. (2018) *Experimental Practice: Technoscience, Alterontologies and More-than-Social Movements.* Durham, NC: Duke University Press.

Rae, H. (2002) *State Identities and the Homogenization of Peoples.* Cambridge: Cambridge University Press.

Shilliam, R. (2011) *International relations and Non-Western Thought: Imperialism, Colonialism and Investigations of Global Modernity.* Abingdon: Routledge.

Shuster, M. (2012) Language and loneliness: Arendt, Cavell and modernity. *International journal of Philosophical Studies* 20 (4), 473–497.

Stroud, C. (2001) African mother-tongue programs and the politics of language: Linguistic Citizenship versus Linguistic Human Rights. *Journal of Multilingual and Multicultural Development* 22 (4), 339–355.

Stroud, C. (2010) A postliberal critique of language rights: Towards politics of language for a linguistics of contact. In J.E. Petrovich (ed.) *International Perspectives on Bilingual Education: Policy, Practice and Controversy* (pp. 195–221). Charlotte, NC: Information Age Publishing.

Stroud, C. (2015) Linguistic Citizenship as Utopia. *Multilingual Margins: A Journal of Multilingualism from the Periphery* 2 (2), 22–39.

Turner, J. (2016) (En)gendering the political: Citizenship from marginal spaces. *Citizenship Studies* 20 (2), 141–155.

Williams, Q. and Stroud, C. (2015) Linguistic Citizenship: Language and politics in post-national modernities. *Journal of Language and Politics* 14 (3), 406–430.

Wynter, S. (2003) Unsettling the coloniality of being/power/truth/freedom: Toward the human after man, its overrepresentation – an argument. *CR: The New Centennial Review* 3 (3), 257–337.

Index

Note: 'n' refers to chapter notes.

CPSIA information can be obtained
at www.ICGtesting.com
Printed in the USA
JSHW061902190722
28281JS00003B/138